Edward Thomas completed his PhD at Edinburgh University. He has lived and worked for several years in Sudan and the Sudanese diaspora. He works in London, researching and teaching about Sudan.

INTERNATIONAL LIBRARY OF AFRICAN STUDIES

Series ISBN: 978 1 84885 217 4

See www.ibtauris.com/ILAS for a full list of titles

ISLAM'S PERFECT STRANGER

The life of Mahmud Muhammad Taha,
Muslim Reformer of Sudan

Edward Thomas

I.B. TAURIS
LONDON · NEW YORK

Published in 2010 by I.B.Tauris & Co Ltd
6 Salem Road, London W2 4BU
175 Fifth Avenue, New York NY 10010
www.ibtauris.com

Distributed in the United States and Canada Exclusively by Palgrave Macmillan
175 Fifth Avenue, New York NY 10010

International Library of African Studies 26

ISBN: 978 1 84885 004 0

A full CIP record for this book is available from the British Library
A full CIP record for this book is available from the Library of Congress
Library of Congress catalog card: available

Printed and bound in Great Britain by CPI Antony Rowe, Chippenham
from camera-ready copy edited and supplied by the author
Typeset in Garamond by Vibhu Mishra

Dedicated with love to my parents

Contents

Acknowledgements

People who knew Mahmud Muhammad Taha generously committed their memories to me; I am extremely grateful to everyone who spent time answering my questions: 'Abdallah al-Dabi, Professor Abdullahi An-Na'im, Dr 'Abdelwahab El-Affendi, 'Abd al-Rahman 'Ali al-Shaykh, Ahmed Omer, Dr Al-Baqir Mukhtar, 'Ali Lutfi, Amna Muhammad Lutfi, Asma Mahmud, 'Awatif 'Abd al-Gadir, Batoul Mukhtar, Bona Malwal, Eltayeb Hassan, El-Nour Hamad, Fatma Ibrahim, Fatma Yusuf Gway, Dr Girgis Iskander, Ibrahim Yusuf, Khalid Muhammad al-Hasan, Mahmud Amin Siddig, Mona Zanoon, Muhammad 'Abd al-Khalig, Muhammad 'Ali Malik, Muhammad al-Fatih, Mudawi Turabi, Omer El Garrai, Saadia 'Izz al-Din, al-Hajja Sayyida Muhammad Lutfi, Dr Steve Howard, Yusuf Hasan, Yusuf Lutfi, as well as other people who preferred not to be mentioned. Asma Mahmud, El-nour Hamad and Abdullahi An-Na'im spent several days on my questions. Girgis Iskander was willing to spend hours of his time thinking about my questions and composing long, precise responses: he even translated an entire book to save me time and bother. Al-Baqir Mukhtar and Eltayeb Hassan, completing their doctorates on Republican thought in England, were unfailingly generous with advice and suggestions. Gerhard Lichtenthaler, Jurgen Rogalski and Haydar Ibrahim Ali helped me find copies of Taha's works. Al-Baqir Mukhtar and Girgis Iskander read this book for me before it was submitted.

This book began as a thesis written at Edinburgh University. I would like to acknowledge the financial support of the Spalding Trust, which paid for my fees and the Carnegie Trust which funded a field trip. I am very grateful to them both.

Dr Ian Howard, Dr Carol Hillenbrand and Dr Yasin Dutton of the Islamic and Middle East Studies department all generously contributed their expertise.

James Sharrock and Vibhu Mishra did an excellent job in proof-reading and type-setting the book version, in record speed.

The biggest influence on this book was Dr Paul Lalor, who supervised my studies. I will always be grateful to him and his wife Dr Floresca Karanasou for their kindness, hospitality and warm friendship. I would also like to thank all the people who put me up and looked after me during my studies and field trips. Especially Louise Anderson, George Louis, Mahmud Amin Siddig, Vernon German, Martin Nixon and Nicola Steen. And to Daniela Baro, who inspired me to turn this into a book and to come back to Sudan. Love and gratitude.

Transliteration

This book adopts a flexible approach to transliteration. Words transliterated from Arabic texts follow a modified version of the system adopted by the *International Journal of Middle Eastern Studies*. The book does not use the diacritical marks of that system.

Oral sources are treated differently. In Sudan, the Arabic letter *qaf* is pronounced hard *g*, and the long and short vowel sounds *o* and *e* appear. This is reflected in transliteration of informants' speech and also of proper names and words with special meaning in Sudanese Arabic. For example, *akhwan* appears when spoken and *ikhwan* when written, to represent the same word for brothers. *Tariga* is usually adopted instead of *tariqa*, to represent a word usually translated as "Sufi order".

Arabic and other foreign language terms used in quotations and citations follow the usage of their authors.

Introduction

It is narrated on the authority of Abu Huraira that the Messenger of Allah (may peace be upon him) said: Islam appeared as a stranger, and it will return as a stranger. Then blessed are the strangers! (*Sahih Muslim*, 1:272)

This well-attested *hadith*, or saying of the prophet Muhammad, was a favourite saying of the subject of this biography, Mahmud Muhammad Taha (often called *ustaz* Mahmud). He was a junior nationalist politician who became, after a spiritual transformation in a colonial jail, the charismatic leader of a small group of religious and political activists called the Republican brothers and sisters. They called for a mystical, inclusive reinterpretation of Islam, and became a picturesque and articulate feature of Sudanese street life in the 1970s and 1980s. Taha's views were opposed by Sudanese Muslims who were then taking control of the state, and this led eventually to his execution in 1985.

Checking the reference for the saying, Google transported me to a number of websites produced by militant groups and another evidently run by amateur terrorist-hunters who as a public service posted on the web incriminating booklets written by Muslim bomb-makers and their recruiting sergeants, one of which quoted the saying about Islam's strangeness. Some narrators of the *hadith* have people asking the prophet who the strangers are – and different answers are given, such as "those who withdraw from the tribe [the family or the familiar]" or "those who forbid evil when people are corrupted".

Taha's favourite saying is a way for people who want to shake up traditional versions of Islam and attack the grand compromise between the leaders of Sunni Islam and Muslim political leaders – a compromise that allows Islamic *shari'a* law to work as a slow moving but flexible body of law and ideology. The grand compromisers dispense with the radical possibilities of Islam and conserve the authority of the state and of traditional religion. Some groups today want to challenge that grand compromise through violence, and the saying helps them to do it.

Taha engaged in nasty scuffles with colonial authorities when he was a young nationalist leader, and sometimes took sides in insurgencies and wars, but he opposed violence in later life – when he became a vegetarian, insecticide was too violent for him. He wanted to do away with a traditional and sedately oppressive version of Islam and transform it into an all-inclusive perfecting process that stretches from pre-history to heaven[1]. Taha believed that the prophet Muhammad lived out this perfection and that all Muslims were called to live it out too. He said, however, that the prophet accommodated human frailty with temporary, concessive regulations for human affairs. These concessive laws included the permission for slavery, and discrimination against non-Muslims and women – allowing Islam to make a temporary reforming alliance with unjust hierarchies rather than trying to revolutionise them.

Most Muslims believe that these *shari'a* laws are eternal, and many believe that *shari'a* institutions are definers of Muslim culture and identity. In contrast, Taha claimed that the Qur'an had an eternal ethical message that would supersede the provisory legislative content that shaped much of the *shari'a* system. The world would only come to this supreme ethical message through a supremely ethical man, and Taha, drawing on the mystical Sufi tradition of Islam, aspired to a personal perfection that would inaugurate an age of goodness – he wanted to be a perfect, blessed stranger.

The antagonism between *shari'a* and Sufi versions of Islam recurs through Islamic history and many of the people who played out this antagonism with Taha and his followers made knowing reference to ancient Middle Eastern polemics and prosecutions for heresy. This book tries to present Taha as part of a tradition kept alive through ancient texts. But it tries to situate him in Sudan where he lived, rather than in the Middle Eastern cities where the old texts were mostly written. It looks at Taha as a legal performer as well as a legal reformer, and looks at the jails, judges and police that he dealt with – and at Sudan's statutory, customary and *shari'a* legal systems. Sudan has never had one set of laws for the whole country, partly because it is an enormous, ecologically, economically and linguistically diverse country. The book tries to relate

Taha's life to the historical experience of an African country on the edge of the Arab and Muslim world, where the interplay of religion, culture and ethnicity has major consequences for the division of wealth and power.

Taha's life was lived in the economically developed core of Sudan, the northern Nile valley. Sudan's colonisers and the Nile valley elites who inherited the colonial state viewed Sudanese people of its underdeveloped periphery as backward, Islamically-incorrect folk-religionists if they were Muslim; and pagans if they were not. Sudanese elites aspired to identify with prestigious versions of Islam which they believed were situated in the cities of the Middle East and the Gulf. In peaceful times this perception would give rise to small investments in educative missions for the pagans and the Islamically-incorrect. In bad times, the state resorted (and still resorts) to prodigious violence against these marginal groups: enslavement, forced migration and sexual violence that have cruelly reshaped millions of Sudanese lives. Taha's twentieth century Nile valley vantage point shaped his views of Sudan's diversity – rather than seeing diversity as a resource or a joy, his early writings look for ways to civilise his compatriots into a version of Islam grounded in high Middle Eastern culture. But in many respects, Taha ended his life as a martyr for the rights of the people of Sudan's periphery, probably also believing on the gallows that his death might be the start of something that flipped Sudan into utopia. He did not transform Sudan magically, but he immediately became an important reference point for many Sudanese intellectuals wanting to conceptualise Sudan's diversity in Islamic terms.

I have tried in this book to relate Taha's sometimes unsettling views about Islam and Sudan to his life story, and I hope that the book gives a reasonably rich description of Taha's context – looking at ethnicity, class, literacy, migration, domestic arguments and architecture. It detains readers with songs, recipes, stories and jokes, cuttings from the newspapers and school curriculums – all in the hope of explaining how Taha's views were shaped by his time and surroundings.

Terms

A brief explanation of three terms that may cause confusion might be useful here: "*shari'a*," "Sufi," and "Muslim Brother". (Chapter 12 of this book sets out Taha's views on *shari'a* in detail, and includes an account of the development of Islamic law).

In this book, *shari'a* is a synonym for Islamic law and its legist tradition that extends into a version of Islamic spirituality that stresses obedience and the unknowability of God. Not all authorities would agree with this: some identify *shari'a* with the sources of Islamic law, and contrast the infallible sources with the laws that were codified by jurisprudents. *Shari'a*, in this account, consists of the Qur'an and the *sunna* (all that the prophet said, did or tacitly approved). Some upholders of a restrictive definition of *shari'a* further limit the term to cover only the legal content of the sources. I hope that this book gives a thorough account of the way that Taha used the term in his writings – he believed *shari'a* included the eternal and the provisory and concessive, and that the relationship between the eternal and the provisory was being worked out in his life and he hoped in the life of all. He was not averse to spiritualising *shari'a*, but his *shari'a* spirituality was not the mix of submission and incommunicability of the legists – it was other-worldly, unsettlingly optimistic, resolving conflict and contradiction in a sea of light.

The *shari'a* tradition is sometimes depicted as a puritanical antagonist of Sufism, which is in turn, is depicted sometimes as a gentle exotic theosophy and sometimes as a vernacular, latitudinarian religion of the Islamic periphery. In Sudan, the historical relationship between the two traditions was not always hostile. The Sufi mainstream in pre-colonial Sudan sometimes taught *shari'a* and sometimes scorned it. That mainstream was organised around local orders or organisations called *tariqa*s. Sufi celebrities institutionalised their spiritual prestige with community leadership, educational activity and trade. *Shari'a* was invoked by states in the Nile valley and Darfur, but it was usually trumped by customary law. Successful merchants used it in one state to modernise commerce before it fell to foreign powers. *Shari'a* was used by Ottoman-Egyptian colonialists (their regime was called the Turkiya) to negotiate their authority over Muslim Sudanese, to marginalise local *tariqa*s and to exclude most Sudanese non-Muslims from legal protection. The *shari'a* tradition decisively entered the idiom of the state in 1820, but it did not destroy other Muslim forms. Small *tariqa*s retained their importance in local settings. New, larger *tariqa*s centralised spiritual authority and extended their followings beyond the local, inspiring Muhammad Ahmad, the Sudanese Mahdi, whose movement reached across most of Sudan to overthrow the Turkiya in 1885.

Sudan's British colonialists redeployed a Turkiya version of *shari'a* as an authoritarian measure against the Sufism they viewed as quixotic and rebellious. However, they eventually solicited the support of Sufi leaderships in an attempt to extend their control over rural Sudan. Sufi elites, reconstituted as colonial agents, became the backbone of a patrimonial relationship between the state centre and the periphery, and eventually inherited the state. These elites used their affiliation to Arabness and Islam to explain their good fortune. As a result, Sudanese nationalism acquired its Arab-Muslim colouring. Challenges to the state from junior elites were often articulated through *shari'a*, and the post-colonial state accordingly sought to extend the authority of *shari'a* laws and affiliate itself to the *shari'a* tradition.

Sudan's first Islamist movement was called the Islamic Liberation Movement when it was founded in 1948, and changed its name to the Muslim Brotherhood in 1954. The Muslim Brotherhood gave rise to a number of other parties, including the Islamic Charter Front (1964) and the National Islamic Front (1985) – who were mainly led by the same, Muslim Brother-linked leaders. In this book, all these parties and movements are referred to as "Muslim Brothers" or "Muslim Brotherhood," to give readers a sense of political continuity – although the Brotherhood itself is a different organisation from the parties.

Outline of chapters

Taha's biography is presented in a more-or-less chronological order. Chapter one (1911–1921) deals with Taha's first ten years; chapter two (seventeenth century to 1911) relates the time and place of Taha's childhood to the wider Sudan. Chapters three and four (1921–1936) look at Taha's schooldays in his home town of Rufa'a and in the capital Khartoum, and the changes his society underwent in the heyday of British colonialism. Chapter five (1936–1945) deals with his marriage and the end of his private life. In chapter six (1945–1946), Taha founds an activist political party and goes to jail. He spends chapter seven (1946–1951) in jail and in an ascetic retreat, and begins to reflect on the inclusive character and transformative power of religion. In chapters eight and nine (1951–1958), Taha returns to life in the mainstream, making money, watching Sudan become independent and occasionally talking about his prison revelations, which attract some hostile attention. This hostility does not stop him from publicising his beliefs in chapter ten (1958–1964). In chapter 11 (1964–1969) he returns to an ascetic life, writes books, begins to attract young intellectuals, and is accused of apostasy by radical exponents of the *shari'a* tradition. Chapter 12 discusses the books that Taha has written and places them in the context of the *shari'a* and Sufi traditions in Sudan. Chapter 13 (1969–1976) goes on to discuss how Taha reinvented Sufi ideas and organisational methods, and relates Taha's experiences to a Sudan ruled by a military regime that tried to reconfigure power away from the Muslim patrician system into a multi-cultural autocracy. Chapter 14 (1973–1982) deals with Taha's attempts to spread his message outside his urban base and to engage with the wider Sudan. Chapter 15 (1977–1983) describes how Sudan's military regime became dominated by new-style religious politics, and looks at the confrontation that developed between Taha and the Muslim Brothers. In chapter 16 (1983–1985) that confrontation ends with Taha's execution. Chapter 17 (1985 onwards) looks at the aftermath of that execution.

Chapter 1

Remembering childhood

How wonderful are the days of the *khalwa*
And marvellous the green childhood.
(Al-Tigani Yusuf Beshir, a favourite poet of Taha's,
quoted in El Shoush 1963:29)

Chapters one to five look at the society that Taha was born into, and
the first three decades of his life. This chapter gives an account of his
earliest years. Here he is called Mahmud, to distinguish him from his
father, Muhammad Taha.

Rufa'a and Heglig

Mahmud did not know exactly when he was born – either in 1909 or
1911. His birthplace was in the populous and fertile Blue Nile region,
in the most economically developed part of the northern Nile valley.
Mahmud's contemporaries disagree as to whether he was born in Rufa'a,
a small east-bank town about 200 miles south of Khartoum, or Heglig
(al-Hijaylij), a hamlet ten miles north of Rufa'a. Heglig was where his
father had a farm on the rainfed lands of the Butana, away from the
river; and Rufa'a was then a town of several thousand people which lay
on the river, and where many of his relations lived[1]. He spent his early
boyhood between the two places, going to Heglig to plant and harvest
when the rains came (between July and November).

Mahmud's parents

Muhammad Taha al-Malik Fadul, Mahmud's father, married twice, and
Mahmud was born to his second wife, Fatma Mahmud. Her family was
from the far north, but had settled in Sifita, a village on the west bank

of the Blue Nile. They had five children together: Batul and Kulsum, the daughters, came first, and Mahmud was followed by a brother Mukhtar, born in 1913. Ahmed al-Mustafa, born in 1915, lived only a few months. Mahmud also had a half brother named Ahmed wad al-Birr. Muhammad Taha, the father, was a farmer of modest means and some respectable connections. He had houses in Heglig and Rufa'a. The Rufa'a house was plain – a courtyard of 1,500 square metres, and two rooms of unbaked mud with old-fashioned windholes instead of windows. Houses had separate quarters for women and men, built in a mud courtyard enclosed with a high wall.

Muhammad Taha lived near the house of Muhammad Lutfi, a young school teacher who went on to be an important figure in Rufa'a education – and whose daughter would one day marry Mahmud. Next door lived Zahra 'Abdallah, who would breast feed the young Mahmud when his mother was busy. The men-folk would gather in Lutfi's house for their meals together[2].

As well as a farm, Mahmud's father had an oil press that he worked with his sons and possibly his slaves or hired men. The press was the simplest kind, made out of a hollowed tree and powered by a camel. The extra income probably meant that the family was comfortably off, and the sesame oil also spiced up Fatma's social life. Sesame oil is used for cosmetics as well as cooking, and women came to Fatma's house for communal make-up sessions. The women rubbed their skins with ointments and sat under a thick black blanket around the embers of aromatic woods and spices[3].

Heglig

In Heglig, where Mahmud spent the rainy summer season, men worked their fields and then collected a plate of stew from their wives, eating together with male guests staying in the village *khalwa*. (Women ate separately, with the children). *Khalwa*s were originally retreats for village mystics, but they became religious and cultural centres for small communities. The *khalwa* was a place for congregational prayer, a guest house, a kindergarten, and a place to eat a meal and idle away an evening in male company.

Heglig folk memories recall the poor diet of their village – the diet affected people's night vision so badly that they needed guide-ropes to get home from the *khalwa* after their evening meal. It was only when vitamin-rich mustard-cress was introduced that the problem cleared up[4]. A study of diet in the area in the 1940s showed that people depended heavily on one crop, sorghum, most commonly eaten as a sour bread pancake called *kisra*. The roasted grains were used to treat nausea and charred stalks made a flavour enhancing potash called *weikab*[5]. Sorghum stalks made toy flutes for boys and girls turned the leaves into trumpets[6].

Rufa'a was a town where girls and boys mixed together into late childhood, and Mahmud's sister-in-law remembers that he played with the boys and girls of his part of the town, Daym Graydab (Qaridab). They played games like *shilayl*, which has children hiding and finding scraps of bone or cloth, shrieking nonsense chants[7]. Mahmud also played football – a recent arrival in Rufa'a promoted by a famous and far-sighted educator, Babikr Bedri[8]. Rufa'a boys played an enthusiastic, barefoot game[9]. When the Rufa'a boys went to Wad Medani (the provincial capital) for the annual competition, there were so many of them that they were sometimes put up in the jail[10].

Affectionate attachments

In 1915, Mahmud was five. It was a year of famine and disease. A meningitis epidemic struck Rufa'a – meningitis was called "the axeman". Mahmud's mother was struck down and died. On a rainy day, Muhammad Taha took the children by camel to Heglig, away from Rufa'a's sad memories. Mahmud stayed there until his father died in 1920. Then, the children were taken to live with their maternal grandmother, Zeinab Hamza, who lived with one of her sons in Rufa'a[11].

Mahmud himself would later tell people that he was brought up by someone called al-Rabb Biyjud, a name which translates as May God Be Bountiful. Anyone hearing her name in northern Sudan would guess that she was a slave. Slaves were captured in the south or the Nuba mountains, where people spoke African languages and followed Noble Spiritual Beliefs (otherwise called "paganism", "animism" or "African traditional religions" – this term is taken from Sudan's 1973 constitution). Their African names were replaced with Arabic names – Good Morning, or Rose, or Friday – often intended to make their Arabised, Muslim owners feel cheerful or pious. By the time Mahmud was born, a colonial law had abolished slavery, but the authorities encouraged slaves to stay with former owners, because some British officials believed that liberation would make slaves idle or licentious and seriously hamper agricultural production. Some underplayed the cruelty of slavery:

Between many of the Sudanese slaves and their Arab masters there
had developed in the course of years an affectionate attachment like
that which prevailed between the Negroes in the southern states of
the USA and their owner[12].

Al-Rabb Biyjud was a *dada* in Sudanese Arabic, a "mammy" in southern
US English. When Mahmud was a boy, she was reportedly young and
beautiful, with no family but Mahmud and his siblings. She called
Mahmud *al-darraj* (an unobtrusive helper) because he would help a
rheumatic aunt with her walking. Mahmud believed in later life that she
sacrificed the chance of marriage in order to devote herself to him and
his brothers and sisters. According to Mahmud's daughter:

> He [Mahmud] called her *ummi* [my mother]. She gave up her life
> altogether when the *ustaz*'s mother died. She preferred to live and
> bring up the *ustaz* and his brother and sisters ... she said that if she had
> married a man, he might not have treated them well. She lived her life,
> all of it, for them. The *ustaz* respected her very much and considered
> her his mother, no-one else was his mother[13].

Al-Rabb Biyjud fasted and prayed as a Muslim[14]. She lived with Mahmud
until she died in the 1970s, and he buried her himself.

Mahmud and the Rikabiya tribe

Mahmud acknowledged to a close friend and follower, Ibrahim Yusuf,
that the death of his parents and his experience as a boy farmer made
him depend on himself[15]. Perhaps this emotional independence helped
him develop novel ideas about society and religion, and helped him to
stand up for his ideas when they were repeatedly challenged. Yet his early
years brought him into the rituals and collectivities of the rural Sudan,
and gave him a rural boy's sense of loyalty to place. The death of parents
did not necessarily interrupt this process[16].

Mahmud had his face scarred with the markings of his Rikabiya tribe,
three roughly vertical lines on each cheek. These scars, called *shillukh*,
appear in the pharaonic art of Sudan and had a complex of meanings
– ornamentation, tribal identification or affiliation to a particular Sufi
tariqa[17]. In the nineteenth century, when Arabised ethnic groups increased
in prestige, and some non-Arabised groups were routinely enslaved, the
shillukh of Arab groups became a mark of belonging to a tribe that was
free from the fear of slavery[18].

After the 1950s few northern Sudanese were marked with the tribal *shillukh*. But when Mahmud was a boy, tribes were important because the British-dominated colonial government controlled rural populations by promoting the authoritarian potential of tribal leaderships, sometimes foisting new tribal identities on small groups, or rewarding obedient notables with tribal chiefdoms[19].

Mahmud's tribe was not a colonial invention, however. Its genealogy goes back to the fourteenth century when Ghulamallah ibn 'A'id, claiming descent from the prophet Muhammad, came to Dongola in the far Nubian north. His descendants included Muhammad 'Abd al-Sadig, one of the first Sufis in Sudan; and Hasan wad Bilayl, a Dongola miracle worker who was Mahmud's ancestor. The Rikabiya people had a history of migration, and their presence in the rangelands of the Butana goes back to 'Abd al-Sadig's day. In the early eighteenth century the Rikabiya may have been strong enough to make a bid to dominate the Butana, a sparsely populated area about the size of Ireland, but the lands came under the sway of Shukriya tribe, who claimed to have origins as Arabian camel-nomads and who dominated the area until Mahmud's day[20]. The Rikabiya still had prestige, because of their claim to be descended from the prophet and because 'Abd al-Sadig's own progeny led a *tariga* called the Sadigab[21].

The *khalwa*

Around the time that his mother died, Mahmud entered the *khalwa* as a pupil. Probably he attended two, a main one in Rufa'a and another in Heglig in the rainy season[22]. The *khalwa* was run by a *faki*, a man with some knowledge of the Qur'an[23]. *Faki*s were given food by the villagers, and some had small-holdings which their pupils helped to farm. The Qur'anic text supplemented their income in other ways – they sold verses as charms, they inked verses on a wooden slate and washed them off, selling the washings as medicine[24]. Like kindergartens, *khalwa*s give men their first memories: the fire that was built in the brief chill before dawn, to light the wood-slates where the boys wrote with pens made of sorghum stalks and memorised their lessons; the *faki*'s blows when they made mistakes. Boys learned to weed fields and say their prayers, and they would be let off learning altogether at harvest, when they worked their fathers' fields[25].

The first year or two of *khalwa* is sometimes called "the bitter course" because pupils are hit for each mistake. Mahmud may have passed beyond the blows to the stage of memorising the Qur'an – he was bright and religiously inclined. Although he never claimed to have memorised the whole book, he always recited the Qur'an from memory when speaking in public, and scarcely wrote a page without quoting it.

But Qur'anic learning was not the main point of the *khalwa*. It initiated boys into communal work and social hierarchy[26]. Colonial authorities had little respect for the education offered in *khalwa*s, although they eventually used them as a cheap method of extending pre-school education. Some officials recognised the *khalwa*'s function as a place for children to be socialised. "A *khalwa* is valueless, we are told, for education, but it surely has some value as a school for manners", wrote Rufa'a's assistant district commissioner (DC) in 1934[27]. When the British came to Sudan, they counted 68 *khalwa*s in Rufa'a district alone[28].

Mahmud's earliest feelings about all this religion are not clear. Sayyida Lutfi, his sister-in-law, and a near witness to Mahmud's childhood, does not remember any more than perfunctory religious observances:

> Only old people belonged to *tariga*s in those days. An old person, when he got old, would go on the pilgrimage [to Mecca], would go to the *tariga* and the prayer sessions. The father would not force his son to go to his *tariga*. All our boys were polite and said their prayers and fasted[29].

According to Mahmud's sister-in-law, Sayyida Lutfi, Mahmud was a respectful youngster, always asking permission to go out to wedding parties. He would not lie nor let his friends lie to protect him[30].

Mahmud and Muhammad

Rural education was based on a religious text, but in a largely illiterate society there were other ways of communicating religious belief. The prophet Muhammad appeared in dreams and he was invoked in ardent hymns and ecstatic dances. Even his sandals appeared as a formalised squiggle on the pupil's slate in the *khalwa*. The prophet's birthday was celebrated, with all the *tariga*s of the town setting up tents where the *shaykh* would sit and receive his guests. Boys recited the Qur'an, ate sweets, and speeches were made in classical Arabic[31].

Like many groups in Sudan, the Sadigab clan of the Rikabiya claimed the prophet as their ancestor. At the *mi'raj*, a celebration of Muhammad's night journey to heaven, Sadigab tradition involved a trip to Faw mountain in the Butana to repeat the formula "There is no god but God," 70,000 times, in the hope that one time it would be said purely, and their praise would be accepted. A handful of the most devout would have themselves incarcerated in stifling little mud enclosures and abstain for ten days from food, drink and sleep. Then they would go back to the Sadigab *masid* (a Sudanese word for a religious centre) and stand in a big circle for *zikr* (repetition of the name of God). They would almost bend double, so the word "God" was pronounced as a grunting cry from their insides[32].

After the ceremonies, people would sing hymns about the glories of *wali*s, saintly departed *shaykh*s. Their tombs would be visited for prayer – one of the few openings for women to participate in Sufi practices. One *wali* was *shaykh* Taha wad 'Abd al-Sadig, the Sadigab leader, who died in the 1915 meningitis epidemic that took the life of Taha's mother. His followers built a domed tomb for him in Rufa'a – he was the last to die in that epidemic, and some believed his death had killed "the axeman", meningitis[33]. Although he was very young when *shaykh* Taha died, Mahmud recalled *shaykh* Taha's death in the last speech of his life, saying it had redeemed his followers from the power of disease[34].

One source for the history of Rufa'a at this time is Babikr Bedri. His chatty and shrewd memoirs depict him as a devout Muslim and daredevil soldier in the Mahdist armies, as well as a sometimes cynical observer of Sufi devotion. The Anglo-Egyptian administrators believed that the *faki*s were fanatics who could stir their followers to Mahdist rebellion and they tried to limit their influence, but they were careful to respect religious observances. When a woman in Rufa'a had a vision of a *wali* standing in the grounds of the district commissioner's house, she wanted to build a shrine there. The DC contacted Bedri, who paid the woman to have a vision in a less important place[35]. Bedri did not like it when his rakish brother Yusuf found religion and devoted his life to meditation on the mystical names of God. He would have preferred for his brother to go back to his drink and women. His brother-in-law Abu Zayd kept up with the Names, went mad and killed a slave girl[36].

Sufism in Rufa'a linked tribes, religion, education and even madness – it was central to everyday culture. It is difficult to trace Mahmud's relationship with Sufism in his early life, but it played an enormous part in his later life. He looked to *wali*s for guidance and came to believe that the prophet personally directed his meditation.

Land and food

The Nile allowed for sedentary farming and in Heglig, ten kilometres from the river, farmers could live somewhat precariously off the rains. Colonial authorities pressured farmers to increase production for the export economy they were trying to develop. But fluctuating yields led to a famine around 1914, just before Mahmud's mother died. In Rufa'a, Babikr Bedri met a farmer starved out of his wits. The Sudan government had to draw on Indian stocks of corn to provide seed for farmers, and some merchants made fortunes out of the price changes[37].

Mahmud, his father, and his father's slaves farmed the Heglig rainlands in the rainy season in the years after his mother's death and the famine, raising fodder and sorghum, harvesting at the end of the rains. Sorghum prices fell by more than half in the year after the famine, and everyone could eat in "the twenty year", when prices fell to twenty rials[38]. Mahmud enjoyed farming – he told Ibrahim Yusuf that it taught him self sufficiency – and he later won school prizes for gardening[39]. The food he grew was the food of plain subsistence, a food which he preferred to eat all his life, for its taste and its association with Sudan and with simplicity.

Sorghum was the staff of life for all the groups of the area, although the diet included pulses, green vegetables and dates. *Ful* beans, an Egyptian staple now widespread in Sudan's Nile valley, were more expensive than meat in some areas[40]. The diet was based around *kisra* and *mulah*, a stew usually based on dried fermented okra. The widespread use of fermented foods is a mark of the west African influence on Sudanese food, according to Dirar, a Sudanese nutritionist. In the nineteenth century, colonialists brought new foods to Sudan that now make up the diet of modern Khartoum – wheat bread, *ful* beans, salads, and Egyptian-style meat and onion stew. This diet was little known in rural Sudan at the start of the century, but it was spread through big colonial institutions (like schools and railways) and then enthusiastically promoted by the Sudanese elite which took over the country in 1956.

Dirar's history of indigenous foods shows how Middle Eastern foods with prestigious imperial connections became the food of the elite and began to encroach on the diet of ordinary people in the course of the twentieth century[41]. This interplay between the Middle Eastern and the African is one of the central dynamics of Sudanese history, and the power imbalances it generates have skewed relationships between individuals and between groups. Mahmud's tastes were fixed at a young age – his favourite food was *kisra* and *mulah*, the simplest meal of the village. In later life, he seems to have preferred it because it was poor man's food, and he had ascetic preferences[42]. Although he lived his life at the fringe of an urban elite, he kept to the tastes of his rural childhood.

Conclusion

Mahmud was born just after the brutal nineteenth century turned into the tumultuous twentieth. But his older acquaintances who reminisced about Heglig and Rufa'a remember it as warm and old-fashioned. The hospitality and poverty, the religion and the farming, the smell of incense and smouldering sandalwood: all crop up in their memories. They did not talk so much about the famines, the winners and losers of the newly internationalised agricultural market, and the former slaves still tied to their employers. And any redeeming flaws that the young Mahmud may have had are forgotten in a later haze of saintliness and eminence.

Mahmud's home, farm, school and religious beliefs all brought him in contact with a wider world – the world of Africa, the Middle East, Islam and European imperialism. He retained many of the tastes, values and relationships of his early life. He associated them with the goodness of simplicity, and when he later turned ascetic, he returned to those tastes and values for inspiration. However, the material simplicity, and local forms of allegiance and association of this time and place could be deceptive. Perhaps the colonisers were deceived by simplicity too – their understanding of rural Sudan was based around static ethnic and religious stereotypes. But Taha's society was anything but static – it had passed through a century of violent and confusing social change, and was being jerked into a world where money infiltrated every transaction, and class every relationship. The next chapter tries to explain the enormous changes that Mahmud's world was undergoing.

Until now, Mahmud Muhammad Taha has been called Mahmud, to distinguish him from his father – Sudanese people have patronymic surnames. With his father's death behind him, he will now be called Taha.

Chapter 2

Sudan from 1500–1900

This chapter looks at Sudanese society between 1500 and 1910. It concentrates on the northern Nile valley, where Taha was born, and relates that area to the rest of Sudan, Africa and the Middle East

Pre-colonial Sudan

Since pharaonic times, the Nile valley has had centralised states, but from then until Taha's day, other groups maintained small-scale subsistence societies outside the state. In the sixteenth century, a group known as the Funj set up an agrarian state in the northern Nile valley. Funj trade, in slaves and exotic goods, developed towards Mediterranean markets, and their rulers began to adopt its Islamic forms. Funj sultans garnered the support of Arab settlers in Sudan, and converted to Islam. They used Islamic symbolism to enhance their prestige, but their monopoly trading system was not based on *shari'a* law. Muslim merchants introduced *shari'a* courts to deal with commercial disputes in the early seventeenth century: their independent jurisdiction helped weaken Funj power[1].

Darfur in the west had a stratified society and central authority from the seventeenth century. It had ethnic, Islamic religious and trading links with west Africa, but gradually was drawn into the Nile valley and the Mediterranean periphery as its trade with Egypt, dominated by slaves, became economically important. The slaves were captured by huge state sanctioned expeditions, in the western plateau of south Sudan, called Dar Fertit, an area inhabited by stateless tribes[2]. The Azande state, whose border lay on the Congo-Nile watershed, appeared in the seventeenth century[3]. Although it had slaving interests, it played no part in the Mediterranean system, and had no affiliation to Islam.

The small-scale societies that surrounded these states were often defined by slavery. Tribal names like Nuba, Berti, and Bergu come from a word in the tribal language for slave[4]. These groups often succeeded when isolated from state power, behind swamps and in highlands. Local histories describe how similar communities adopted state forms to protect themselves from the encroachments of the state slavers of the Funj and Darfur[5].

Islam in the northern Nile valley

Some small-scale communities followed their own Noble Spiritual Beliefs, but Sudanese state elites adopted the prestigious religions of the Middle East. Sometimes, their devotion was only nominal – the Muslim Funj rulers only respected *shari'a* enough to eat pork in secret, while their subjects ate it in public[6]. The Islam that engaged most religious imaginations in Sudan was a Sufi religion of miracles and dances, although *shari'a* was always part of the scene.

Ghulamallah ibn 'A'id was a Yemeni who claimed descent from the prophet, and one of the earliest Muslim names in Sudanese history. He arrived in the fourteenth century and taught Islamic studies in the far north of Sudan. His son Rubat was the forebear of four brothers, the sons of Jabir, who had a school for *shari'a* in the late sixteenth century[7]. Jabir's grandson Muhammad Sughayirun was invited by a Funj sultan to start a school for Islamic studies in the Funj territories[8]. Another of Ghulamallah's sons, Rikab, gave his name to Taha's Rikabiya tribe. His descendants included Muhammad 'Abd al-Sadig, a sixteenth century contemporary of the sons of Jabir and founder of the Sadigab *tariqa* at Mundara, some 120 kilometres east of Rufa'a in the Butana. One of Rikab's descendants was Hasan wad Bilayl, a Dongola miracle worker who founded Taha's Rikabi clan, the Bilaylab.

Elephant tamer, avid polygamist and man of prayer, Muhammad 'Abd al-Sadig was sharply distinguished from his *shari'a* cousins. Like other flamboyant Sufis, he was a *malamati* (blame-seeker), who committed outrageous sins in order to be condemned by the world, thereby increasing their dependence on God. The *Tabaqat*, an eighteenth century biographical dictionary and one of the oldest Sudanese textual sources, stresses the antagonism between legists and Sufis in its account of his life. One of 'Abd al-Sadig's outrages was to marry over ninety women including two sisters, in defiance of *shari'a*. A *shari'a* judge named Dushayn declared the marriage null.

When *shaykh* al-Hamim came to the Friday service in Arbaji, justice
Dushayn declared his opposition ... [he said] "You have married five
and six and seven. All this has not been enough for you. And now you
marry two sisters at the same time." The *shaykh* said "What do you
intend to do?" The Judge said, "I intend to dissolve your marriage
because you have defied God's book and the Way of the Messenger
of Allah, Peace and Blessings of Allah be upon him." The *shaykh* said,
"The Messenger of Allah has given me his permission"[9].

The *Tabaqat* lets 'Abd al-Sadig keep his wives, and gives the judge
a nasty rash. "This negative view of the judge reveals a clear bias of
the popular mind in favour of the Sufi institution and its *shaykhs*,"
comments Mahmoud[10]. In the *Tabaqat* 'Abd al-Sadig represents Sudan's
Sufi mainstream against the interlopers of the *shari'a* tradition. However,
other Sufi contemporaries, like Idris wad Arbab, condemned his
malpractices[11].

*Tariga*s thrived under the Funj. The Blue Nile, Taha's birthplace,
was home to many of the localised *tariga*s that benefited from Funj
patronage[12]. Their education and mediation services attracted followers,
and their centres became linked to trade routes. Some Sufi families
enriched themselves through trade and landowning at this time –
asceticism was often a virtue of the *tariga* founder not inherited by his
sons[13]. The trade and "worldliness" of these mystical groups opened
them up to the greater Arab and Islamic world, and gave a distinctive
character to northern riverain Sudan.

The end of the Funj sultanate

By the early nineteenth century, the Funj state had begun a process
of affiliation with the wider Muslim world. In the Nile valley, this was
accompanied with a sense that Arab lineage was a mark of prestige. When
the Funj state began to disintegrate in the eighteenth century, tribes,
merchants and holy men acquired more political power, and the tribes
that dealt best with the breakdown of central authority were nomads
who claimed Arab origins, such as the Shukriya of Rufa'a[14]. Following
the nomad example, sedentary and urban groups began to ascribe to
themselves Arab ancestry, and the idea of a past Sudan roamed by
rugged nomads with pious ancestors began to take hold.

Groups which claimed Arab lineage increased in prestige, as
other groups lost it. Ethnic differences acquired new socio-economic
importance, closely associated with slavery and freedom. Merchants

began to share the privilege of slave-ownership with the Funj elite, and the ideology of slavery was adjusted to allow for this. Slave owners became concerned with defining just who could be made a slave, a preoccupation of Islamic jurisprudence, which does not allow the enslavement of free Muslims. Arabness, skin colour, and Islam all acted as charms against enslavement, and the Muslims of the north "created derogatory ethnic labels to refer to non-Muslim groups in the south"[15].

The Turkiya 1820–1885

In 1820, invading Ottomans from Egypt overthrew the collapsing Funj state and occupied the northern Nile valley and parts of the south (they occupied Darfur for eleven years from 1874). The Turkiya (as the regime was known) was intended as a modern African colony providing gold and slaves for Egypt's economic development. It brought Sudan closer to the markets and societies of the Middle East, and entrenched class and ethnic distinctions through an economic policy based on the commercialisation of slavery, commoditisation of land and through the spread of cash transactions. It negotiated its authority over the Arabised Muslim population of the north in Islamic terms, importing prestigious Middle Eastern forms of Islam and setting up *shari'a* institutions to challenge the power of the *tariqa*s. *Shari'a* forbade the enslavement of Muslims, so Turkiya slavers took their human booty from the diverse, small-scale non-Muslim societies of the south. Sudan was divided into "a juristically Islamic, directly-administered northern zone and an anarchic southern slave-catchment area"[16]. Egypt imported slaves, but they also flooded into the north, and became the mainstay of its production, where previously they had been a domestic luxury for royals and merchants[17].

Slaves and cash

In the north, Arabised Muslims contended with dramatically changed agricultural systems of production. Farmers without access to cash sold previously inalienable land to cash-rich merchants with Turkiya connections, in order to meet new demands for cash taxation[18]. *Shari'a* inheritance law divided and individuated rural land, and this also facilitated land commoditisation[19]. Merchants used the *shayl,* a usurious form of agricultural credit, to bring free peasants into debt-dependence, and sometimes replaced landless peasants with wageless slaves[20]. The militarised atmosphere and the changes in agrarian life impelled many farmers to leave the land-poor area of the far north and work as slavers or petty traders. They were called *jallaba*, and their migration fuelled the demand for slave labour. Shuqayr, a witness to the Turkiya, explains:

> When the Egyptian soldiers came to Sudan with their firearms, gunpowder began to be used much more. A single Arab could terrify a whole tribe of blacks with a rifle ... raiding and capturing blacks became the trade of many[21].

Unlike the far north, Taha's Blue Nile region had vast tracts of land needing cultivators, and few indigenous people emigrated. However, many Ja'alis (a tribe heavily affected by the commoditisation of their formerly communal lands in the north) were given land by the local notables in Rufa'a, the Abu Sinn family of the semi-nomadic Shukriya tribe, based in the Butana rangelands[22]. Indeed, Daym Graydab, Taha's Rufa'a home, was named after one of these Ja'ali groups[23]. But many Ja'alis joined, and eventually supplanted, the European entrepreneurs who took over the state's slaving work in the south after 1850. It took ten years of furious violence for them to establish the *zariba* system, a network of trading and slaving stations owned by merchant houses in Khartoum.

The Turkiya had chosen the frontier between Islam and the Noble Spiritual Beliefs as an ideological dividing line between slavery and freedom. But for Sudanese Muslims from the Arabised villages of the Nile, this ideological divide was constructed from ethnicity as well as religion. A ruling of the caliph 'Umar (d 644) against enslaving Arabs was touted as a guarantee of freedom for people who claimed Arab ancestry, and "Arabs" packed their genealogies when they travelled, to show to anyone trying to capture them[24]. The *shillukh* or tribal markings acquired new senses – by identifying a face as Arab and not "black", they became a charm against enslavement[25]. Islam legitimated the violence – even *zariba*s owned by Egyptian Christians flew banners with Qur'anic exhortations to *jihad*, or religiously justified warfare. (Most interpretations of *shari'a* allow the enslavement of captives taken in a *jihad*)[26].

The slaves left little testimony. Like Shuqayr (quoted above), some captured slaves cited the military superiority of the slavers as the reason for their capture[27]. Slaves also recorded their thirsty captive trek to market[28]. When slaves were sold, their treatment might improve markedly – usually it did not. Women slaves who bore children to their masters had some status, but others could be forced into prostitution, providing entertainment, cash and slave children for masters[29]. Slaves were given strange names, some ironic, like Lucky, or some free of irony, like Sea of Lusts[30]. Slaves were often taken as tax and were sometimes left unburied at death to save money[31].

In Rufaʿa, by the end of the nineteenth century, almost all households had slaves, and they performed much of the agricultural work. When Taha was a boy, slavery was legally abolished although many slaves stayed and worked in their masters' homes without wages – runaways were officially pressured to return to their masters. Slave owners even used manumission – frequently mandated by *shariʿa* – against their slaves, as a cheap pension-scheme. When slaves were too old to work, they were freed to fend for themselves, their owners receiving spiritual benefits and saving the cost of the slaves' upkeep[32].

The slave trade helped to entrench colour prejudice in Sudan. Nineteenth century travellers described local colour distinctions: "blues" had the darkest purply shine to their skin while "yellows" had the lightest colour[33]. The Funj were a dark skinned elite, but by the colonial period, the Mediterranean premium on fairer skins became clear from an unhappily precise measure – the price of female slaves, which depended on age, beauty and colour. Muslim slave-owners paid high prices for lighter skins[34]. In Turkiya Sudan fair-skinned women cost 20-70% more than their dark-skinned sisters[35].

Kissing cousins

In the first years of Islam, *shariʿa* rules transformed Arabian society with the practices of the metropolitan near east. These ancient cities based their economies on individual property rights, and required female chastity in order to safeguard inheritance. The prophet Muhammad mandated a form of their patrilineal marriage and inheritance law, whose individuation of property served capital accumulation[36]. According to Tillion, the aim of Muhammad's laws was not to oppress women but to destroy the tribe "and thus to equalize, modernize, revolutionize and democratize Arab society"[37]. Endogamy (cousin marriage), says Tillion, was the principal strategy by which tribes attempted to circumvent the revolutionary effects of *shariʿa* inheritance law on their common ownership of capital. Kissing cousins kept land in the family.

Northern riverain Sudan is now an area where endogamy is widely practised, but endogamy may be a relatively new phenomenon. Spaulding argues that as *shariʿa* law spread in the last days of the Funj, women were gradually excluded from landholding[38]. Elsewhere, he shows that marriage preferences in one small community in the late 1860s were decidedly exogamous, while in the twentieth century endogamy became the norm[39]. A study of Sudanese folk-tales showed that the most widespread fairy tale reported by Sudanese students interviewing village grandmothers was that of Fatma the Beautiful. Fatma's parents ask her to marry her own brother. She runs away with all the girls of the village, telling them that the men of the village had decided to marry each girl to her brother, and after long adventures, marries a kind young man[40]. Fatma's parents propose a dramatic solution to the problem of excessive sub-division of inherited land, and the whole story explores the boundaries of marriage for children to reflect on. This little skit on endogamy, land and love is related to the need to protect land that has become the commodity of an individual, and perhaps this need came about as a result of the Turkiya.

Official Islam

The Turkiya regime in Sudan was Africa's first colonial state. Like the European colonisers after them, the Turkiya claimed to provide dignified cultural standards and just laws that Africans had not managed to provide for themselves. This culture and law was needed to justify the confiscation of wealth to fund a state apparatus, and it implied new class divisions. The religious policy of the Turkiya was part of this justification; it imposed official Ottoman Islam, based on the *shari'a* tradition. Turkiya *shari'a* courts jeopardised the religious authority of Sufi *shaykh*s, but *shari'a* extended slave and land ownership and enriched the merchants who had pressed *shari'a* commercial law on the Funj state[41].

Shari'a jurisdiction was slowly extended from Turkiya personnel to Sudanese Muslims[42]. However, *shari'a* law has some drawbacks for colonial administrators: its very high evidentiary standards protect defendents and sometimes thwart prosecutors; and its regulation of credit and commerce restricts the accumulation of capital. For that reason, the Ottoman empire began to modify *shari'a* rules in the nineteenth century with legal content drawn from western legal traditions in order to reconfigure economic power in their empire, and allow for its integration into the world markets created by western empires. Like subsequent European colonial states, the Turkiya used discrete legal systems for the centre and the hinterlands. Muslim subjects of the centre were ruled by *shari'a* and by new, non-*shari'a* legislation. In the hinterland of its Sudanese colony, the Turkiya ruled through chiefs, turned into taxmen by the new administration[43]. It made tribes into commodities, selling hereditary chiefships to slavers and merchants with access to cash[44]. Funj Sudan had had more informal styles of rural community leadership under centrally appointed overlords[45].

Mamdani, discussing the nature of colonial states in Africa, uses South Africa's apartheid state as a model. This model promised, in the words of Cecil Rhodes, "equal rights for all civilised men" – and secondary rights for those classed as uncivilised[46]. It produced a "bifurcated state", a state where the "citizens" of the directly ruled centre attained rights assigned by new laws, while the "subjects" of the countryside were ruled indirectly. Instead of legally assigned rights, they had "decentralized despotism" – traditional tribal leaderships reconstituted as hierarchies under the colonial government[47]. This bifurcation, argues Mamdani, has been inherited by the post-colonial state, and its effects will be examined in subsequent chapters.

The book and the law

"Decentralized despotism" was to some extent a colonial innovation. In Sudan, the colonialists used Islamic and local law and custom to buttress its authority. The state ruled using a version of *shari'a* from the Middle Eastern metropole, that accommodated the needs of the state, that spoke to the religious and cultural aspirations of some influential Sudanese, and that could incorporate foreign legal material when that was economically necessary. In Sudan, that version of *shari'a* was anything but conservative. It thoroughly revolutionised economic and social relationships, in order to serve the economic and military demands of the Egyptian state.

Turkiya Islam brought a range of new practices to Sudan – warfare for the faith, and slave-ownership as the right of an ordinary Muslim. They made *shari'a* part of the idiom of the state, as El Zubeir Rahma, a slaver who controlled much of the south and eventually controlled Darfur, makes clear:

> I became king there ... and I ruled over the land in accordance with the Book and the law of Mohammed. I then undertook the civilisation of the country, making it fit for habitation, and causing it to progress along the paths of commerce and peace[48].

The idea that "The Book and the law of Mohammed" legitimated a state, however predatory, was crucial to Turkiya ideology, but was not crucial in pre-colonial Sudan. When Sudanese opponents of the Turkiya began to resist it, they did not criticise the self-serving nature of Turkiya law; they preferred to criticise the fact that the Turkiya did not keep to the letter of *shari'a*. For example, the regime permitted usury and imposed a poll tax on Muslims, in defiance of *shari'a*, which applies it to non-Muslims only. This point was stressed by the Mahdi, who eventually overthrew the Turkiya and its "evil legists"[49]. He was not the last Sudanese to use Islamic correctness to challenge the state.

The first successful challenge to Turkiya rule came after the regime threatened the survival of its central economic institution – slavery. In the 1870s, the Egyptian khedive, at the urging of Christian, commercial and humanitarian interests in Europe, began to repress the slave trade. European governors in the south destroyed the *zariba* system, and the defeated *jallaba* began to search for a leader.

The Mahdiya, 1881–1898

Muhammad Ahmad al-Mahdi successfully seized control of the apparatus of the modern state built by the Turkiya. He used a version of Islam that drew on contemporary, back-to-the-scriptures reform movements, Nile valley Sufism, but also on millenarian versions of Islam that were popular in west Africa. He used organisational methods that had been pioneered by new Sufi groups in Sudan. He managed to unite the aspirations of disaffected groups from the Nile valley and the west: bankrupted traders and slavers, marginalised Sufi leaders, over-taxed peasants and pastoralists, westerners and Nile valley people turning to religion after sixty years of violent economic and social change.

Islamic reform movements

The eighteenth and nineteenth centuries saw Islamic reform movements in Muslim societies linked to Sudan. The Arabian reformer Muhammad 'Abd al-Wahhab (1703–1792), helped a military leadership unify local tribes and conquer Arabia. 'Abd al-Wahhab's version of Islam challenged official Ottoman religion with a call to return to the textual sources of Islam. His rigorist interpretation of the scriptures stressed the invincibility of the law and influenced Islamic studies in Mecca, a meeting place for scholars and Sufis from all over the world. African Sufis in Mecca returned home to use 'Abd al-Wahhab's idea of allegiance to a saving law to build new political structures in West Africa. Their laws offered guarantees against enslavement for Muslims in the age of the Atlantic slavery[50]. At the beginning of the nineteenth century the economic hopes of marginalised tribes were mobilised by reformers' denunciations of non-Islamic or partially Islamised societies to begin a century of *jihad* across West Africa. The resulting wars used the ideology of a pristine Islam to create a state and enslave people who failed to meet the state's definition of Islamic correctness. These wars created Islamic states based on a slave mode of production across sudanic Africa (the belt running south of the Sahara between Sudan and the Atlantic).

However, Sudanic reformers differed from 'Abd al-Wahhab in that their legitimacy was not based on book-knowledge alone, but also on mystical visions, where Sufi saints of the past girded them with swords ('Abd al-Wahhab was hostile to Sufism)[51]. Islamic mystical experience encouraged millenarian expectations across sudanic Africa during the nineteenth century[52]. More activist forms of Mahdism encouraged migration to the east, seen as a parallel to the prophet's migration to Medina and an effective expression of dissent. One of these migrants was probably the great-grandfather of 'Abdullahi al-Ta'ayshi, a West African who had attached himself to one of the Baggara tribes. The Baggara are Arabised, Muslim cattle nomads who lived on the borderlands between north and south Sudan. Al-Ta'ayshi was a man in search of a deliverer. He first thought that El Zubeir Rahma Mansur, the slaver and conqueror of Darfur, would save him: El Zubeir rejected him. A few years later he went to join Muhammad Ahmad's *tariqa*.

Muhammad Ahmad was a Sufi shaykh from a Nile valley *tariqa* at a time when the power of local Sufi leaderships were being challenged by Turkiya religion and by the rise of new, literate, centralising *tariqa*s (see below). He told a *shaykh* of his own *tariqa* that he was the Mahdi, but that claim had been spurned[53]. He then began to seek the support of religious families in Kordofan for his claims. In 1881, 'Abdullahi al-Ta'ayshi acclaimed him as the Mahdi and helped him to mobilise disaffected Western tribes and other supporters to challenge the state.

Moon of my nights

The Mahdi successfully exploited the millenarian themes of west African Islam, but also deployed new understandings of Islam that had become part of Sudanese life. Sudanese Sufism, like that of other peripheral Islamic societies, was a vernacular religion which used the charismatic appeal of the *shaykh*, and behind him the prophet, to engage with people's hopes. Early Sufi theosophists had interpreted the person of Muhammad as a pre-existent creative emanation of God, and this theme was turned into ardent love poetry that enjoyed a vogue across the northern half of Africa[54]. These poems became popular in the thirteenth century, but according to al-Bashir, the earliest Sufi poetry in Sudan celebrated the charisma of local *shaykh*s, rather than that of the prophet. One woman poet wrote in colloquial Sudanese Arabic of her longing to visit Mecca with her *shaykh*, Sharf al-Din wad al-'Araki:

> Sharf al-Din I live by God and you,
> who touched the [prophet's] window with your hand
> oh let me be the sole of your shoe
> and blessed by you each day[55].

Al-Bashir argues that Sudanese poets adopted classical Arabic in the nineteenth century, when passion for the *shaykh* deferred to a more "orthodox" passion for the prophet Muhammad. Songs celebrated the prophet as "lord of being", "the light" and "the guider", part of an emotional repertoire which allowed people to link their deepest feelings to their sense of the prophet's presence in their lives[56]. This change happened as the Turkiya brought Sudan under the influence of metropolitan Middle Eastern religion.

Devotion to the prophet instead of to the *shaykh* was not, however, a consequence of Turkiya policy. Indeed, the Turkiya adopted a hostile attitude towards Sufi song, as one poet complained:

> Listen and see, oh audience
> they [Turkish rulers] said don't praise the Chosen [Prophet
> Muhammad][57].

Although Sufism was promoted in other parts of the Ottoman empire, it was repressed in its Sudanese colony. Perhaps the Turkiya, trying to mediate religion through the colonial state and its *shari'a* law, was agitated by the claims of other mediators, even the prophet:

> The moon of my nights has a delighted forehead,
> he has deep-black and large eyes and split teeth.
> His nose is straight like a sword
> and his neck is more beautiful than that of the gazelle[58].

What brought Sudanese Sufism out of its parochialism was not so much the arrival of *shari'a* courts, as a new development within Sufism. Holy families with their local power bases were vulnerable to advocates of a more literate Islam. The challenge came in the nineteenth century with the introduction of centralised Sufi *tariqa*s to the northern Nile valley. Activist, literate, missionary and with some prestigious Meccan connections, these groups had come under the influence of Ahmad ibn Idris (d 1837), a Moroccan based in Mecca. His movement tried to invigorate folk-Sufism with the textual tradition of Islam. The movement made Sudan into a country where writing could be an full time job: the Majdhub family of reformers wrote prolifically in the nineteenth century and in the twentieth century some family members produced some of Sudan's most famous secular poetry[59].

The new Sufis successfully challenged the locally organised *tariqa*s in Sudan, with their parochialism and latitudinarian tolerance for non-Islamic behaviour. The most important of these new *tariqa*s was the Khatmiya, founded by Muhammad 'Uthman al-Mirghani (1793–1852) in the 1820s. He set up a network of followers through marriage alliances, mosque-building and indefatigable propaganda. His *tariqa* was different from the older ones because it spread across the Nile valley and the east of the country while retaining central control. This centralised, well connected group was able to communicate effectively with the Turkiya authorities, while smaller groups were politically marginalised.

The Sufi leaderships of the Nile valley were custodians of its Arabised and Islamic culture. They were initially hostile to the Mahdi's millenarianism, and responded equivocally and tardily to the Mahdi's call. But he managed to include some of them in his coalition, building a set of links between western Sudan and the northern Nile valley that was important for the nationalist movement in the twentieth century. The Mahdi mobilised the military power of tribes like the Baggara, who were overtaxed by the state but had probably never thought of taking it over. He promised the uprooted *jallaba* that he would reinstate the slave trade, whose abolition had crippled the Turkiya system[60]. In 1885 he took Khartoum.

The Mahdist state

The Mahdi died six months after his triumph. His was succeeded by 'Abdullahi al-Ta'ayshi, who inherited the institutions of the old regime and built an independent Sudanese state which survived for 12 years in the rush of the European scramble for Africa. Al-Ta'ayshi needed to co-ordinate the Mahdi's disparate coalition, and put down localised resistance in the Nuba mountains, and the western borderlands of Darfur and Dar Masalit[61]. Tribal leaders or even whole tribes of doubtful loyalty were controlled by a policy of forced migration. Al-Ta'ayshi's own nomadic Ta'aysha tribe were forcibly displaced to Omdurman where initially they depended parasitically on the sedentary population. This caused tensions with the most reluctant members of the Mahdist coalition, the riverain tribes. These highly Arabised and Islamised groups had been developing into Sudan's elite, but now they were supplanted by a group of nomads from a tribe of low status[62]. In 1891 al-Ta'ayshi had to suppress a coup attempt led by the Mahdi's family, who led the riverain tribes.

Al-Ta'ayshi maintained the momentum of the Mahdist revolution with a series of *jihad*s against neighbouring states. But this ended in 1889 when an invading Mahdist army was routed just over the Egyptian border. Defeat in Egypt and a great famine sapped the regime, which became increasingly identified with al-Ta'ayshi's family. Tribal deportations ceased, and tribal autonomy returned to the periphery. In 1896, the Anglo-Egyptian regime in Sudan began to prepare for the reconquest of Sudan, reaching Omdurman in 1898.

Reconfiguring power

The Mahdiya entrenched the centrality of the state in the lives of ordinary Sudanese. The migrations that were a result of the commercialisation of agriculture in the Turkiya were replaced by more dramatic migrations by diktat. (Forced displacement subsequently became one of the main policy measures that the Sudanese state would use to discipline the people at its periphery). The regime weakened the tribes in order to strengthen the state, even ordering that the genealogies that had become the touchstone of tribal legitimacy be burnt[63]. Peripheral tribes with a history of autonomy, such as the Nuba and Masalit, were forced to submit. However, the Mahdiya was not able to extend its influence in the south. It made initial attempts to win the trust of southern tribal leaders through the release of slaves. It tried to carry on slave-raiding in the region, but eventually withdrew from the south because it was fighting border wars on so many different fronts[64].

Mahdiya military policy showed an adept understanding of state power, with a profusion of security forces. Only slave troops and bodyguards were allowed firearms, a means of controlling Sudan's huge army, estimated at 250,000 men[65]. Male slaves were a state monopoly[66].

The Mahdiya maintained the Turkiya tax bureaucracy, replacing Turkiya taxes with a two and a half percent tax on agricultural produce, inspired by the Qur'anic alms-tax, the *zakat*. Farmers also had to meet the food needs of marching armies. When the border wars abated and the state was consolidated after 1891, an additional ten percent tax was levied on merchandise[67]. Taxes and economic blockades by the regime's hostile neighbours weakened trade, but a market economy survived the Mahdiya.

The Mahdiya acknowledged the new forms of land ownership, even the enforced sales of Turkiya and maintained the state's powers over land use. The Mahdiya entrenched the state's control of finance and production, starting the first African indigenous mint[68]. It nationalised all shops, mills and oil presses, and monopolised all exports, buying Sudanese raw material at a discount and selling it high[69].

Cultural revolution

The Mahdi identified himself as a religious leader, and his version of Islam demanded a number of changes in Sudanese society. Women's slow disappearance from town life has been traced back to the last days of the Funj, and the Mahdi continued this process, imposing the veil on women. Women who took part in the rural economy could not work the fields and wear the veil, and slave women went unveiled as a mark of their inferior status, underlining the point that a working woman was a social shame. Divorce rights and freedom of movement for women were also restricted. The Mahdi prohibited jewellery, circumcision and marriage feasts, mourning, the ululation and wailing of women, and he fixed the bridewealth at two Egyptian pounds (£E)[70]. These social changes breached older traditions which involved women in landownership, production and community social events. They also brought their lives into line with the urban Islamic societies of the Middle East. Some societies resisted the intrusion of *shari'a* courts in their lives, but changing attitudes to women were taken up in unlikely places. The Baggara adopted the severest form of female circumcision in the late nineteenth century because of its prestigious associations[71]. The rite is still associated with Islam, Arabness and the urbanised centre of Sudan[72].

The uses of conformity

The Mahdi's religious policy followed the same centralising tendency of the Turkiya. The official liturgy bore his title: *ratib al-mahdi* (the prayer-book of the Mahdi). The Mahdi abolished the Sufi *tariqa*s and the schools of law, and those who rejected his Mahdiship were declared infidels. He changed the five pillars of the faith: the confession of faith included his name; and *jihad* took the place of pilgrimage to Mecca, which was forbidden.

The Mahdi was not the first person to try and build a centralised religious organisation. He had much to learn from the Turkiya's use of state controlled religion, and also from the centralising techniques of the Khatmiya *tariga*[73].

*Kafir*s and caliphs

For aspiring Muslim reformers in Sudan, the reconfiguration of religion needed new standards of Islamic correctness, drawn from religious texts. "Incorrect" Muslims could be stigmatised as unbelievers, and stripped of legal rights. This process has an Arabic name, *takfir*. Christians and Muslims used the fact that Southerners were not Muslims to justify their enslavement, but the term had banal uses too – it could sometimes liven up squabbles between *tariga*s. Al-Mirghani's Khatmiya used the term *kafir* (infidel) against *tariga*s like the Majdhubiya, who opposed the Turkiya[74]. Likewise, the Mahdi used it against his "Turks" and the slavers used it against their prey. *Takfir* marks the Islamising of discourse and the entry of textual standards of belief. It can be used to polarise society in order to build support for militant action and Islamic state formation. The Mahdi used *takfir* and the centralising potential of new *tariga*s to set up a national movement opposed to the Khatmiya, who were bitter enemies of the Mahdi from the beginning, and whose leadership spent the Mahdist period in Egyptian exile.

Like west African reformers, the Mahdi energised his call for a *shari'a* state with the fillip of mysticism. The Mahdi made fluent use of Sufi symbolism in his letters to Sufi leaders, which dwelt on asceticism, on the revival of the way of the prophet, and on his vision of the prophet calling him to the Mahdiship. He drew parallels between his own life and the prophet's. When he retreated to the west it was a *hijra*, like the prophet's migration to Medina; like the prophet, he called his followers *ansar*, and his deputies were *khalifa*s. Although the Mahdi used some of the themes of textually-correct religion, such as *takfir*, he relied also on the power of the vision where the prophet Muhammad girded him with a sword in the presence of Sufi saints, and told him to lead a *jihad*.

The Mahdiya falls to the British

By choosing the title of Mahdi, Muhammad Ahmad signalled to his followers that they were living at the end of time. His new ideology allowed him to substitute war for pilgrimage as a pillar of the faith. It allowed him to present the discontent of bankrupted traders, marginalised Sufi leaders and over-taxed peasants and pastoralists towards a complex, centralising state as a contest between light and darkness. But in the end, the state itself was the winner. Rural Sufi leaders conceded religious authority; Baggara pastoralists were deported en masse to the urban centre; merchants had their property nationalised; slavers had to sell to the treasury – in every case the state gained authority and coherence. The Mahdiya did not have the consolidation of the colonial state as a stated objective – its objective was to end time and usher in an era of justice. But the strengthening of the state was one of its main bequests to its conquering successors.

Irish republicans and British public school-boys

The Mahdiya was the first African state to expel a colonial power. This dramatic event made the Mahdi world famous. British leaderships had a strong antipathy for the Mahdiya, which they linked to the killing of Charles Gordon in the Mahdi's battle for Khartoum. Gordon was a British general in the service of the Egyptian khedive, whose heroism was a talisman for the British public school system, and a popular theme of Victorian empire literature. But the Mahdi drew other responses: the Muslim reformer al-Afghani in Paris used the Mahdi for anti-British polemic[75]. African-Americans vacillated between hate and admiration for the liberating slaver; the *New York Times* reported that Irish-Americans intended to travel to Sudan for a crack at fighting the British[76].

All the same, the Mahdiya state fell in 1898 when the British general Herbert Kitchener led an Anglo-Egyptian army to Omdurman, killing an estimated 15,000 Mahdist troops. The British claimed that they came to Sudan to rescue it from al-Ta'ayshi's barbarity, but intra-European imperialist strategies were a more substantive motive, allied to the late Victorian desire to avenge the death of Gordon.

Tribes and state

The second colonial period in Sudan began a decade before Taha was born. Although the British and Egyptians were nominally co-rulers, British dominance was overwhelming. The British were reluctant, however, to acknowledge that they had acquired a country with a state – they persisted with the colonial view of a country made up of a patchwork of warring tribes which needed the just hand of British administration to survive. Like the Mahdists, however, they slotted themselves into a state system that maintained class structures and a taxable cash economy. Sudan was to be used to provide raw materials for the British economy, and Britain initially used Egypt to finance the reconstruction of a country ravaged by wars and famines[77].

The Mahdiya had tried to diminish the authority of the tribes in order to create a new and centrally controlled identity for Sudan, but the British regime, like the Turkiya, went to great lengths to categorise the country into tribes, even creating some new ones. Tribal leaders were their taxmen, and they found it hard to find non-tribal political structures for "detribalised elements": the slaves and other groups displaced by the wars of the period. Slavery was a vexing issue for the colonialists – the campaign to abolish slavery had been a powerful propaganda tool for their campaign against the Mahdiya, but the British believed that the abolition of the slave trade had been a major cause of the fall of the Turkiya, and wanted to change things slowly. They feared that "detribalised" bands of slaves would turn to prostitution and thieving and quietly encouraged slaves to stay with their masters.

One of the first concerns of the conquerors was to ensure that land was registered. The Mahdist period had widened state intervention in systems of land ownership, with population displacements and land grants to loyal tribes[78]. The British consolidated the movement towards the commoditisation of land, begun before the Turkiya, and eventually built up a large agricultural export sector. Initially, British reforms required an increase in slave labour in some areas – in Rufaʿa, slave numbers actually increased by ten percent to 5,311 between 1905 and 1912[79]. But eventually, cash agriculture replaced slaves with waged workers.

Like the Turkiya, too, the British adopted a central religious policy with a "Board of Ulema" (*shariʿa* legists) imported from Egypt. Their network of *shariʿa* courts was supported by a *mufti*, who could make official rulings on *shariʿa* questions (*shariʿa* jurisdiction was restricted to family law – all other law was developed by the colonial authorities, largely from Indian colonial law or Sudanese custom)[80]. British authorities associated *shariʿa* with Sudan's developed core – it was not at all part of law in the south, and administrators resisted it in Darfur. The *shariʿa* system was supposed to counteract the dreaded "*faki* influence" which might stir another revolt. Indeed, for the first decade of British rule, Sudanese resistance was phrased in Mahdist idiom – the most serious revolt took place at Katfia on the Blue Nile, near Rufaʿa, when grievances at government land reforms turned into a revolt of Mahdist sympathisers which ended in the public execution of their leader in 1908[81].

The British soon made their peace with the Sufi *tariqa*s, through the good offices of al-Mirghani, the Khatmiya leader who had spent the Mahdiya in Egypt. He was given a knighthood in 1915, a token of the support he had given the government. By that time, Britain was at war with Turkey, the major Muslim power, and the Sudan government was trying to garner the support of Muslim Sudanese against the Turkish enemy. The Mahdist movement (the traditional enemy of the Turks) was rehabilitated. The Mahdi's son 'Abd al-Rahman signed the "Sudan Book of Loyalty" an effusion of support for the British war effort. The small-scale Sufi *tariqa*s, who had been marginalised by the Turkiya and given their loyalty to the Mahdiya only to see themselves abolished, emerged again. In some respects, the experience of powerlessness had strengthened them, as they had been forced back on their local constituency during the Turkiya and Mahdiya, becoming "a succor and a shield for the lower classes"[82].

Darfur and the south

Darfur was first incorporated into the Turkiya's Nile valley state in 1874. The Mahdist state's control of Darfur was tenuous, barely weathering two revolts there; and the Mahdiya depended heavily on the policy of forcing the displacement of Westerners to the capital. When the British conquered Sudan, they initially felt that recolonising Darfur would be too burdensome for their administration, but they swiftly took control in 1916, fearing that Darfur might be a bridgehead for the Central Powers in Africa. They subsequently followed a policy of neglect – almost no investment was made in the region. Many British administrators believed that the neglect was benign. Keeping people under the authority of tribal leaders and the version of tradition that those leaders improvised for the British was in their best interest. The British administrators favoured tribal identities, even resisting the imposition of the *shari'a* courts they used in the northern Nile valley – in Darfur, they thought they would be "detribalising". Tribal chiefs were counterbalances to indigenous religious leaderships and the relatively powerless Egyptian sector of the government, and they also fitted with the paternalist British approach to the country.

In the south, the British also made tribalism the cornerstone of policy. There, administrators sometimes needed to search for a chief who could mediate the authority of the state, act as tax collector and decide land questions. But chiefs were hard to find. In 1920, some provincial governors concluded that "there were no tribal institutions of a political nature to foster and there were no sufficiently strong figures to act as Paramount Chiefs"[83].

Chiefless communities of the south stymied the British policy of making a chief into a tax collector. The Nuer of the Upper Nile resisted the British until the late 1920s, inspired by a group of prophets. The British felt that the prophets "had to be eliminated before proper chiefs could emerge and administrative processes take root"[84]. The population was concentrated in small areas and bombed by the British air force until they agreed to be assigned chiefs and sub-chiefs.

The astonishing social diversity of the region and limited government funds were factors in the policy of neglect which the British operated in the south. The British believed that minimising contacts with the economically developed north would protect the south from slavers and unscrupulous traders[85]. Southern policy, developed in the 1920s, effectively banned Northerners from the area and handed responsibility for services to European missionaries. The British picture of a protected, backward zone may have enthused young administrators, but it infantilised the people of the south – one administrator wrote in the 1940s:

> What is needed is for the southerners to remain quiet, contented and peaceful, with few desires and few worries, happily singing in the sun to their cattle[86].

Southerners were to pay dearly for Britain's southern policy.

Conclusion

When Taha was born in 1911, Sudan's astonishing diversity had survived almost a century of colonisation and war. But the nineteenth century had associated power, wealth and prestige with certain groups. Islam and Arabness helped to construct a privileged Sudanese identity linked to the state. However, southern groups, with their Noble Spiritual Beliefs, their African languages and their diverse social organisations, were not able to cope with the concentration of power amassed by state forming elites and their clients. Many were enslaved and formed the agricultural labour force for the more fortunate, landowning section of the privileged northern group. Those who escaped enslavement found their home territory a place of war. The distinction between people organised in a state and those outside it ended up as the difference between slavery and freedom – the memory of slavery has created a distinction which is still "the basic criterion for stratification of the village"[87].

The state in Sudan could influence, for good or ill, the lives of many people. Yet one curious fact of the nineteenth century's headlong rush towards centralised power is that the state went under an assumed name. Because the state was explained in highly coloured religious language, it sometimes pretended to be something else – a midwife for the end of the world, or an international slaving corporation spreading religious law, for example. This may have helped the British towards their misconception of Sudan as a seething mass of stateless tribes, but it helped many Sudanese towards misconceptions too.

Sudanese Islam also underwent rapid transformations in the nineteenth century: the small-*tariqa* Sufism of the Sadigab, the memory of the Mahdiya, the *shari'a* legists of the colonialists. The *shari'a* system had a bumpy ride through the century before Taha was born – but in spite of the many manipulations it suffered, many people still believed it was something immutable and necessary for the state. Nineteenth century interpretations of *shari'a* helped to create the slave-free stratified society of Rufa'a. However, that society is remembered by many of Taha's contemporaries as a simple and unified society – a warm, aromatic home. What he made of the place and time in which he was born is the subject of the rest of this book.

Chapter 3

Escaping the village shop

"I could at best have been a village shopkeeper in Heglig, if my mother had not died and we had not moved to Rufaʻa", said Taha to one of his followers in later life[1]. Rufaʻa was only 15 kilometres away, but it was one of the leading educational centres in Sudan.

Education
Before the twentieth century

The first educational institutions in the Blue Nile were established by the Funj, who encouraged *khalwa*s with land grants and tax privileges[2]. These *khalwa*s, originally Sufi retreats, became centres for community services and access to the power of religion. They taught boys Islamic studies, and some schools even attracted students from outside Sudan. Turkiya education policy maintained the *khalwa* system, but also brought colonial schools to Sudan, aimed at training personnel to work in colonial administration. Turkiya educators established schools in major towns, teaching geometry, grammar, handwriting and religion to a few hundred boys, the clerks of tomorrow[3]. European missionary societies also opened schools under Turkiya supervision.

There were no Turkiya schools in the Blue Nile region, although the *khalwa*s continued their educational work, with some official encouragement. *Khalwa*s became more involved in the provision of social services during the Turkiya, because the political and judicial functions of *tariqa*s were whittled away by the colonial state (see chapter two)[4]. The Mahdiya swept away the small educational edifice built by the Turkiya. The Mahdiya had a complex relationship with the small *tariqa*s and their *khalwa*s. Their (reluctant) political support was crucial to the Mahdi's campaign against the Turkiya – but the Mahdi's hostility to non-Mahdist

Islam, and the long wars of the period, undermined *khalwa* education[5].

Education in the condominium

Under British rule, Turkiya-style schooling was re-established. By 1906, the authorities had introduced an education tax in the five northern riverain provinces. Over three percent of province budgets went on schooling[6]. School building followed the colonial concentration of development in the riverain areas and urban centres of Kordofan and the coast, reinforcing regional imbalances[7]. For example, by 1936 Darfur had four sub-primary schools for a population of half a million people[8]. In the south, social services including education were run by missionaries, partly to keep costs down but also to help the south to resist northern cultural penetration.

The British were ambivalent about the value of education. Educated Sudanese administrators kept down staffing costs, and education was part of a "civilising mission", but it could create an articulate class that might threaten the colonialists' authority. Condominium policy was formulated by Lord Cromer, the British representative in Egypt. He wanted primary education that would create a native class of artisans and administrators. The English language was to be avoided because "it could furnish the subject races with a very powerful arm"[9]. However, James Currie, the first British education secretary, argued that secular education would counteract the influence of *faki*s. In the first years of the condominium, the British viewed the *faki*s as suspiciously Mahdist. Until 1912, violent anti-colonial resistance in northern Sudan often had Mahdist overtones, and secular education was expected to "exorcise" this influence[10].

At the same time, the Gordon myth, central to the propaganda of conquest, brought a different model of education. Kitchener decided to commemorate Victorian England's martyr with an elite school for "the sons of leading men". This educational institution, he said, would win Britain "the first place in Africa as a civilising power"[11].

Rufa'a schools

Small-scale *tariqa*s maintained their popular support in the rural Blue Nile throughout Sudan's long nineteenth century. They had to compete with Turkiya *shari'a* courts; with new, large-scale *tariqa*s; and with the Mahdi's hegemony. This competition forced small *tariqa*s to concentrate on their role as providers of spiritual and social services.

According to 'Ali Lutfi (Taha's wife's brother), Rufa'a's extensive

experience of *khalwa* education encouraged Babikr Bedri to establish a
secular school there in 1903[12]. Bedri had been a Mahdist soldier and then
a merchant: he set up Rufa'a's first secular school, in spite of opposition
from local *fakis*, who may have feared a loss of income or status[13].
Secular education was popular with the townspeople. When Bedri tried
in 1910 to teach boys to memorise the Qur'an, as they did in the *khalwa*,
parents refused, preferring a modern education for their children. British
support for this kind of education was more ambivalent – in 1910 Bedri
was unable to get an English teacher for his school, which would have
upgraded it to a post-elementary primary school. Currie the education
secretary was afraid of the spread of English[14]. It was several years later
that a primary school was built in Rufa'a.

Bedri's biggest innovation was to open Sudan's first girls' school
in 1907. Sufi educators, including one family of *shaykhs* in Rufa'a, had
occasionally taught girls in the past, and very occasionally a woman would
rise to *tariqa* leadership[15]. Girls' education influenced gender relations
in Rufa'a, where the social exclusion of women did not have the same
air of respectability that it acquired in other Nile valley towns[16]. Some
women of Taha's generation read the Qur'an and the newspapers[17].

Taha's schooldays

Taha entered a secular elementary school around the time that his father
died. The syllabus covered arithmetic and Arabic reading and writing. He
was successful enough to gain entrance to the post-elementary primary
course, which lasted another four years.

Taha was an old schoolboy. Most pupils entered elementary school
around the age of seven, but he was ten before he joined. Assuming
that he was born in 1911, the later of two dates he gave for the year of
his birth, he would have started elementary school in 1921 and finished
primary school in 1932. The course only lasted for eight years in total,
so he may have spent some years working, as one contemporary, Girgis
Iskander, later heard claimed[18].

Sudan's ten primary schools charged fees, although one fifth of
the students had free places. It was a small school when Taha went
there – in 1933, a year for which figures are available, Rufa'a primary
had only 34 boys and four staff[19]. The curriculum was based around
religion, arithmetic, literacy and dictation. In primary school he began to
study English, a subject available only to the 1,300 boys in all Sudan who
reached post-elementary education[20]. It was taught with endless grammar

analysis[21]. The British were more reluctant to allow history teaching, for fear of "encouraging Moslem feeling"[22].

Muhammad Lutfi, Taha's neighbour in Rufa'a and future father-in-law, took over as headmaster, just before Taha joined the school. He was one of Babikr Bedri's teachers and he rose to become an educational inspector and opened his own girls' school. In later years Daym Graydab became called Daym Lutfi, in his honour. Lutfi's daughter, Sayyida, does not recall whether Taha was a pupil of her father's. But Taha knew the Lutfi girls, who were allowed to leave the house on their own. Sayyida herself often spoke to Taha, although he was not a close relative, and girls were not supposed to speak to boys outside the immediate family. Taha agreed with her that it was a fine thing for girls to have their freedom[23].

Some of Taha's schoolfriends remained close to him throughout his life. Amin Muhammad Siddig came to Rufa'a primary from El Geteina, a village on the east bank of the White Nile. Amin Siddig's father was a Khatmiya *faki*, and he had open-minded views and was pleased to have his son improve himself[24]. Like Taha, Amin Siddig succeeded at primary school and was one of the fortunate few to make it to the country's only secondary school – Gordon Memorial College. Other students of Rufa'a primary, like Muhammad al-Hasan Muhammad al-Khayr, who was a few years below him at school, stayed friends with Taha and eventually became supporters of his political and religious movement[25].

Rufa'a in the 1920s and 1930s
International markets

Taha stayed in Rufa'a until 1932, when he was at least 21 years old. It was a small, spacious market town, with a few foreign merchants, some grander houses, and trees in the streets. Taha's house was built of unbaked mud, but other houses were made of baked brick[26]. In Taha's day, the rains were part of the agricultural cycle, and the dry lands around the town would burst into green life at the end of summer, when the rains came[27]. At that time too, many people worked their own land with their former slaves, before the growth of an agricultural labour market.

In the 1920s, huge irrigation schemes were being built in the Gezira, the triangle of land below the confluence of the two Niles that had been chosen as the leading cotton growing area of Sudan. After the first world war a global cotton boom brought unfamiliar riches to many farmers across the water from Rufa'a. The Gezira plain was particularly suited to irrigation, and the colonial regime set up a syndicate owned by shareholders to provide raw cotton for the English textile industry. Gezira lands were registered and then leased to the government, which sold tenancies to farmers via the syndicate. Much of the syndicate's profit went to expatriate shareholders, but in the cotton boom of the early 1920s, local farmers had a happy encounter with international markets:

> the Gezera farmers were rolling in money as never heard or seen before in the Sudan. There were bank notes for 50, 100 and more pounds ... Some used their money wisely and acquired land and houses; some went merry and sought the dancing Marissa girls [*Marissa* is a local sorghum beer]. We heard that the farmers used to stick a 100 pound banknote on a dancing girl's forehead[28].

Dancing Marissa girls

The "dancing Marissa girls" were another product of British policy. The British abolished slavery in 1899, but passed laws to keep notionally liberated slaves with their masters, believing that real abolition would destroy the agricultural labour system. But by the 1920s the regime's cash agricultural schemes had created a market for agricultural labour – the British used wage labour to induce former slaves and west African migrants into the schemes, and slave numbers in Rufa'a and the Gezira declined sharply[29]. Colonial labour officials found it hard to attract the settled population of the Gezira into the uncertainty of wage labour[30].

The development of wage labour in this period impelled the government to enforce existing legal measures against slavery – even though slave-holding groups protested. Their religious leaders ('Ali al-Mirghani, 'Abd al-Rahman al-Mahdi and Yusuf al-Hindi) wrote a letter to the director of intelligence that claimed Sudanese slavery was benign and complained that freed slaves turned to drink, sloth and prostitution[31].

The need for manpower in the new economy won out – but, the new economy offered few opportunities for female slaves, other than domestic service, prostitution or alcohol-brewing[32]. Some of them became dancing *marissa* girls. *Marissa* is a thick, sour sorghum beer that has long been a staple of Sudanese diet (nineteenth century nursery rhymes had 'Abdullahi al-Ta'ayshi asking for a drink)[33].

British administrators, tribal shaykhs and the intelligentsia

Rufa'a's British administrators in the 1920s had to manage the development of the commercial class – other important relationships were with tribal leaders and with a group one administrator called the

"Intelligentsia". Who were these administrators? By the time Taha was at school, the military conquerors who began Sudan's second colonial administration had largely been replaced by the men of the Sudan Political Service (SPS). The SPS promised a life of adventure and importance to young British men from public schools and good universities (many wrote grateful memoirs). Some of them, particularly in remote parts of Sudan, "completely identified with the people in their charge" (to quote Wilfred Thesiger, one of the most famous and grateful)[34]. However, they identified the interests of their charges with a version of tradition at odds with the modernising shifts that radical Mahdists, dancing Merissa girls, educationalists and Gezira capitalists felt changing their lives.

J W Robertson, whose first posting was in Rufa'a in 1922, and who rose to be the civil secretary, wrote an affectionate, paternalist diary of his first days in Rufa'a. People were "like children"; the children themselves had cheeky, smiling faces, and "all salute as we go past and jump down from their donkeys and stand to attention"[35]. (A previous DC had beaten people who did not dismount)[36]. Robertson paid court to the local shaykhs (he washed the foot sores of Shukriya mayor shortly after he arrived).

There were several tribal groups in Rufa'a at the time. Taha's home in Daym Graydab (a better part of the town), was populated by Rikabiya people, who said they were the prophet's descendants, and 'Arakiyin, from a Sufi family as distinguished as the Sadigab, up the river. Other groups had come from the north, during the Turkiya migrations. These tribes had mostly good relations with the Shukriya, whose dominance of the region was established in the days of the Funj[37].

The leaders of the Shukriya were the Abu Sinn family (collectively called the Sinnab). They had a small police force, and wide judicial powers. Both Turkiya and British authorities gave the Sinnab responsibility for taxation and land registration[38]. John Longe, who was DC in the early 1930s, noted the power of the *shaykh*s:

> the people of Rufaa are so 'tribal' in their outlook and thus so loyal to (or afraid of) their sheikhs that grievances which elsewhere would quietly reach the D.C.'s ears would in Rufaa be hushed up until at last when the burden had become too heavy to bear, the whole district would rise up in protest[39].

Longe identified one group who were not afraid of the tribal leaders:

... the "Intelligentsia" of Rufa'a town. These last are mostly of
the schoolmaster type both active and retired and are the first to
criticise "NA" [Native Administration, or the use of tribal leaders in
administration] if the opportunity arises[40].

Longe's diary illustrates one of the dilemmas of colonial rule, the fact
that the country was run by conflicting sets of laws, with civil law at
the urban centre and a colonialist interpretation of tribal law in the
countryside. Tribal law did not fit comfortably with the experience
of many Sudanese (when Muhammad Lutfi tried to set up his own
school, Sinnab opposition reached the level of death-threats)[41]. Turkiya
and British authorities reconstituted tribal leaderships as rural ruling
classes in order to manage their colonies cheaply. This "decentralized
despotism" (Mamdani) was a policy of the Turkiya and of the British,
as well as authoritarian post-colonial regimes, and it was clearly being
resisted by Rufa'a's anomalously large educated class in the 1920s.
Longe's "Intelligentsia" complicated the affection of many SPS personnel
for traditional Sudan. Some administrators like H A MacMichael had to
restrain their contempt for the educated junior "employee despising his
origins" (MacMichael wrote an encyclopaedic chronicle of the Arabs in
Sudan)[42]. Longe preferred the "rustic arab" to the "semi-educated man",
but admitted that he fought against his bias towards rural simplicity[43].

But the rural was not simple. Taha lived in a complex and changing
society. By the time he left Rufa'a in the early 1930s, he was affiliated to
one of the classes in his stratified small town. This class, the intelligentsia,
were sometimes called the *effendiya*, an Ottoman term for the bureaucratic
class. They could belong to the higher ranks of the bureaucracy, or be
affiliated to the landowning and religious elite, or they could be small-
town teachers and engineers. The group was defined not by class but by
their European or Egyptian work clothing, and their modern education.
Their modest salaries, and the relative scarcity of consumer imports
in Sudan, meant that they did not develop radical new consumption
patterns which were used as class markers – like the tastes of the Cairo
effendiya for orientalised "Louis Farouq" borrowings of French styles and
architecture[44].

Instead, the Sudanese *effendiya*, like Sudanese elites before them,
adopted Egyptian styles that were common before Europe was chic
there. Domestic architecture was becoming Arab – an architecture which
emphasises the seclusion of women and the inward-looking nature of

an endogamous society. Nineteenth century Cairo's bourgeois housing had private apartments hidden up narrow stairs, down dark corridors and behind wooden screens. "The principal aim of the architect is to render the house as private as possible, particularly that part of it which is inhabited by the women"[45]. In the Blue Nile, walled brick houses with closed women's quarters began to replace the conical grass hut in the nineteenth century[46]. This was the home for an *effendi*, simply furnished with beds strung with rope and a chest for clothes[47]. The food was Sudanese, *kisra* and *mulah*, although *effendi*s were likely to come across wheat bread and *ful* beans, foods sponsored by the colonial power and common in colonial institutions such as schools[48].

Conclusion

Taha's education saved him from a life of farming, or the counter of a village shop. There was a saying in Rufa'a – "education divides people" – and Taha was joining a new social division[49]. The *effendiya* were in a difficult social position: they were aware that the colonial state was setting up a kind of civil society at the centre, but knew that their civil rights were equivocal, while those of the British were inalienable. And they chafed at the dominance of tribal leaders, rustics who had not attained the same level of cultural dignity as they had themselves. The dignity which the *effendiya* awarded to their culture was a confused one, too. Some of it was borrowed from the British, who often denigrated the act of borrowing, and some of it came from a competing Arab and Muslim culture. As will be seen below, the British tried to limit *effendiya* influence, and constantly worried that the awkward position occupied by the *effendiya* would create disaffection that would undermine British rule. Many years later, when Taha became disaffected, he formed a small nationalist party, and some of his first followers were drawn from the Rufa'a intelligentsia.

Chapter 4

Training an *effendi*

In 1932 there were little more than 1,300 boys in ten Sudanese post-elementary primary schools[1]. If Taha had finished his education there, he might have hoped for a job as a junior clerk or elementary teacher, at about £E 50 a year[2]. Instead, he was one of about 400 students, almost all from the elite, who attended the country's only secondary school, where he enrolled as an engineering student. This chapter describes his studies and the political and cultural atmosphere of the time.

Gordon College
A better class of boy

Girgis Iskander, one of Taha's school friends in Khartoum, says that Taha worked for the government after he finished school in Rufa'a[3]. Other contemporaries believe he went straight from Rufa'a to Gordon Memorial College. If Taha's guess about his age was correct, he was in his early twenties when he arrived there in 1932, a little above the average leaving age of 20½ years[4]. He was small (about 1.6 metres) and slight. He came from a minor town, yet for the Khartoum and Omdurman students, he was a country boy. Gordon College gave him an introduction to life at the centre of the Sudan, and brought him into contact with ideas from all over the Arab and Islamic world and the British empire. What kind of place was it?

Girgis Iskander recalls the highly selective admissions procedure to the college. Students were streamed by ability, although the college would make exceptions for the sons of tribal leaders. Official college reports categorise students by class and ethnicity. Students were listed as Arab, Berberine, *mustawtan* (Sudanese of mixed Egyptian or Levantine origin) and *sudani*. The last term, Sudanese, described non-Arabised or recently Arabised groups, the Southerners who lived in the north. "Arabs" overwhelmingly dominated the school (see table below), and most students were sons of merchants or government officials, two groups near the centre of the colonial state. Teachers complained that the sons of officials were duller than the sons of "illiterate peasants"[5]. The 1935 report called for the recruitment of "more sons of sheikhs and landowners from all the northern provinces"[6].

The college helped entrench the dominance of Sudan's developing elites. The authorities wanted to include provincial *shaykh*s of the Native Administration in the elite, as a counterbalance to the educated bureaucratic class they were creating. By denying admission to students from the south and the west (there was only one Darfur pupil) the authorities helped concentrate development in the riverain centre and the towns of Kordofan and the coast.

Ethnicity and class at Gordon College, 1932–1935[7]

i. nationality

Year	Arabs	Sudanese	Mustawtans	Berberines	misc	total
1932	342	11	85	32	-	470
1933	308	10	79	24	-	421
1934	277	9	74	22	2	384
1935	240	8	71	23	2	344
1936	208	· 9	55	17	2	291

ii. parentage

Year	officials	officers	farmers	headmen	merchants	craftsmen	total
1932	177	20	137	13	99	24	470
1933	159	17	102	13	102	28	421
1934	185	11	74	7	86	21	384
1935	169	16	61	1	78	19	344
1936	147	22	49	1	64	19	291

Curriculum

Bray, Clarke and Stephens' work (1986) on African education and society defines three goals of education: instrumental, expressive and normative. Instrumental goals give students work or life skills; expressive goals seek to create group cohesion and identity; normative goals standardise beliefs and behaviour[8]. This section looks at the second two goals, and compares outcomes British teachers intended from a Gordon College education with *khalwa* educational outcomes.

*Khalwa*s were good places to learn about group cohesion and identity, and the teaching monologue gave students a set of moral and theological certainties. The *khalwa* initiated pupils into a traditional society, where individual choice counted for less than custom. Gordon College also taught group cohesion. The SPS juniors who taught there encouraged team sports: football taught fair play and competitive spirit, whereas the *khalwa* weeding sessions taught more about collective effort and the good-humoured management of tedium. In contrast to the *khalwa*, the colonial school aimed to provide students with technical competence that would serve the state and the developing capitalist economy. Colonialists were aware that by detaching young men from traditional society, and giving them a new set of aspirations, they might create a disaffected group. But this group was necessary for the state's existence.

The college students followed a two year general course and then spent two years on a specialisation – science, engineering, teaching, accounts, or *shari'a*. English language instruction took up almost a quarter of the course, along with history, geography, religion and classical Arabic[9]. These cultural studies were peripheral to Taha's engineering course but they were the normative core of the syllabus. Taha studied the History (it had a capital H) of Sudan, Greece, Rome and Persia, and the Arabs, and the Geography of Africa, Egypt, Sudan and Europe[10]. Religion aimed "at imparting a sound education in ethics and morals rather than a mere memorisation of a number of rules and laws"[11]. It was taught by Egyptians from al-Azhar University, who also taught the course for *shari'a* judges.

Taha and his contemporaries were introduced to two traditions, colonial and Islamic. The disjunction between the grand narratives of each tradition troubled some sensitive students, including Taha. However, there were also continuities: both grand narratives stressed the power of the text and the authenticity of the past over the present. Taha attained a fluent understanding of these traditions, but in later life, he began to look for authenticity in the present, as subsequent chapters show.

Taha's life at Gordon College

Taha's school day was carefully mapped out – roll call at 6 am, baths, exercises, the first period and then breakfast. There were five more periods before lunch (*ful*, lentils or an unpleasant meat and vegetable stew) and then work stopped for the afternoon heat. In the evening there were games, homework and supper[12]. Outside the curriculum, school societies organised debates on undemanding topics like the pen and the sword. Others produced magazines, or performed Shakespeare in

Arabic. There were sports and music classes, lectures and visits[13]. Fifty boys joined the social service society, which started literacy courses in the *daym*s, the slums around colonial Khartoum where groups displaced by war and enslavement lived. This attempt to educate the poor failed, however, because their *daym* students stopped attending the classes[14].

Taha's name only appears once in the school reports – he won a prize for gardening in 1935[15]. Students could choose to work on gardens by the Nile banks close to the school instead of doing physical training in the morning, and Taha chose to continue his farming. Another village boy, Amin Siddig, felt that Khartoum boys looked down on his poor clothes and unlaced shoes, while the village boys thought they were more straightforward than the townies[16]. One fellow student, Girgis Iskander, remembers Taha as "silent, quiet, dignified", a young man who took his religious duties very seriously and prayed regularly[17]. Taha was something of a recluse, thought Girgis Iskander:

> A quiet polite small person (we were probably smaller then) devoted and probably devout. After school he would only be praying or studying on his prayer mat. Never heard him laughing or making noise. He commanded respect and a degree of awe. To the ordinary student he was rather stiff but there was no nonsense[18].

Amin Siddig entered the college to study *shari'a* but changed to accounts. His father, the *faki* from Geteina, was very unhappy, but Siddig could not stomach the obsequiousness of the *shari'a* section students towards their religious teachers. Siddig told his son about the his own youthful japes at the college, but he also remembered Taha's seriousness – Taha would not allow his fellow students to dodge fares on Khartoum's public transport[19]. Taha may have been aloof, but his time at the college brought him into contact with some of the brighter minds in northern Sudan, who were allowed the "literary education" denied to the rest of the country's students.

The British did not like the "'half-baked *effendi* ideas [which] resulted from exposure to European learning"[20]. But some *effendi*s had an erudition that alarmed the British, like Moawiya Nur, a student at the college in the 1920s. He gave up a medical career to take a degree in English literature in Beirut, and had minor success as a writer[21]. Taha was one of Nur's many admirers[22]. Nur's story ended unhappily – his education, said his admiring teacher Edward Atiyah, had alienated him from his own society, and the British did not know what to do with a man who understood their literary canon better than they did themselves. After several bouts of mental illness he died[23].

Atiyah, a Lebanese Oxford graduate who later worked in the colonial intelligence service, taught at the college in the late 1920s. His autobiography described the college atmosphere of young intellectual eagerness in a colonial backwater. The students followed the careers of Mohandas Gandhi, and the Turkish and Arabian nationalists Mustafa Kamal and Ibn Sa'ud in the Egyptian press. Alongside anti-imperialist articles and Fabian papers the students read film-stars' gossip[24]. The English masters were remote, the non-European teachers felt suppressed, and discipline was sometimes harsh – a flogging by a drill sergeant in front of the warden and a tutor[25].

Girgis Iskander points out that the students' antipathy to the colonial authorities was mild, and that they "were greatly influenced by the older generation, who held the British in veneration"[26]. But there were occasional problems. In 1931, a strike with political overtones closed the college. The students protested against a cut in graduate salaries. The strike involved a sugar boycott, inspired by Gandhi, who began his boycott campaign against the salt tax in India in 1930[27]. Gordon College was a centre for young nationalist thinking in Sudan – Mekki Shebeika, a Sudanese historian who was then an assistant housemaster for Rufa'a students, describes the college after the strike as follows:

> The trials of the days of the strike, the threat of expulsion and the fear of not getting a job, and the discussions between [the authorities and the students] were a practical lesson, where [students] learned nationalist principles, patience, struggle, discussion of general questions – these lessons qualified many of them to take part in the nationalist battlefield in days to come[28].

The nationalist battle was looming, but for the moment, radicalism had become unpopular in Khartoum, as the next section of this chapter shows.

Urban nationalism and rural power

The nineteenth century enhanced greatly the status of Sufi, commercial and tribal elites in Sudan, and those elites realised soon after the British conquest that that their future lay with the new colonialists. Initially, the British distrusted the "fanaticism" they perceived in Sudanese Islam, and tried to counter its influence by reviving the *shari'a* court system created by the Turkiya. But they had to canvass support from Sufi leaders in 1914, when Britain declared war on Turkey, a leading Muslim power which had partial and nominal suzerainty over the Anglo-Egyptian Sudan. The British feared that the Muslim subjects of their empire would revolt, and in Sudan and elsewhere, they tried to build a network of collaborating elites. Those Sufi leaderships who had spent the nineteenth century building big centralised organisations were able to offer an attractively wide spectrum of political support, but the British also patronised smaller *tariqa* leaderships, by incorporating them into rural power-structures. 'Abd al-Rahman al-Mahdi (the Mahdist leader), 'Ali al-Mirghani and Yusuf al-Hindi (leader of the Hindiya *tariqa*) were the most important religious leaders of the period, and they helped draw their rural constituencies into the new agricultural modes of production needed to create an export economy[29].

Mahdism had served Muhammad Ahmad's radicalism and al-Ta'ayshi's autocracy. When the British came, it changed again, under the leadership of his son, 'Abd al-Rahman. At first the British restricted his movements, but after the declaration of war against the Ottomans in 1914, they gave 'Abd al-Rahman land grants, and he astutely built up a fortune that financed the revival of his movement. The northern Nile valley was not a promising place to build support – it was dominated by the Khatmiya and the small *tariqa*s, who often looked on the Mahdiya as a tragic time of national division. Instead, 'Abd al-Rahman went west, where Mahdism was more popular. In the 1920s and 1930s 'Abd al-Rahman's paid agents organised support in Darfur and Kordofan. To neutralise British suspicions, the agents informed on unruly local *faki*s to the intelligence services. In the early twentieth century, centralised religious groups continued the nineteenth century process of undermining local religious leadership to their advantage[30].

Economic power

During the Turkiya, Khartoum entrepreneurs had dominated Sudan's trade. Although the Mahdiya's isolationism and monopolistic practices affected trade, Sudan still had a commercial elite when the British arrived: these merchants petitioned Kitchener to allow multinational trading companies to return to Sudan[31]. By the mid-1920s, the government had created a class of agricultural capitalists. The Gezira cotton farmers, who featured in chapter three worked with the government-sponsored plantation syndicate. Bigger cotton lords had even better fortune – they owned private pump irrigation schemes, often on land given them by the state. 'Abd al-Rahman al-Mahdi and 'Ali al-Mirghani figured prominently among these men.

The British decision to sponsor elites who had come to the fore in the nineteenth century meant that the latter's claims to the superiority of their culture and religion were vindicated in a flood of cash. This cash allowed them to expand their political activity.

Detribalised groups

The British continued the Turkiya process of sponsoring tribal leaderships and re-working their authority. They found it harder to deal with groups which did not fit their categories of traditional leader, and nomad or peasant tributary. Some of the groups which the British saw as anomalous were an established feature of Sudanese society, like the commercial elite. The government patronised them when they sought economic development but restricted their activities in times of political turmoil, when "tribal" society had to be maintained[32].

Other "anomalous" groups were created by colonialism. The *effendiya* were described in chapter three. They, and the men who worked in colonial enterprises like the railways, the Gezira scheme, and the postal service, were bringing a commercial and infrastructural unity to Sudan that was necessary for colonial economic policy, but sat uneasily with the British identification of the interests of administered people with "traditional" ways of life. The urban working classes were particularly puzzling to the British – many were ex-slaves who lived in the *daym*s, the slum areas where Gordon College students had tried and failed to promote literacy. They sometimes adopted ethnic identities from the old slaving frontier, or occupational identities, like the postal workers of Daym Telegraph. The British appointed "tribal" chiefs for these fluid micro-societies, and used them to organise the labour supply of the *daym*s[33].

The 1924 revolt

The dislocated and dynamic experiences of "detribalised" groups undercut the British picture of a traditional, tribal Sudan. The first decade of British rule saw localised Mahdist risings, but the next major challenge to the British settlement in Sudan came from detribalised Sudan. In the early 1920s a group of educated junior officials from established commercial families began small-scale secret agitation for union with Egypt, and against the construction of a religious and tribal elite[34]. They became the White Flag League (WFL). They met with political successes only when they gained the support of 'Ali 'Abd al-Latif, a cashiered army officer of slave origin. He was able to mobilise the support of military cadets, junior clerks and skilled manual workers, such as the post workers, who introduced new organisational tactics to Sudan, distributing political leaflets by post[35]. Many of 'Abd al-Latif's supporters were detribalised, Muslim Southerners[36]. A contemporary British report described them as:

> negroids ... outside the orbit of normal control or of appeal to tribal and national sentiment ... This class has shown itself readier in the past than most others to avail itself of the educational facilities offered since the British occupation, and is, consequently, strongly represented in the lower ranks of officials, military and civilian, and similar capacities in commercial life[37].

Hadarat al-Sudan was the only Arabic newspaper in the country, owned by Sufi leaders including 'Abd al-Rahman al-Mahdi. It mocked 'Abd al-Latif's slave origins, and they dismissed his followers as "the scum of society" who "disturbed people of status, merchants, businessmen and men of good origin"[38].

The events of the period have been widely documented elsewhere – an army mutiny in 1924 was put down with bloodshed and Egyptian personnel were expelled from Sudan[39]. The 1924 movement is important because it redefined the term "Sudanese" as a nationality. Previously, a *sudani* was an ex-slave, and the "nationality" given in official forms denoted ethnicity (see, for example, the description of the nationalities at Gordon College in chapter three). Sudan's first nationalists, from the capital's "good families" were inspired by Egyptian nationalism and the wider Arab world[40].

But 'Abd al-Latif resisted this Arab identification. He gave a new meaning to the word "Sudanese" as a nationality rather than the subaltern ethnicity of British official reports. This meaning was taken up by elite actors, like 'Abd al-Rahman al-Mahdi, who called for a "Sudan for the Sudanese"[41]. 'Abd al-Rahman could not oppose the nationalists by calling for a British Sudan, and so he appropriated a term which had been applied to disadvantaged ethnic groups. However, this borrowing was also a re-invention – 'Abd al-Rahman and the elite nationalists began a process of defining a nationality in terms of Nile valley culture[42]. The Sudanese elite had learned well the lesson of nineteenth century Sudan – that large populations would accept the authority of an Arab-Muslim state, a centralising force that draws on a constructed Islamic past in order explain its power over a heterogeneous political present[43]. 'Abd al-Rahman al-Mahdi and his supporters reconstituted the Arab-Muslim state as an imaginary "nation" – a population linked by common culture, language or ethnicity.

The Sudanese elite were in a good position to propagate their views. The British responded to the 1924 uprising with a campaign to diminish the power of restive urban groups by empowering "traditional" leaders, reconstructed in their own image. New judicial and administrative powers were awarded to native *shaykh*s. School discipline became harsher and school entry was restricted – the primary section of Gordon College was packed off to Rufa'a, "part of a policy of discouraging educational activities in urban centres in favour of remote rural areas"[44]. They closed the military school, and began to encourage football in schools, government departments and the railways "to keep the minds of the public off the events of the past few months"[45].

Football, poetry and nationalism

As the workers turned to football, the beneficiaries of the new order – tribal and religious leaders – consolidated their power. Al-Mahdi and al-Mirghani competed for influence with the British, and began to look for urban power bases too, forming mutually hostile intellectual coteries and patronising education with the money they had built up from their religious activities and government land grants.

Older graduates gravitated towards the wealth and power of the patricians and became embroiled in their personal and sectarian rivalry. However in the late 1920s younger men began to organise independently. They formed secret urban study groups, which discussed literature and politics. Literature, they believed, dignified their struggle: many (like Taha himself) saw 'Abd al-Latif as too uneducated to lead the country. Classical Arabic poetry in Sudan was first produced by the more literate Sufi *tariqa*s of the nineteenth century – in the twentieth century, Sudan's small legist class and the first graduates of Gordon College began to write nostalgically about an Arab and Islamic past that was not wholly their own, and to denounce the lax morals of the Sudanese present that was[46]. In the 1930s, new influences began to enter elite culture, as the first Sudanese returned from literary educations in Beirut and Cairo. They were influenced by Arab and European literary trends, and turned from the imagined past to the complex present. One of Taha's favourite poets, Al-Tigani Yusuf Beshir, wrote romantically about Sufism and the loss of faith; others wrote on socialist themes in new metres[47].

El-Affendi suggests that the intelligentsia saw Egypt as "the citadel of Islamic culture ... against the submersion of Sudan in the jungles of heathen Africa"[48]. Egyptian culture had a much more significant impact on educated Sudanese after 1936, when an Anglo-Egyptian treaty restored limited Egyptian influence to Sudan, and brought in a wide variety of Egyptian literature, to which the intelligentsia became addicted[49]. But by the 1940s, some poets were discussing their African identity in Arabic[50]. In spite of the evidence of diversity, Sudan's literary movement was oriented towards the cities of the Middle East. Muhammad Ahmad Mahjub, later a prime minister, described the study groups as follows:

> The objective towards which the literary movement in this country should be directed is to establish an Islamic-Arabic culture supported and enriched by European thought and aimed at developing a truly national literature which derives its character and inspiration from the character and traditions of the people of this country...[51]

Younger intellectuals had access to radical political ideas. When al-Fajr, one of the study groups, began publishing in 1932, they produced some rudimentary class analysis, supporting the marginalised against the patricians and *effendiya*[52]. Their magazine dealt also with Middle Eastern and European literature, and Islamic thought[53]. Al-Fajr's followers wanted to be an educational vanguard for Sudan, but culturally, they and other 1930s nationalists continued the process of affiliating Sudan with Middle Eastern forms. Like the British colonialists, they had a hierarchical understanding of different cultures, and the cultures of Sudanese people at the margins of the state came low on their list. The societies of the south were not studied or understood, while French novelists and Egyptian religious reformers had intellectual attention lavished on them.

This, in part, was due to a British policy of minimising northern influence in the south. The British policy of Native Administration kept Sudanese people in self-contained ethnic units. Southern policy protected the south from what the British saw as a predatory Islamic and Arabic culture and commercial system, and this policy more or less banned Northerners from the region. The ban also prevented African influence seeping north, and fastened the grip of Arab and Muslim identity on the questing young intellectuals who played an earnest role in the definition of Sudan's national identity (some of them went on to lead the country).

Conclusion

Girgis Iskander, Taha's schoolmate, admits that it is difficult to know what influenced Taha at this time. "He was deeply religious, more so than the others, with a dash of nationalism"[54]. Nine years after he left the college he began his own nationalist movement, a movement that saw itself as an intellectual vanguard. He does not seem to have responded to the government sponsored religion on offer from the Egyptian *shari'a* teachers at Gordon College, but his schooling introduced him to colonial and Islamic super-structures of knowledge.

Sudanese identity was fluid in the 1930s, but Sudanese elites pressed for an Arab-Muslim identity and rejected 'Ali 'Abd al-Latif's reworking of Sudaneseness to include peripheral or poor urbanised groups. Like other *effendi*s, Taha was unsympathetic towards 'Ali 'Abd al-Latif, believing him "too immature and uneducated to lead a revolution"[55]. During Taha's school years, Sudanese nationalism was dominated by patrician power, and its younger radical wing was reflective and literary rather than activist. Many "radicals" stressed Islamic and western culture; they had an elitist educational mission, they stood for social justice; and opposed the power of the patricians. Although their passivity irritated Taha, who went on to found an activist party, he and other radicals were influenced by their literary and educational approach[56].

Taha's move to Khartoum gave him technical skills and brought him in contact with many new ideas and identities, and with people much richer than himself. Taha's education also isolated him. There were no Southerners, and few *sudani*s at Gordon College, to challenge the idea that Arab and Islamic culture were a norm for Sudan. Taha's educators eagerly worked up the distinctions between the Sudanese, and then ranked the cultures they had defined. As Girgis Iskander explains:

> No, I don't think the students knew or cared about any African religion ... I am not deriding the Southerners if I say they did not exist in the GMC at our time. They were out there in the Southern jungle segregated by the Colonial order ... Many students could only think of Southerners as slaves or servants. Rather disgusting to think about it[57].

Chapter 5

Starting work and getting married

In 1936 Taha was a qualified engineer in his mid-twenties. In the nine years that followed, Sudan's politics were overshadowed by the war in Europe and Africa. Taha got work, made money, married and had a son. He was not widely known, but he began to participate in Sudan's independence struggle, and was part of the British war effort. He moved from Atbara to East Sudan and Omdurman.

Going to work
Engineering jobs

Mr Souper was Khartoum's municipal engineer and the senior engineering lecturer at Gordon College. About 15 of his students graduated each year, and he used his contacts to arrange their employment. Some of them found it hard to get work in the aftermath of the worldwide slump[1].

New commodity exports, especially Gezira cotton, paid for Sudan's administration and development until the late 1920s. Then, world depression hit cotton prices, government expenditure, and Sudan's capitalist development all at once. The anti-nationalist measures after 1924 restricted Sudan's economic expansion – the newly empowered tribal *shaykh*s were inefficient tax-collectors, and although they extended individual land ownership, they did not get involved in agricultural development. But by the mid-1930s, the worst was past, and a new governor-general pressed for economic development. The British needed fairly quick returns, and so they concentrated development around a "growth pole", the areas of central Sudan which were able to respond most quickly to investment[2].

By the time that Taha left Souper's classroom in 1936, economic conditions were better, and the railway was looking for staff[3]. Taha joined a small and prosperous salariat, going to work on Sudan Railways, a big enterprise at the forefront of colonial modernisation. At this time, Taha made his only trip outside Sudan, a brief visit to Egypt[4]. Then he started work in Atbara, a town created by the Anglo-Egyptian authorities as the railway centre of Sudan, being the point on the Nile nearest the Red Sea.

Clubs

Atbara was once the dusty home to the Egyptian Army railway battalion. When that army was expelled after the nationalist uprising of 1924, there was a need for replacement labour, which was largely supplied by thousands of Nubians and Ja'alis, villagers from the land-poor northern region of Sudan. This was the area most affected by migrations of the Turkiya period attendant on the changes in land inheritance. Atbara was smaller but newer than the capital, and it was responsive to modern ideas and structures. The people who moved there had to improvise new forms of social organisation: its historian Sikainga says that although people from different areas lived together, they founded regional clubs which "all used the Western model of organization; each had a written constitution, which provided for annual election of committees and offices"[5].

The government allowed these new forms of social organisation, and indeed sponsored one of the most important social groupings of the period – the (school) Graduates General Congress (GGC), founded in 1938. The GGC campaigned for more state funding for education and training, still lagging at around three percent of the budget, and lower than that of neighbouring British colonies[6]. Graduates could mobilise urban residents and workers in big colonial enterprises, some of whom began to petition the GGC for political assistance in disputes with the authorities[7]. One person, grateful that the Congress had founded a school in his area asked who his father was, thinking Congress was the name of a rich man[8].

However, the graduates deferred to Mahdi and Mirghani domination of the commercial life and patrimonial political structures that the British had determined for Sudan, and as a result were highly factionalised between Mahdists and the Ashigga'. The Ashigga' were members of a study group increasingly linked to 'Ali al-Mirghani. Like the early leaders of the WFL, they supported close ties with Egypt in order to free Sudan of British power. The Mahdists had a traditional hostility towards Egypt and instead called for Sudanese independence.

Taha's views in the 1930s and early 1940s

Evidence of Taha's views in the 1930s and early 1940s is scanty. Contemporaries recall his sense of identification with workers, and his hostility to the fact that Sudanese politics was becoming a dialogue between native and colonial elites, rather than between the Sudanese people. He may have developed an antipathy to patrician dominance – 'Abd al-Rahman al-Mahdi once complained to Muhammad Lutfi, who became Taha's father-in-law, that Taha would not kiss his hand[9]. In the early 1940s, Taha was unhappy with the Ashigga' dominated GGC which was drawing closer to Egypt[10]. Some of these ideas are found in his party's first publication, *al-sifr al-awwal*, which appeared in 1945 (after the events recounted in this chapter).

Taha's first work criticised the GGC's intellectual laziness and its co-operation with colonial powers, and repeated the "Sudan for the Sudanese" slogan – a nationalist phrase full of ironies that was discussed in chapter four. The slogan was invented by the WFL, taking the colonial ascription of ex-slaves as a triumphant form of self-description. The elite refused to join that revolt, but by then, the slogan had become an inescapable one for Sudanese nationalism, and its elite leaders promptly co-opted it. They, however, defined the "Sudanese" that Sudan was "for" in terms of their own Arabised and Muslim cultural identity, in effect using the slogan against the "Sudanese" who were excluded by this culture. Sudanese intellectuals took the western idea of the political rights of a nation – a linguistic, ethnic and cultural unit – and conflated it with their own recent history of the state. In nineteenth century Sudan and before, large-scale communities and states were constructed using Islamic idioms and political structures borrowed from the Middle East. This process enhanced the status of groups associated with Islam and Arabness. In the twentieth century, the Arab-Muslim Sudanese state became the Arab-Muslim Sudanese nation. Taha's first work did not challenge the idea of an Arab-Muslim nation, as will become clear in chapter six, but he was committed to a Sudanese nationalism that did not depend on a colonial power.

Taha's activism

Taha praised GGC educational activism when he began writing in 1945[11]. Although he does not seem to have joined the GGC, he was one of the founders of a club for graduates in Atbara[12]. Yusuf Lutfi visited him there in 1942, Taha was organising public meetings and attending literary circles where people would read the Egyptian press and study books together[13]. He believed that he was targeted by the regime for his activities. His schoolfriend, Amin Siddig, was also harassed by the security services, and had difficulty gaining employment after he left the college[14]. Some contemporaries present a picture of a mercilessly fervent activist. When Taha found people at the graduates club playing cards and dominoes, he would knock over their tables and tell them that intellectuals had a duty to oppose the injustice of colonialism, and should not while away the time on games[15].

Taha had good relations with some workers and artisans, although he himself was a professional[16]. Rail workers and professionals had adjoining clubs in Atbara, and when Taha became president of the club for senior workers, he broke down the wall between them. 'Ali Lutfi, who tells this story, sees Taha as one of the first union organisers in Atbara, the centre of Sudanese trade unionism, which began to develop after the authorities granted permission to workers to form clubs in 1934[17]. Al-Fajr's literary and educational activists welcomed their establishment, and saw them as a prelude to trade unions, which were not permitted until 1948[18]. Atbara's artisans club opened in 1935, and by the early 1940s they were discussing the need for union action – prices were rising but the wages were not[19].

World war

In July 1940, three people were injured when Italian bombers attacked Atbara[20]. The world war had come to East Africa, with an Italian front in Ethiopia threatening British power in the Red Sea. German and Italian propaganda was reaching Gordon College[21]. The Sudanese elites, including the GGC, made declarations of loyalty, and political agitation was laid aside until British and Sudanese forces defeated the Italians in March 1941. Before that battle, the military asked Sudan Railways to build a line to Tessenei, just over the Ethiopian border[22].

Taha believed that the British authorities had labelled him as a trouble maker. At some point during the war they transferred him to the Tessenei line as a travelling engineer on the eastern section of the railway[23]. Taha regarded this obscure posting as a demotion[24]. According to Amna Lutfi, who married Taha at this time, she and Taha went to live in Atbara again, probably around 1943, after a period of wandering around Eastern Sudan in a railway car.

Marriage
A visit to Rufa'a

The people who remember Taha's life at this time are not exactly sure of dates. But before Taha left the railway, he went home to Rufa'a and got married. His wedding was in 1940 or 1942, which would have made him about 30 years of age, old for a Sudanese bachelor. His bride was a good catch – Amna Muhammad Lutfi, the daughter of his headmaster. She was educated and had a certain freedom from traditional restrictions on women. Even in his early years, Taha had approved of the liberal domestic arrangements of Lutfi's home and Amna's father's commitment to girls' education[25].

The Lutfi girls married well. Amna married an engineer, and her sister Sayyida wed a doctor – both men travelled around colonial Sudan doing prestigious jobs. The female graduates of colonial schools had begun to join the professional classes, but many of them had to contend with the prejudice that a working woman was not respectable enough to marry. By the 1940s, educated women had premium marriage value, but not all of them used their education in the labour market[26].

Taha was a good catch too – from a modest but respectable branch of the family (the couple shared a great-great-grandfather). He had made it to Gordon College and got a well paid job with the government. Amna's father, now an inspector of education, was an admirer of his young student and neighbour, and Taha paid £E 40 for Amna's bridewealth (two or three times the going rate), and almost as much on her trousseau. (Bridewealth is a payment from the groom to the bride usually held in trust by her male guardian).

The wedding was a fairly big occasion for Daym Lutfi, and the celebrations lasted for three days. Amna wore a robe of silk and gold and danced the bridal dance shyly. Their procession visited the river, and a shrine to *sayyid* Hasan, a Sufi saint who had appeared in a vision in Rufa'a[27]. *Sayyid* Hasan built up his father's Khatmiya *tariqa* in Sudan, and was the grandfather of 'Ali al-Mirghani, the patrician. The visit was a nuptial formality, but it shows that Taha had not disavowed his veneration for Sufi saints in his hostility to the politics of their children.

Indeed, as will be seen in chapter ten, Taha was an admirer of Mirghani spirituality.

Some of Taha's own family were still in Rufa'a. His half brother, Ahmad was working as a driver, and his full brother, Mukhtar, had become a Sufi *shaykh*. He probably joined the 'Arakiyin, one of the old, small-scale *tariqa*s of the Blue Nile. Although Mukhtar had not progressed in colonial schools, he knew all sorts of things, like how to repair a watch or a car, and he was an innovative educator. He tried to re-invent the *khalwa* tradition, by starting a university which taught crafts and technical skills as well as religious studies[28]. His mosque had seven or eight shops around it, where students could learn and ply a trade[29].

Mukhtar's modern Sufi centre was near Lutfi's house. On Sundays and Thursdays his followers held the *zikr* (congregational recitations of the name of God) This Sufi ceremony often involves a big cowhide drum. Mukhtar's drum kept Muhammad Lutfi awake at night, and he would complain to Mukhtar about the noise, but Mukhtar just carried on. Lutfi got so used to the drum that one night when it was not used he went next door and asked Mukhtar to start drumming, to help him sleep[30].

Thread talk

Shortly before the Mahdiya fell, a Sufi *shaykh* in Rufa'a called Farah wad Taktuk said that the Sudanese would soon be ruled by a green-eyed race, who travelled in houses and spoke with threads – *al-safar bil-buyut wal-kalam bil-khuyut*[31]. He was prophesying the trains and telegraphs of modern colonial Africa.

After Mahmud Taha and Amna Lutfi wed, they left Rufa'a to live in the foothills of the Ethiopian highlands in a travelling house, a railway car fitted out for itinerant engineers. With them was al-Rabb Biyjud, who carried out domestic tasks[32]. Taha believed he was repaying his obligations to al-Rabb Biyjud by including her in his own kinship network – many female ex-slaves stayed with their masters at the time, however, because they had few other options. It was an isolated but curiously modern lifestyle for al-Rabb Biyjud and Amna. They lived in Taha's railway car while he worked on the railway lines in his pith helmet, jacket and shorts.

Amna returned to Rufa'a in 1944 to have her first child. He was a son, named Muhammad after his grandfather. A photograph survives of a slight child with a long face and large, serious eyes. At some point the couple returned to Atbara for a time, and Taha probably continued his involvement in political activities. But around the time that Muhammad was born, Taha decided that his political activities and his support for workers' rights were seriously hampering his career. In 1943 or 1944, he resigned from the railway and got a job with the Sudan Light and Power Company (half owned by the government), which ran the trams in the capital. Taha told people in later life that he left the railway because his views about workers conditions conflicted with those of the British[33]. He also wanted to join the independence struggle[34].

Omdurman

Sudan's capital lies at the confluence of the Blue and White Niles, and is made up of three cities. To the north-west of the confluence lies Omdurman, a bazaar town and the capital of the Mahdiya: it was the preferred residence of most Sudanese. Khartoum North, to the north east, was an industrial area developed by the colonialists, and Khartoum itself, below the confluence, was the British administrative capital with an uptown "Arab market". Over the railway tracks were the slums. The world war was ending: it had caused new migrations in Sudan, as the economy swelled to meet the demands of the military and people moved, or were forced to move, to fill jobs. Sudanese troops fought in African theatres of war, and the experience made many prefer the city over the village on return[35].

Economic forces did not cause Taha's migration, and he and his young family did not move to the crowded slums: he chose to stay in Omdurman. The end of the war brought him fortune – he bought up a load of scrap metal from an army base, which suggests that he had money to speculate with[36]. He stayed in a house in al-Morada, next to the Mahdist arsenal that the British had converted into a football stadium[37]. The house had been let by Amna Lutfi's father from Dardiri Muhammad Osman, a schoolmate of Taha's who had become a leading figure in the GGC. Taha's house was quite comfortable, and he now had chairs and a sofa instead of the traditional *angareb* or wooden bed strung with rope. Some war veterans moved to the area, along with rural people drawn to Sudan's cash nexus by the fortunes of war. Taha and his family moved to a house nearby, in Bayt al-Mal, a short time after they arrived[38].

Taha arrived in the capital at a time when the British were looking to include the *effendiya* in the running of the state. Since the late 1930s, the British had become aware that their sometimes contemptuous attitude

towards Sudanese elites was untenable. Some administrators believed
that

> we must make up our minds to mix on much freer terms with
> them in our homes and our clubs and so reach the stage when by
> freer and friendly exchange of ideas we can better understand their
> aspirations[39].

Sudanese nationalists hoped Britain would repay Sudan's loyalty
during the war. Mahdists accepted the government's good intentions
when in 1945 it offered to include elites in an Advisory Council, along
with the religious, commercial and tribal elites. Others, like the Egypt-
unionists who dominated the GGC, preferred to use the spectre of an
Egyptian Sudan to threaten the British into concessions. Taha was
unhappy with Mahdism and Egyptian influence: with like-minded
friends from his schooldays, he began to discuss alternatives. His house
became a place for them to meet and talk, and out of their discussions
was founded one of the first political parties in Sudan, the Republican
party. Its story is taken up in the next chapter.

Conclusion
The end of private life

Taha's time as an engineer in Khartoum was the end of his life as a
private person. After the war he became involved in nationalist agitation
and soon became a political prisoner. What were the experiences that
shaped these 35 years? The evidence is scarce. Taha's contemporaries
describe a serious man who was strict with himself, and generous with
his money and friendships. He had done well at his job and made a
range of contacts among the *effendiya* and industrial workers, but he had
not forgotten Rufa'a, where he returned to marry, and where his son
was born. He told friends later in life that he was searching for a way to
express his ideas in religious ways, but had not found one. He put his
energy into the independence struggle instead[40].

Taha learned about new methods of social organisation in Atbara.
He had joined a colonial elite, but he had worked harder than many in
order to do so. He was an orphan boy from a small farm, who found
the strength of character to get to Gordon College and well paid work.
The long journey of his youth gave him an independent streak, as he
acknowledged to Ibrahim Yusuf. He had a young activist's disdain for the
nationalist institutions on offer at the time, although he shared many of

their aims, and some of their limitations. Independent, forthright, and forceful, Taha was a candidate for the leadership of something. He spent his next 40 years finding out what that candidacy might be.

Chapter 6

The Republican party

Chapters six to ten cover the period from 1945 to 1964, looking at the period from the perspective of marginal political groups, examining their exclusion from power, their organisational methods and ideologies[1]. Chapter six looks at the events of 1945 and 1946. Taha started agitating for independence, but his party met with limited success, until he managed to gain the attention of British prosecutors. He served two jail sentences, which changed his life forever.

The struggle for independence
Independence for the elite

The rivalry between two colonial masters spiced up Sudan's nationalist struggle, otherwise a largely bloodless transfer of power to Sudanese elites led by Sufi landowning patricians. British colonialists had transformed existing tribal and political-religious elites into a patrimonial system and created new elites: graduates, military officers, and big agrarian capitalists. The British used ethnic classifications still recognisable in Sudan today. Areas linked to favoured ethnicities benefited from British rule much more than others. Sudan's export economy was based on the northern Nile valley, and people from other areas could only enter this "cash nexus" by migrating and selling their labour there. The Arab and Islamic culture of the cash nexus became linked explicitly to its economic success, and under British rule partially Islamised or Arabised groups adopted practices that they thought would make them more Islamic or Arab.

The nationalist movement was a narrow one. Only urban people with sufficiently close experience of the workings of the colonial state could effectively challenge it – the elites, and ordinary people drafted into colonial enterprises. In 1956, just over half a million people worked in the modern sector, out of a population of just over ten million[2]. Yet the modern sector of the economy, with its huge income differentials, accounted for over half the country's cash wealth[3]. Urban and rural Sudan were developing away from each other: in the years following World War II, many songs and school plays clearly depicted the quarrel between the urban and the rural[4].

Each of the co-domini had one of the big patricians as a client. The patricians managed relations with their own clients, maintained their economic privileges and their rural constituencies, and tried to develop urban support. They had similar economic interests, and that made their rivalry dishearteningly factional, and meant that smaller urban political groups looked for something new. They turned to institutions created after the arrival of the colonial state. These schools, clubs and unions were places where smaller parties could build up a following. The schools that the British and Egyptians built after the war at nationalist prompting provided recruits for nationalist agitation. In 1946, schoolboys around the capital wore badges calling for the evacuation of British forces, provided by Egyptian agents working through their educational missions in Khartoum[5]. The intelligence services worried about the frequent demonstrations and "the underlying restlessness of the student class and of the smaller intelligentsia"[6].

Across Africa, colonialism inspired the growth of new social formations and associations, created out of the new institutions and experiences that the colonists brought[7]. In Sudan, social clubs created new social bonds by improvising western models of organisation. British security men monitored these developments, "dealing firmly with attempts to wreck existing social clubs with the introduction of politics"[8]. Yet these clubs mushroomed after the war – the number of football clubs in the capital doubled between 1936 and 1946, to 60[9]. Clubs eventually became part of Sudanese urban identity, allowing people to organise themselves by categories which they could choose and help to define. They were a secular urban counterpart to the traditional northern Sudanese community organisation, the Sufi centre. Workers clubs were organised by class and occupation; football clubs were often organised by neighbourhood, sometimes reflecting the neighbours' common ethnic or geographical origin. Their relative autonomy meant that political actors outside the state could use them as a forum for their views.

A house in Omdurman

In 1945, Taha was staying at al-Morada, in Omdurman. Amna Lutfi's brother Yusuf lodged there while attending an Omdurman school. He remembers the house as a busy place, full of young *effendiya* friends of Taha who came to eat and talk politics. Taha was doing well, he was working full time for the municipal trams, and he had a busy social life. He still had old-fashioned religious tastes: he was fond of listening to *maddah*s (itinerant hymn singers), who came to chant the Qur'an. *Maddah*s played an important part in the religious entertainments of a village, but many who came to the towns were little more than beggars[10].

Around October 1945, Taha and his friends held the first meeting of a new party, *al-hizb al-jumhuri*, or the Republican party. Six people attended and five of them became office bearers on the executive council. The party had a western style constitution (see Appendix 1), like a trade union or club, rather than the informal and charismatic structure of a Sufi *tariqa*. It was briefly active in the mid-1940s, but it never had more than 23 members in those years[11]. Many of these men had had a Gordon College education, and jobs in Khartoum. Two of them described themselves as writers and poets – one of these, Muhammad al-Mahdi al-Majdhub, was from a Sufi holy family, the Majadhib of al-Damer. Many of them had a connection with other literate Sufi *tariqa*s of the nineteenth century, like Amin Siddig whose father was a Khatmiya *faki*, or Zanoon Gubara, who came from the village of al-Shaykh al-Tayyib, a nineteenth century scholar who had his own *tariqa*. Zanoon Gubara had travelled to London, Cairo and the Soviet Union, so he had a fairly wide range of experiences: others like Taha had not seen much of the world outside Sudan[12].

Taha and his young friends took religion seriously. When they joined, they swore a vow not to steal and not to engage in sex outside marriage[13]. And they were hyper-active. They would eat a meal together and then write a pamphlet which would be printed on a roneo that Taha had in the house. The pamphlets were wrapped up in a cloth and given to young Yusuf Lutfi to smuggle out of the house – the colonial security services were thought to be watching[14]. Then they would go to work, spreading the message. What was it?

The Republican party message

Among many common traits, the Ashigga' and the Mahdists – who were increasingly identified with the new Umma party, funded secretly by 'Abd al-Rahman al-Mahdi – shared a commitment to monarchy, led either by 'Abd al-Rahman or Farouk of Egypt. Taha and his friends saw their shared monarchism as evidence of the two groups' complicity with the colonialist powers, and their distance from the people. They chose the "Republican" name to emphasise their reliance on the Sudanese people – the Arabic word *jumhuri* connotes public rule slightly more strongly than its Latin/English translation.

Al-sifr al-awwal

The party's manifesto was called *al-sifr al-awwal* ("The first volume"), and appeared in October 1945. Its main message was the need for a redirection in the independence struggle, delivered with intemperate remarks about the professional politicos taking over the GGC, which it attacked for restricting political activity to the exchange of memoranda with the government. Instead, said the manifesto, the GGC should address the people. The political problem of Sudan would be resolved by educating people to self-confidence; economic problems would be resolved through self reliance. Modern education alienated the youth from manual work, instead of teaching them free thought and respect for labour. The manifesto contained a section on the rights of women, which stressed their maternal vocation.

Al-sifr al-awwal reads like a writer's first work, incautiously flitting between political satire and gnomes of philosophical and religious wisdom – the virtues of free thought, the relative values of western civilisation and Islam. The manifesto is a Muslim one in many respects, introduced with a Qur'anic exhortation to faithfulness in affliction, and full of optimistic expectations of religious education:

> The Republican party wants a life lived under the guidance of true religion. It wants to return life to what it was like in the days of 'Umar – the great 'Umar ['Umar ibn al-Khattab, the second caliph or successor of the prophet Muhammad, d. 644]. The days when men were human, as human as Adam, the days when people feared God and feared nothing else ... and the Republican party's way [to that goal] is education[15].

The manifesto devotes much of the short section on economics to the question of development of the south: "for whom twentieth century civilisation has ordained a life barefoot and naked, hungry, sick and ignorant"[16]. In addition to this sense of an educative mission

for southern "ignorance" the manifesto calls for the (re-)education of
the north, and it calls for no discrimination between citizens. Sudan is
mentioned more often than religion[17]. It was noted in chapter five that
elites who previously identified themselves as Muslim Arabs began to
identify themselves as Sudanese, expecting all other Sudanese to join
them in a cultural and linguistic unit. This process influenced Taha, who
wrote about the nationalist movement leading the country to a new dawn
"under the guidance of Islam, with a consciousness of Arab excellence"[18].
The party's 1945 constitution had called for deeper relations with Arab
and neighbouring countries, and for the maintenance of Sudan's borders
– that is, the unity of the south and the north.

Republican activism

While the patricians and the nationalist leaders manoeuvred to control
the state, the Republicans took their message to the public squares,
cinemas and cafés. The pamphlets that Yusuf Lutfi smuggled past
the police outside Taha's house were collected by the members who
distributed them in coffee houses and cinemas. Activists made brief
speeches and then dived off to another venue, so that in one night they
covered three or four places, making the party appear bigger than it
was. The activists' choice of venue was also a choice of audience – the
younger, male citizens of modern Sudan, who shared their exposure to
the modern and the foreign, paying for their leisure in cafes and cinemas.
Sometimes the police picked up the party men, and they spent a night in
custody – they even sent a telegram to the speaker of the British House
of Commons to complain at the government's "war against freedom
of expression"[19]. This telegram poses a minor chronological problem
– all Republican sources surveyed here date the party's formation to the
twenty-sixth of October 1945, when the manifesto was published, but
the telegram is dated the first of October. It seems likely that the party
later took the manifesto's publication as the date of foundation, but that
they organised informally before this.

The party's secrecy allowed them to produce and disseminate instant
and aggressive analysis of the political scene. One pamphlet was in
English, entitled "Islam: the way out". Another, al-nadhir al-'uryan ("The
naked warning") appeared in 1946, and attacked the GGC, the Umma
and Ashigga' for resorting to the power of the patricians, instead of
developing an authentic ideology; and for playing off one colonial power
against the other, instead of building up the power and self confidence

of the Sudanese people. Independence would only mean "exchanging the English for English in Sudanese skins"[20].

Taha believed that the Khatmiya and Mahdist sects had served a purpose in giving a national consciousness to northern Sudan. However, they now dominated and divided Sudan's nationalist movement, whose competing parties "repeat ... the ugly song of sectarianism"[21]. Like other Muslims from the Nile valley, Taha was suspicious of Mahdism. He felt that the Mahdiya was a chaotic period, and disliked the Mahdi's shrewd son 'Abd al-Rahman, who used his religious prestige to appropriate his followers' labour on plantations given to him by the British.

'Ali al-Mirghani was also deeply involved in the colonial economy and represented the concerns of economic elites to the colonial regime, but Taha saw him as true Sufi who had personally abandoned wealth[22]. He and Amin Siddig paid al-Mirghani a visit around 1945. Siddig would not bow in his presence, even though he was the son of a Khatmiya *faki*. Al-Mirghani could cope with young hotheads, however; he seated Siddig personally, to the consternation of the deferential Mirghani entourage[23]. Taha thought that al-Mirghani was a casualty of the patrician system's success, who was trying his best to prevent a Mahdist takeover. A 1946 pamphlet, addressed to the "calamitous" Umma and Ashigga parties, read:

> [One of] you exploit one patrician [al-Mirghani] who does not know what he wants, and [one of] you is exploited by another patrician [al-Mahdi] who knows what he wants. Both of you are at the brink of an abyss[24].

Taha had sympathy for al-Mirghani the Sufi, but he had no time for the *shari'a* establishment set up by the colonialists. In 1946, Sudan's *mufti* issued a judgement against "political" preaching in mosques. Taha was already using mosques as a forum for his ideas. The party responded with a pamphlet entitled *muftina wa muftihim* ("Our *mufti* and their *mufti*"), which compared Sudan's obedient Muslim establishment with Palestine's *mufti*, then at the forefront of the anti-colonial struggle[25].

In March the police picked up some inflammatory pamphlets published by Communists and Republicans. Taha was interviewed by the criminal investigation department and in May, he was summoned by the police magistrate to execute a bond of £E 50 to keep the peace. The magistrate was W C McDowall, a Glaswegian who arrived in Sudan at the beginning of the war and had been kindly disposed to the "bright and friendly" young *effendis* he had met at his first posting in Eastern

Sudan[26]. He tried a few young educated agitators from different parties in Khartoum, and later recalled:

> [Their] seditious speeches were never taken too seriously and were generally dealt with by fines or short terms of imprisonment. I received occasional threatening letters, including two death threats, which I passed on the Sudan Police[27].

Taha refused to be bound over, and accepted instead a one year jail sentence, served in Khartoum's Kober prison. He began to figure in the political intelligence summaries, compiled monthly by the security service and sent to province governors.

> The Republican Party, hitherto an insignificant handful of slightly unbalanced young men who attracted no particular public attention, achieved in June, an unexpected prominence, as a result of the prosecution of their President, Mahmud Mohamed Taher, for distributing in May a highly seditious and dangerously inflammatory pamphlet ... he refused [to be bound over] ... and was accordingly committed to prison ... Every effort was made, unsuccessfully, to explain to him and to his friends that he was not being required to denounce his Republican principles but merely to undertake to propagate them by legitimate means. He preferred the role of 'political martyr' and has been hailed as such by the [graduate] Congress and the local vernacular press. As a result of this advertisement, the Republican Party's shares have boomed and its membership risen to nearly 100 [sic][28].

Before 1945, the police were responsible for prisons. After the war, prisons were given their own department, and an effort was made to "encourage industry and self-respect among prisoners, and so to develop the reformative element of imprisonment"[29]. The post-1945 emphasis on social intervention led to the establishment of a "criminal lunatic asylum" and children's prisons with scout troops[30]. Prisoners had to work in quarries, farms, and domestic service. Taha differentiated between his political imprisonment and the cases of other offenders, and he believed that he should not be obliged to work in the prison. He also refused to stand up for British officers. After one day of this behaviour he was put in solitary confinement on bread and water. Taha's friends began agitating for his release at their usual haunts. The civil secretary was obliged to make a press statement on the Taha affair[31].

Using the newspapers

Taha's stand against the authorities won him some publicity. *Al-Ra'y al-'Amm*, the leading newspaper of the day, gave details of his disobedience in jail[32]. When he was unconditionally released after 50 days, the intelligence services wrote it up as the governor general's "act of clemency"[33]. But the nationalist movement sent telegrams and poems of congratulation to the party leader who had "gone in a man and come out a hero"[34]. Republican writers believe that he was released because the authorities "did not want to make a hero out of Taha", in the words of an un-named British official whom they frequently quote[35].

Success and freedom

Taha's first brush with the law was a marvellous success. The nationalist movement in Sudan was a timorous one by African and Middle Eastern standards: most of the senior nationalists had too much to lose, and all the riches of the state to gain, and the younger radicals were easily dismissed as "smaller intelligentsia" and easily dealt with in police courts. But Taha called the magistrates' bluff and came off the winner. His self-projection as a political martyr paid instant dividends, as police membership estimates show.

Taha's success may have made the party more aggressive. The deputy secretary of the party, Amin al-Tinay, disagreed with Taha and formed the Liberal Republicans. "How many men constitute a party?" asked the Ashigga' press snootily[36]. The Liberal Republicans wrote to the British foreign secretary to demand independence. But when Amin al-Tinay's journalist brother wrote up Amin al-Tinay's opinions as those of the Republicans, Taha went and confronted the journalist at night[37]. In another incident, Taha and Amin Siddig (who kept a gun) threatened a broadcaster from the radio station in Omdurman who had broadcast a negative report on the party[38].

Perhaps the trial gave Taha a sense of the dramatic potential of the law courts, and the publicity value of martyrdom. All the same, few people from Taha's class were prepared to go to prison for their convictions, and he could have been kept in for a year and come out with nothing. He was one of the "smaller intelligentsia", of the derisive police dossiers, but he was a man in his mid-thirties with a career, and a husband and father too. In June 1946, when Taha was in prison, Amna went back to Rufa'a and had a daughter, called Asma[39]. Taha's family had to come to terms with the fact that their young *effendi* was away making a bid for political influence.

Taha was out of prison at the end of July 1946, but not for long. He was important enough to be a guest speaker at the Umma party Bairam festival in September – the Bairam recalls the patriarch Abraham's sacrifice of his son. Security men heard both of Sudan's colonial rulers condemned roundly[40]. The intelligence services believed that the Republicans were now part of the Independence Front, a grouping led by the Umma party that opposed links with Egypt[41]. In February, the Republicans had described the Umma and Ashigga' parties as "more calamitous for this country than calamity upon calamity"[42]. Now that he had acquired some celebrity, Taha may have been looking for their recognition – the British security men started to mistake him for an Umma fellow-traveller.

The Rufa'a incident, 1946
Female genital mutilation

In September, Taha involved himself in another legal challenge – this time a new law against female circumcision, or genital mutilation. This practice scarred the overwhelming majority of northern Sudanese women, and was and is widely seen as a prerequisite for marriage[43]. The British campaign against circumcision began in the 1930s, and had the support of Sudan's elite. In March 1945, the Sudan medical service published a booklet with explicit and harrowing warnings of the dangers of the practice[44]. The *mufti*'s foreword to the booklet said that infibulation, the severest form of circumcision, was un-Islamic and should be ended, citing classical Muslim legists for support[45]. 'Ali al-Mirghani and 'Abd al-Rahman al-Mahdi attacked the "vicious custom"[46]. In 1946, the Advisory Council (a policy making body comprised of northern notables) approved the law, which interdicted even the relatively mild *sunna* circumcision, which most of the *mufti*'s legists were prepared to support[47].

Ina Beasley was a colonial educator who arrived in Sudan in 1939. She involved herself with the government campaign and recorded some contemporary perceptions. Two of her closest collaborators were from Rufa'a. Batoul Muhammad 'Isa was a midwife who left Rufa'a's girls' school in 1926[48]. A second collaborator, Nafissa 'Awad al-Karim, was unmarried. She had an intimidating fluency in classical Arabic, which was deployed against male audiences[49]. Taha would almost certainly have known of this campaign, which was welcomed by Beasley's women informants:

"Why were we not born twenty years later?" some of the Girls'
Training College students used to say. "It is all very well," said the
old women. "We have always been told we are stupid and that men
know all about religion. They told us this was part of our religion and
we have undergone all this suffering. Now suddenly they say it is not
our religion and we ought not to do it. That it is our fault that it goes
on. All right, but first you must assure us that without it we shall get
husbands for our daughters"[50].

Douglas Newbold, a senior official and dedicated opponent of the
practice, reported this stock male response after a debate with Gordon
College students, all of whom agreed that "women were the only obstacle
to reform among the educated classes"[51]. Beasley responded scathingly
to the self-exculpation of Sudanese men:

The young men might sulk and be resentful that their barbarous habits
were brought to the light of day just when they were beginning to
claim their fitness to hold high office and achieve self government[52].

Beasley's subordination of the right of self-determination to the
rights of women accurately represents Republican perceptions of the
colonisers. They believed that the British were using the law to portray
the Sudanese as too backward for independence. In a tract published in
1945, the Republicans pointed out that the practice, which they did not
promote, could not be excised from Sudanese society by legislative fiat,
but only by education. They agitated against the law on the streets and
in the mosques[53].

Fatma Amasayb

Fatma Amasayb, later a television actor, was circumcised in Rufa'a in
1946. In September, her mother Minayn bitt Hakim was the first person
to be arrested under the new law against circumcision. R H Dick, the
local DC, sentenced her to four months in jail[54]. Taha was in Rufa'a at the
time, fresh from his victory in Kober jail. He confronted the authorities
again, in a Friday sermon in the mosque:

This is not a time for worship in seclusion or in houses of prayer,
people, this is a time for struggle [jihad] ... any of you who see a victim
and does not vindicate him, God will not vindicate him to his enemies
... and he has not even a nail-paring's worth of faith[55].

Taha led a demonstration from the mosque to the *merkaz* (local administrative centre) where Minayn was detained. The crowd freed her, but she was re-arrested that night by a policeman relative and handed over to 'Abdallah Abu Sinn, the Shukriya mayor of Rufa'a. Minayn was held in Hassa Heisa, across the Nile. The next day, the schools and market closed as Taha led about one thousand of Rufa'a's angry menfolk to smash up the *merkaz*. Abu Sinn's life was threatened[56]. Although the ferry was stopped, the demonstrators were jam packed into commandeered rowing boats. At one school, the boys left their classes to join the demonstration – a young Hasan al-Turabi, later closely involved in Taha's execution, also joined in[57].

They reached the *merkaz* in Hassa Heisa and began stoning it, with three British officials inside. According to 'Abd al-Rahman 'Ali al-Shaykh, the demonstrators threatened to kill Dick, the DC[58]. His father 'Ali al-Shaykh was a Rufa'a's elder who threatened to circumcise Dick's wife himself, with Taha translating the ugly threat[59]. The telephone lines to the provincial capital were cut down; Dick feared for his life (according to the nervous diary kept by Winifred Johnson, the wife of a local inspector on the Gezira irrigation scheme) and he told two British visitors to run for it[60].

The crowd released Minayn, and the next day a company of Nuba troops came from Wad Medani, the provincial capital, to Rufa'a. The non-Arabised soldiers could presumably be trusted to fire on "Arab" demonstrators. According to al-Shaykh, Taha led a crowd armed with sticks, swords and even rifles to the *merkaz*, chanting "Death, death, death and martyrdom". The troops fired low, and a number of people were hit.

The situation was defused by 'Abd al-Karim Abu Sinn, a local *nazir* (tribal leader), who negotiated the crowd's dispersal. He was sensitive to the criticisms levelled at his family, and to the nationalist (as opposed to the tribal) feeling of the crowd: "I don't speak to you as a *nazir khatt*, but as a fellow citizen", he said. One of the crowd's demands the day before had been that Native Administration should be abolished, because the involvement of 'Abdallah Abu Sinn in Minayn's second arrest had roused existing resentment against him[61].

Taha, his brother Mukhtar, and several others were arrested and taken to Hassa Heisa, and demonstrations died down immediately. In October, 16 of them were tried in Wad Medani. The judge was Muhammad Abu Rannat, later the first Sudanese chief justice, and known as "the black

Englishman" amongst some Sudanese, because of his accommodating attitude to the colonial power[62]. Taha refused to defend himself, and was convicted of inciting hatred against the government[63]. He got two years and his co-accused received lighter sentences. Taha's father-in-law, Muhammad Lutfi, who had joined the demonstration, was in court to see the verdict. He was very relieved at the leniency of the sentence, went home and told his daughter Amna, and thanked God[64].

Back in the capital

A few Republican activists in the capital were arrested after they made speeches in their leader's defence outside cinemas and cafes[65]. But the security men were no longer worried about the Republican party. They did not even bother to prosecute Amin Siddig, the party's secretary, when he published an "actionable" article in *Sawt al-Sudan*: "public interest has subsided and [Taha] is regarded as having got his deserts," they said[66]. Taha's imprisonment won him immediate and widespread publicity. *Al-Ra'y al-'Amm* carried the story throughout October. 'Abd al-Wahhab Zayn al-'Abidin, who was the secret head of the Communist movement in Sudan, and active as the secretary of the GGC, wrote a defence of Taha with the secretary of the United Front of pro-Egyptian parties. They were hauled in by the police to explain themselves, and according to the account of their interrogators, they back-tracked[67]. Social clubs in several towns closed in protest.

Taha's reactionary protest had mobilised broad support in his home town, but his followers were still talking to a tiny urban audience: using newspapers meant that Republicans could only address the four percent of Sudanese people who were literate[68]. In 1947, the aggregate circulation of Sudan's nine newspapers was just over 15,000, and even then many of the copies were bought by the government, partly as a way of influencing their editors[69].

Long term effects

The Rufa'a incident brought Taha publicity, but its long-term effect is assessed negatively by Lilian Sanderson, a campaigner against genital mutilation:

> The Government must have viewed this demonstration with considerable alarm because an army detachment was sent to Rufa'a and a clause was added to the Law, that thereafter no-one could be prosecuted without the permission of the Governor of the province

> ... [Taha] admitted that his was a gesture against a non-Sudanese
> administration rather than support for continued mutilation. It made
> British authorities very cautious about prosecutions in rural areas,
> and thereby probably influenced successive independent Sudanese
> governments not to take more effective action against those mutilating
> girls[70].

Taha's stridency was hampered by his ambivalence – he opposed both
female circumcision and the law against it. In fact, his opposition to the
practice may not have been clear to Rufa'a – one schoolboy participant
later came to the conclusion that he had joined a protest in support
of infibulation[71]. Muhammad al-Mahdi al-Majdhub, a poet and party
member, described Taha as "an Arab rebel for [sexual] honour and
religion"[72]. Taha's opportunistic protest was, nevertheless, an effective
piece of resistance to the colonisers, one which they feared more than
effendiya outbursts on the evils of imperialism. Many African nationalist
movements were no more than educated clubs with cadres numbered in
the hundreds. Rural power was much more awesome to the colonialists.
When the Kenyan nationalist Jomo Kenyatta opposed British legislation
against female circumcision in the 1930s, his Kikuyu organisation grew
from 300 members to 10,000[73].

Like Kenyatta, Taha believed the practice would only end through
education[74]. Taha had the support of a surprising array of Sudanese
opinion for this stand. Fatma Ibrahim, a leader of the Sudanese Women's
Union, and a former Communist MP, believes that the challenge to the
colonialists was more pressing than the campaign against circumcision[75].
Hasan al-Turabi, later a bitter enemy, accepted Taha's nationalist
credentials[76]. Later Republican writers defended the integrity of his action,
although they opposed circumcision: however, the practice continued
even within Republican families for some time after the incident.

Native Administration

The Rufa'a demonstrators' challenge to Native Administration, the
cornerstone of British perceptions and administrative policy is given
no space in official Republican histories. But the incident throws some
light on the conflict between increasingly educated Rufa'a people, and
their Shukriya masters in the Native Administration. Before the Rufa'a
incident, Taha's following was dominated by Khartoum *effendis*; after it,
he had a wider support amongst the people of Rufa'a[77]. 'Abd al-Rahman

'Ali Al-Shaykh said that the demonstrators demanded the removal of the Sinnab mayor who deceitfully surrendered Minayn to the *merkaz* after she had been freed. This demand does not appear in the intelligence report on the event, but it was a direct attack on the colonially constructed rural elites who maintained order cheaply. It may reflect the *effendiya* irritation with the power of men who did not meet their educational standards, mentioned in chapter three.

Conclusion

The representation of this early period of Republican activity is distorted to some extent by Republican historians of the 1970s, when Republican hostility was directed at Muslim Brothers and patrician parties. Later writers concentrate on Taha's early opposition to patrician parties and colonially-sponsored *shari'a* legists. The sources surveyed here suggest that he reserved his strongest criticisms during this period for the intelligentsia's handling of the independence struggle.

The Rufa'a incident may have been an attack on the patrimonial system of rural Sudan, but later Republican historians preferred to stress their opposition to the *shari'a* legists who supported the colonialists' anti-circumcision agenda.

Some Republicans retrospectively suggest that Taha was at this stage more of a nationalist than an Islamic activist. The sources surveyed here suggest that, while he attacked the British vociferously, he was already using Islamic idioms fluently and somewhat opportunistically. His *jihad* for Minayn bitt Hakim was an attempt to mobilise local indignation at a colonialist attack on pre-Islamic customs, indeed a custom which his movement did not support. *Jihad* was a term commonly used by people with grievances against the non-Muslim authorities – striking workers, people who had lost taxes, slaves or land to foreign law. Taha, however, picked a reactionary's fight with the colonialists on a cultural, not an economic issue.

Taha's relations with other political actors in Sudan were complex. His criticism of the nationalist movement was noteworthy for its attention to the southern problem, and for the need for southern unity, as Khalid points out in his history of the period[78]. He was prepared to look further for solutions than many contemporary northern politicians. However, he was not prepared to look further than the Arab-Muslim state. Chapter five discussed how Sudanese nationalism, dominated by a small elite, conflated the idea of the Arab-Muslim state and an imagined

Arab-Muslim Sudanese nation. Like most nationalists, Taha was unable to make this crucial distinction between the Sudan imagined in an urban school and the diverse societies of the hinterland. Tellingly, Taha's British prosecutors do not seem to have noticed his opposition to the new-born political parties: they saw his anti-Egyptian party as a subsidiary of the overwhelmingly Umma Independence Front; above all they saw him as a man who wanted a religious republic – "A small fanatical party of reactionaries"[79].

Chapter 7

Taking the lift to the fields of heaven

"I felt," said Taha "when I had settled into the prison, that I had come there by God's will, and I made my retreat to him"[1]. His retreat lasted through his time in prison and for two years afterwards. The thoughts and dreams he had during this time guided his life and brought him to his death.

Prison in Wad Medani and Khartoum
The vilest social classes

In 1946, Taha was tried and jailed in Wad Medani with 16 others from Rufa'a. With about 50,000 inhabitants, it was the second largest city in Sudan, and the capital of Blue Nile province. Its prison held over 500 prisoners[2]. Prisoners in Sudan's jails were divided into grades, distinguished by their uniform, with the best uniforms reserved for white prisoners. Taha was offered first class treatment, but he refused – although he had made an effort to be treated as a non-criminal political prisoner in his first spell in prison[3]. He wore the third class *'aragi damuriya*, a knee-length robe of cheap cotton which was the traditional dress of rural Sudan before the long Egyptian *jallabiya* became popular in the twentieth century[4]. *Al-Ra'y al-'Amm* denounced the government for putting him in with "the vilest social classes"[5].

Few prisoners were from Taha's *effendi* class – Medani jail was a place where he could mix with another Sudan, the law-breakers of a large provincial town. From the first days of colonialism, the British authorities had used prisons as holding pens for "idle persons" and "vagabonds" (escaped slaves): prisons were urban institutions used to discipline and shame the poorest classes; emphatic class markers that helped make economic divisions tangible and intelligible[6].

If Taha formed relationships with prisoners, they were not memorable enough for him to mention. He was still involved in the struggle – for a brief period he was able to maintain links to the outside, and his brother and others were with him inside[7]. Sudanese social networks made prison walls porous – a relative of Muhammad Lutfi who worked as a nurse in Wad Medani managed to visit him every day. This conduit allowed Taha to continue to write and to follow party activities in jail[8]. He also began a fast, news of which reached people outside the jail. The papers, urged on by the Republican party, reported it as a hunger strike against British rule. Taha, however, told them to stop. His was a Muslim fast broken every night, not a hunger strike, he said.

A strange friend

Taha's links with the outside were discovered, and he was transferred out of Wad Medani to Kober jail in Khartoum. Before he left Wad Medani, however, a strange friend appeared. 'Ali al-Mirghani, the leader of the Khatmiya sect, whom Taha and Amin Siddig had met in 1945 or 1946, asked the British as a personal favour to release the young hothead[9]. "Some malignant fate seems to lead the Sayed [al-Mirghani] only to intervene in cases where the Government cannot possibly yield," sighed the compiler of November's intelligence summary[10]. Al-Mirghani's petition failed, and Taha was transferred out of Wad Medani to Kober prison in Khartoum – Mukhtar and the others were freed after a few months, and Taha spent most of his sentence alone. The governor there remembered him from his stay in May, when his refusal to work had given him some jail celebrity. Taha was given a separate cell, and left alone to make his retreat – or *khalwa* – to God[11].

Khalwa

Taha's first *khalwa* was a Qur'anic basic school: that is one of several meanings of the word, which connotes withdrawal, seclusion, emptiness and contemplation. In central Sudan, these places of seclusion became community centres where people could partake of the blessing of a saint's prayers. *Khalwa*s withstood the centralising forces of the nineteenth and twentieth century: "the deep social imprint of the *khalwa*s was never effaced, many of them surviving as foci of ethnic identity and local government"[12]. They offered spiritual direction to people who aspired to wider spiritual experience. *Shaykh*s directed these aspirants through stages of initiation. The ascetic rigour and esoteric knowledge of the experience made them *khawass* (elect), while run-of-the-mill adherents were *murid*s (aspirants) or *'awwam* (laity)[13].

Retreat allowed the earliest Middle Eastern Sufis to leave the corruption they perceived in their world. They took the terms *khawass* and *'awwam*, used by the earliest Muslim social scientists to describe socio-economic distinctions, to assert a different kind of human hierarchy[14]. Renouncing the world was a way of denouncing it, and esoteric knowledge secretly censured the public science of the state – the *shari'a*. This antagonism has generated much historical analysis[15]. But Sudanese Sufism, born outside the Muslim state, does not fit neatly into these categories. Early Sufi writings stress instead the vivid psychological experiences, charisma and social activism of a few leading figures. Oral and written accounts of their retreats are epic narratives of asceticism, theophany and miracle. Ahmad al-Huda, who brought the west African Tijaniya order to Sudan in the nineteenth century, spent 40 days prostrate on the ground, without food, drink or consciousness[16]. Others made themselves insensate through weeks on the rosary, or fasted fasts of abandoned zeal – a handful of sorghum for ten days, or even no food, drink or sleep for ten days[17]. These intense experiences were often public, and they conferred a celebrity on the men and women who underwent them. For many Nile valley Muslims, that celebrity was *baraka* or blessing, that could burst out into miracles and cures for illness.

Taha's *khalwa* was a public psychological event. However, there are few records of the experience itself – the social and political consequences of the experience are the preoccupation of his own writings and those of his followers. He and they used the celebrity conferred by the spiritual moment to inspire their activism. Taha did not write down what happened in his cell, but it is possible to make some guesses about his experience from remarks he later made to his circle, and from recollections of contemporaries.

Kober

Taha wore his prison *'aragi* and did not cut his beard or hair for four years. Alone in the cell, he fasted by day and spent the night in prayer. His fasts have a legendary quality: three days, then five, then ten, then 29 days without any food or water. 'Ali Lutfi says that Taha's condition drew the incredulous attention of the prison doctor. According to one story, the authorities weighed the water in his shower bucket, and then weighed it coming out the drain, because they could not believe he was not drinking it[18]. Taha's dreams became very vivid to him. Like the dreams of many African Sufi reformers, they involved an encounter with the prophet. Unlike the Mahdi's dreams, there were no swords of truth or calls to *jihad* – instead, there was agrarian calm with a modern twist:

> ... [Taha] said to me that he was in a lift, taken up very high, up to the clouds, and he found huge fields and a man there – Muhammad. He said, "Praise God, you have come to your farm, take your farm. [Taha] accepted the farm[19].

Books

The jail library had books from the classical traditions of Islam – the Qur'an and works by al-Bukhari and al-Ghazali. Al-Bukhari (d 810) is widely regarded as the most scrupulous recorder of *hadith*, oral accounts of the prophet's sayings and actions[20]. Al-Ghazali (d 1111) was a Muslim polymath who left a plum post at a Baghdad University to live in a minaret and meditate, when he found that he could no longer make sense of the legal and theological books which made up his life[21]. Taha had two of al-Ghazali's works, one dealing with the knowledge he had received from God, and one about pitfalls on the way of perfection. He only read the latter, to save him time on his trip to heaven. He told Ibrahim Yusuf that he was not interested in al-Ghazali's knowledge second-hand: "You must find your own knowledge from God"[22].

"He who has no *shaykh*, his *shaykh* is Satan", said Abu Yazid al-Bistami (d 874), one of the earliest Sufi theosophists, in a phrase current in Sudan[23]. Taha had no *shaykh*, but he took the prophet as his spiritual director, his presence mediated through visions and through the writings of al-Bukhari[24].

> In jail [Taha] read al-Bukhari. The most accurate *hadith*. There's a lot of spirituality in it. Al-Bukhari would perform his ablutions and pray two prostrations before writing down a *hadith*. In al-Bukhari he said he found out how the prophet worked [his life] – his ablution, prayer and sleep. The details. He took them from al-Bukhari and lived the prophet in his actions and words, and his spiritual condition[25].

Taha used al-Bukhari's fragments of the prophet's life to live out Muhammad's story in a colonial cell, and he used fasting to enhance his imaginative perception. He later gave a description of the experience to Girgis Iskander, a doctor who felt that Taha's experience tallied with that of many mystics:

He said it was like a nervous breakdown which can be brought about by some physical mechanism like fasting or crushing longing for an unattainable goal. Fasting here is the mere [repression of the] demand of the body for food, and not as prescribed by any religion. This demand for food is pitted against a determination to continue depriving the body of nourishment until the nervous system gives way = nervous breakdown. When such a state is reached, a person might see visual images, "hallucinating", or he might give any verses from a religious text particular meanings[26].

After a while, Taha found the visions unsatisfying. He gave them up to study the Qur'an. Taha was looking for intimacy in his cell, and he found it in the Qur'an's secret meanings unrevealed to anyone before[27]. In 1951, he recalled his decision to continue his retreat after leaving the prison:

Was it the desire for knowledge that kept me in [retreat]? By God, no. It was work for another end which kept me there, an end greater than knowledge, an end for which knowledge is but a means. That end is my self, which I had lost in the heap of delusions and trivialities. It was my duty to seek it [the self] under the guidance of the Qur'an. I wanted to find it, and I wanted to spread it, and I wanted to be at peace with it, before calling anyone else to Islam ... He who lacks a thing cannot give that thing[28].

Authentic self

Theosophical Sufis use scripture as a mystic primer – it allows them to turn textual obscurities and difficulties into a virtue as they puzzle out a meaning intimate to themselves. Other people might long for friends in isolation: Taha longed for authenticity. He articulated his longings in Sufi language, and found Sufi answers – he believed that he encountered God in his cell, and that this encounter transformed him into a different human being, an *asil* (someone who has found his own authenticity). 'Abdullahi An-Na'im, who met Taha 20 years later, described this authenticity:

It was existential, not intellectual. It was a lifestyle, not what he would do. The key is that he is truly a holistic person, everything related to everything else. There were no departments, no divisions[29].

For Taha, authenticity was a stage to a higher spiritual station. If he reached it, his personality would disappear into perfection. He believed that one individual incarnation of perfection would transform the world justice and peace. His *khalwa* taught him that the political transformation he wanted for Sudan could only come about through personal transformation, and he believed that his duty was no longer to attack the British but to purify himself. Taha's trip to the absolute had been sketched out by previous Sufis, who described the highest stage with the picture of a perfect man, *al-insan al-kamil*, who has vanquished human frailty through long processes of failure and forgiveness. Taha seems to have drawn imaginative links between this perfect or perfected man and Jesus; and between Jesus and *al-maqam al-mahmud*, a Qur'anic use of Taha's first name which can be translated as "a laudable [*mahmud*] station" where a human being could directly address God. These ideas were incorporated into the Sufi picture of Muhammad, and sung in the hymns of the *maddah*s, but Taha, like other Sufi theosophists, tried to relate them to himself.

Jesus

Taha's secrets eventually led him to be tried for apostasy. One person he met in Kober was later to become an enemy – 'Ali Taliballah. Like Taha, he was looking for religious answers, and he was close to the Egyptian Muslim Brothers. In 1947, Taliballah was jailed for ten months for possessing a pistol[30]. In 1968, he was a witness to Taha's apostasy. Taliballah told the court that Taha claimed authority over *shari'a*, but a few days later he told the grand *qadi*, Sudan's senior *shari'a* judge, that Taha's claims were even more comprehensive, as the grand *qadi* explained to the press:

> Mr 'Ali Taliballah said that he was with Mahmud Muhammad Taha in prison, and knew from some imprisoned Muslim *effendi*s that Mahmud Muhammad Taha had informed them the night before that he had become the master of time, and that he was called to bear the message of religion, and that he was Christ the son of Mary. The next day, he [Taliballah] went to [Taha's] cell ... and asked him about the truth of this matter. [Taha] said it was true, that he was Christ, and that Islamic *shari'a*, as it had come to the prophet (peace be upon him) had come to an end and that he would be the person responsible for interpreting the true meaning of the Qur'an, and that anyone who died without believing in him, would die an infidel. Mr 'Ali Taliballah says that he was concerned about the matter and wrote to the late *shaykh* Lutfi in Rufa'a to come and visit Mahmud in his prison, out of pity for what had happened to him[31].

Taha was a political prisoner, and as Taliballah testified, Taha's secret

Qur'an taught him about the legal problem of the Islamic state and not only about personal transformation. Taliballah may have exaggerated Taha's claims in the heat of an apostasy trial, but Taha's retreat was a time when he fixed on the need to reform the *shari'a*, to make it fit the needs of a modern state and the modern world (his views are set out in detail in chapter 12) Taha's modernising urge has parallels with contemporary Islamic reform movements. But it differed in two areas. First, Taha's reworking of the *shari'a* radically advocated the abandonment of some *shari'a* norms. Secondly, Taha came to believe that reform, modernisation and revival would only come about through the reform, modernisation and revival of one individual, whose dynamic purity could turn the world over, "like the flip of a coin"[32]. 'Ali Taliballah and many others believed that Taha claimed to be that person, although few close to Taha heard him say he was. His *khalwa* gave him the belief, rather, that such a person must exist, and that he himself must try to become that person, whether or not his attempt succeeded. He was a candidate for the highest office – a will which he wrote at the time expresses his sense of disjunction from the lives of others and the life of his own body. In his will, Taha said that he should be buried unwashed, unshrouded and without prayers said, in an unknown place[33]. (Which is exactly what happened).

Home for more

When Taha left prison at the end of 1948, his father-in-law Muhammad Lutfi came to meet him, and take him back to his wife and two children in Rufa'a. 'Ali Lutfi, Muhammad's son, was a schoolboy then, and his father told him to compose a verse in his honour, about tears of joy. He recited it to an unfamiliar Taha: a small *effendi* wrapped in white Sudanese clothes, the *'aragi* and a white wrap, and a turban. Underneath the turban was long, thick hair and a huge beard, uncut for two years.

The hair and beard remained uncut. Taha decided to continue with his search for the self after leaving prison. He stayed in Muhammad Lutfi's house, with his wife, son and daughter. It was another period of isolation for the family – although Taha was now physically present, he was travelling in his world of mysterious scriptures and visions. The family came and went from Taha's room in the house, where he prayed his days away. But as a retreatant, he had to spend time away from his children – the cares of the world – and from conjugal relations.

Taha's behaviour and appearance caused alarm in Rufa'a. An engineer, and the son-in law of *shaykh* Lutfi, he would wander around the town in a torn robe and worn out shoes, and eat the plainest village food. He would go down to the river in the brief cool dawn, and tell bemused onlookers that he was listening to the waves on the Nile extolling God[34]. Muhammad Lutfi, his father-in-law, paid for all this devotion, maintaining Taha and his young family from his own pocket. Muhammad Lutfi was still an admirer of his former pupil, but people who wanted to criticise Taha would always bring up this neglect of duty[35].

Taha's defence of Minayn bitt Hakim had won the admiration of people in Rufa'a. His first followers had been young *effendis* like himself, but he had persuaded a rural constituency of the power of protest. Now, however, there were plenty of people to criticise him. Amna Lutfi's sister, Sayyida, would tell him to hurry up and get a life. "What's it all leading to," she said, "are you going to stay like that forever?" Taha never answered, not to her or to Amna, but he would smile at her and say "*in sha' allah*", a phrase which means "God willing", but is also used to evade unwelcome questions or requests[36].

Taha continued his search for true religion and the true self. One of his visitors at this time was from the Badrab, a Sufi family of the Gezira. He wrote down what Taha was thinking, that the day of God would come on earth, and humanity would reach perfection in the flesh. He spoke a lot about Jesus and prophecy[37]. Some people put stranger words into Taha's mouth: "He said 'I am Jesus, I am Jesus'"[38]. No-one close to Taha heard him say that, but at this time he did make one arresting, and well-attested, statement to one of his relatives, Mukhtar 'Ali al-Shaykh:

> Everything that happened to Jesus will happen to me[39].

Friends

Living in Rufa'a was a return to small-town Sudan for the young *effendi*. His brother-in-law 'Ali Lutfi stayed in his father's house, a student at intermediate school. One of the duties of young adolescents was to wait on their elders, and 'Ali Lutfi brought Taha his meals, and he has many recollections of this time. Although Taha's dress and manner emphasised his separation from the world of respectable Rufa'a, he met and talked to many people. 'Ali al-Shaykh, the old man who had obscenely threatened the wife of the DC in Rufa'a, would come and upbraid Taha. He had an uncomplicated approach to politics and religion – the Qur'an said "We have made you one nation (*umma*)", and so everyone should support the Umma party that was becoming increasingly identified with 'Abd al-Rahman al-Mahdi's interests. ʿAli al-Shaykh was blunt (sometimes mercilessly so) but Taha was fond of his bluntness – other people in Rufaʿa were criticising him behind his back.

The tanner, who washed his skins in the Nile, was another old man. One day he decided to go and visit Taha, and they struck up a friendship. The tanner could not read, but he saw visions, and he and Taha would discuss what they had seen as Taha assiduously served him tea[40]. He was a staunch defender of Taha: "You don't know what you've got. You've got a treasure here" he would say to people[41]. Pious old men fitted easily into Taha's life but the complications of family life he gratefully left to his father-in-law and his wife. He was living in a world of his own – Yusuf Lutfi recalls going into Taha's room and finding him so lost in contemplation that he could not sense the intrusion. He would spend ninety minutes on each of the five daily prayers, rising after midnight to perform a supererogatory one. Amna Lutfi's uncle once secretly counted his prostrations – 493 in one hour of prayer[42].

The meaning of a *khalwa*

Past Sufis redefined and transformed the class hierarchy of Muslim state societies, substituting for it a hierarchy of piety that they traced back to the Qur'an. Sufi dissidents sometimes used retreat and withdrawal as a means of resistance to the state. Taha used his incarceration against his British prosecutors, taking the routinised oppression of the colonial prison, using it for political publicity and turning it into a travelling machine connecting to the fields of heaven.

Taha challenged the idea of prison as a place for the ideological enemies of the state, but he did not challenge the idea of prison as an institution at the sharp end of a class stratified society, a place where the delinquency attributed to its lowest class could be created and maintained[43]. Although he accepted the indignity of a low-grade prison uniform, Taha was not challenging class structures, he was adopting voluntary poverty, like the asceticism that be admired in ʿAli al-Mirghani. Al-Mirghani slept on a simple Sudanese *angareb* bed, without mattress or pillow. This austerity, thought Taha, was the mark of a true Sufi. He had wealth, but was not corrupted by it[44]. Although al-Mirghani was prepared to use his wealth and influence against the poorest class in the country, Taha saw him as a prisoner of a patrician system that had played a historic role in uniting the people of north Sudan, a system now being used against them.

The next chapter shows how Taha turned from poverty to voluntary wealth. Later in life, however, he renewed his asceticism and gave it a social, rather than spiritual meaning; a means of identification with the poor. Perhaps his prison experience, where he adopted the dress and the food of Sudan's poor in his *khalwa*, made him a keener advocate of the redistribution of wealth. But Taha's "socialism", a feature of his post-*khalwa* writings, never extended to an economic analysis of class and power in Sudan.

Books and class

Taha's reading list is surprising. Who would have thought that British jailers would keep copies of al-Ghazali's "Revivification of the Religious Sciences" for their wards? And what kind of prisoners would read such books in an overwhelmingly illiterate Sudan? Many contemporary Sudanese readers of al-Ghazali were the *khawass* – people who thought of themselves as part of a Sufi spiritual elite. Early Middle Eastern Sufis opposed the class hierarchies which developed in early Muslim states to a spiritual hierarchy of their own invention, redefining terms like *khawass* (elite or elect).

However, the connection between Sufi retreat and resistance was seldom made in 1940s Sudan, where the leaderships of large-scale *tariga*s competed for control of the state. For over a hundred years, successive Sudanese states had tried to co-opt the leaderships of small-scale *tariga*s to help them control rural areas of central Sudan. Sufi leaderships became part of the ruling class. Four religious notables, and many of their relatives, sat on the 75 member Legislative Assembly, which in 1948 replaced the Advisory Council as the native policy-making body of Sudan[45]. By the twentieth century, Sudanese Sufi leaderships were a state as well as a spiritual elite – they were *khawass* in both senses of the word. They were separated from the broad mass of their support by modern education and increasing involvement in the cash economy, and often by the fact that many had moved from a village on the banks of the Nile to a house in one of the major urban centres. According to Abdullahi An-Na'im, urban Sufi elites in the 1940s and 1950s set up study groups where intellectuals from the families met together and discussed esoteric knowledge. They puzzled over the obscure and difficult poetry of classical Sufi poets like 'Abd al-Ghani al-Nabulsi (d 1731) and Muhi al-Din ibn al-'Arabi (d 1240), and recited their poems in a song. Abdullahi An-Na'im identifies Taha with these groups, and describes them as follows:

Probably it is a reflection of a spiritual longing and a strong affiliation with Islamic Sufi traditions and therefore the Middle East. And Arabic would be the language. Given the obscurity of the sources and the subtlety of the meanings it would be a very closed circle of elites who already have a Sufi orientation[46].

Authenticity, past and present

Like many nationalist ideologues of his generation, Taha turned to the literary traditions of the Arab Muslim metropole. Taha's education introduced him to two grand historical narratives – Islamic and European colonial. In some senses, these grand narratives exclude each other. The contradictions between them pained sensitive men like Moawiya Nur, the Gordon College man who immersed himself in western literature, only to have a fatal psychological collapse (see chapter four). But both narratives had similar socio-economic aims – developing class structures and commerce, and dominating non-literate cultures and societies organised outside the state. Culturally, both narratives asserted in different ways the inauthenticity of the present and the eternal value of the past – which is perhaps why British jailers were not averse to copies of Muslim classics.

Taha was deferent towards the past. But he was not a conservative any more, if he had ever been one. He saw the mutability of the present moment as a cause for reverence not fear. His *khalwa* taught him to reject one grand narrative of Islam, the *shari'a* tradition, for the sake of the complex present. In a letter written in 1951, three years after he left prison, he wrote that *shari'a* had to change.

> I do not mean the Islamic legislation that the Muslim legists gabble on about today. That legislation has had its day, has had its social structure, and has served its purposes – to the point of exhaustion. What remains for us is to distil the essence which is still appropriate for our present social structure, and then continue to perfect legislation under the guidance of the Qur'an. I want to be clear: I mean by "Islamic legislation" that which relates to behaviour, and not worship ... and I mean by "our present social structure" a national social structure, and not a racial social structure[47].

Taha's sense of the authenticity of the past was always part of his writing. However, his spiritual experiments in the *khalwa* taught him the importance of present experience, and drew him away from seeking to make sense of his life through books:

It was important to [Taha] that people took up the prophet's way. To free their inner gifts and knowledge. He would tell the literary types this. "Don't read so much – application [is the important thing]"[48].

Publicity

Taha's prayers had a human audience. He no longer appeared in the political intelligence summaries, but his activities were noted by people in prison, in Rufa'a and in the Republican party. In this respect, his *khalwa* was like those of Sudanese Sufi leaders who went on to found *tariqa*s – they used the drama and intensity of their spiritual experiences to organise a following and mobilise a community. Yet Taha seldom spoke about the psychological events of his experience, even to close followers. Taha recognised the connections between his experience and that of older Sufis, but he wanted to distinguish his *khalwa* from that of a Sufi *shaykh* who used the spiritual celebrity of his or her moment with God as the basis of the message. Taha believed that the value of his message was to give ideological direction to the Sudanese nation, not to mobilise folk piety. His brother-in-law 'Ali Lutfi retrospectively compares Taha's mission to that of his tribal forebear 'Abd al-Sadig.

> [Taha] said that Sufism had served its purpose ... it had produced good Muslims. But it could not cope with international knowledge. For example ['Abd al-Sadig] al-Hamim tamed elephants with his stick. That's a miracle, but that is not for the twentieth century, which has reached Mars[49].

Republicans speak of two "lacks" in Sudan's nationalist struggle that were met by Taha. The first was a "lack of zeal", the fact that many nationalists were reluctant to confront the British, and even more reluctant to take their case to the Sudanese people[50]. The Republicans met nationalist timidity with strident activism. The second, the "lack of ideology" was harder to meet. Yet from the start, the Republicans were concerned that "the lack of free reflecting intellect" was the cause of the GGC's lack of political success. Taha told followers that before the *khalwa*, he knew that the answer to Sudan's problems lay in religion, and that it was not the religion of the patricians or the legists, but he knew no more than that[51]. The *khalwa* was a time when Taha constructed a new religious synthesis, which took account of "international knowledge" and "the guidance of the Qur'an". That synthesis, rather than his spiritual celebrity, was what he wished to publicise.

Conclusion
Amna has a toothache

One day around the beginning of 1951, Amna Lutfi had a toothache. She went to see her father about it, and he decided to take her to Khartoum to see the dentist. Amna went in to tell Taha, but he told her to go and get him a razor. When she brought it, he asked her to shave his four-year beard. Amna had never shaved anyone before, but she started the job anyway, and began to tell him about her tooth and the trip to Khartoum. "Right", said Taha, "I'll go with you". Amna dropped the razor and ran to her father saying "Abu Muhammad is going with us to Khartoum!"[52] Muhammad Lutfi was very happy, everyone was happy. From that day, Taha wore no facial hair, not even a moustache (a facial decoration so common in Sudan that one joke even has moustaches on watermelons). Taha had returned from his trip to heaven clean-shaven, to remind him of the eternal youthfulness of God.

This complex, public psycho-spiritual experience defined the rest of Taha's life. He developed ideas about Islam, *shari'a*, and a mystical change that would sweep Sudan and the world, and these ideas will be analysed in subsequent chapters, for he had not yet begun to speak about them. Taha's own words suggest that his most compelling motive for the *khalwa* was to discover himself, and he linked this self-discovery to the Qur'an. But his retreat was also an attempt to recast past truths in present idioms, and the drama of the moment conferred on him a celebrity that could be used to address new groups of people. Not everyone accepted what he had achieved, but Taha felt unavoidably drawn in.

Chapter 8

Giving up abstinence

After four years of ascetic seclusion, Taha returned to mainstream life and personal wealth. He went into private practice as an engineer, gained minor political prominence and raised several families. His Republican party gave up aggressive activism, and began to attract politically aware, pious and progressive young men. This chapter compares their political programme with others on offer.

Omdurman, 1951–1955
Clark Gable

Marriage made Amna Lutfi's life strange. She wandered the foothills of the Ethiopian highlands in a railway car with al-Rabb Biyjud, and lived in the urban centres of the Nile valley, bore two children, watched her husband build himself into a nationalist hero and win the support of Rufaʻa – and then turn prisoner and then again eccentric recluse, leaving her to mind the children and her father to feed them. Now, as Taha shaved his beard and moustache, and gave up asceticism, she went back to life in Omdurman. Taha spent his first days of freedom wandering round shops he had last seen four years before, scrupulously paying off petty debts. Then he went for a trip across Sudan with ʻAwad Lutfi, Amna's brother and an early member of the Republican party[1].

At the end of Taha's *khalwa*, his brother died. *Shaykh* Mukhtar Muhammad Taha, who could mend cars and watches, and who had set up his own small *tariqa* and craft school in Rufaʻa, was struck down in a meningitis epidemic. It was like the one that had swept away his own mother and *shaykh* Taha of the Sadigab. Mukhtar met his end with fortitude. When he was told that a doctor had been called, he refused to see him. "I know it is the end", he said, and died[2]. But Mukhtar had married five times, and he had children by each wife – all large families, now without a provider. Taha maintained all the children, bought them a house in Bayt al-Mal in Omdurman and paid for their educations[3].

Taha rented a big house in Mulazimin, in upmarket Omdurman. The Mahdi family lived nearby and both families sent their children to Comboni College where Italian priests and nuns taught the best families in English[4]. Taha got work with the tram company, his old employer, and had enough money to support his now enormous family. Early in the 1950s, Taha resigned his post in the tram company. He set himself up as a private contractor with an office above some shops in the 'Arabi market of Khartoum. It had two or three rooms opening off a reception area. Instead of the mystic's torn *'aragi*, he was once again wearing the colonialist's shorts and pith-helmet. He began to go to the cinema, where he watched his favourite stars: Clark Gable, Gary Cooper, Humphrey Bogart.

Taha was still somewhat withdrawn from society – he seldom paid social calls. He spent more time in the office, not only working, but also holding meetings for a small coterie of young men interested in his new ideas. The meetings would go on late, so he would only catch the second showing of the film, after 9.30 pm. He took his friends along, and afterwards they would discuss the storyline. Thursday nights (the start of the weekend) he would sometimes take his son Muhammad to an Arabic film[5].

The big question

Sudan in the 1950s was full of diversity and inequality. The market economy was configured around minorities enriched or otherwise transformed by the colonial state at its developed core, while the majority lived in rural areas, under rural laws. The south and the adjacent Nuba Mountains and Ingessana Hills had been administered separately and closed to trade and movement with the north as a result of the southern policy developed in the 1920s. By 1947, the policy was reversed, but the challenges to uniting Sudan under a single state remained enormous. The fact that Arab-Islamic state models were more or less the only ones under consideration aggravated the situation. It was a time when creative constitutional thinkers were badly needed in Sudan – this chapter will examine some of the views of radical parties operating in Sudan at the time, and in particular look at Taha's ideas.

Five years before independence, the British still imagined they had many years ahead of them in Sudan, and the draft constitution they produced in 1951 envisaged a continuing British presence. The Legislative Assembly (an elected body drawn from the elite) adopted this transitional document in 1952 only after safeguards for southern autonomy had been removed. Isma'il al-Azhari, leader of the National Unionist Party (NUP, a grouping of the Ashigga' and other Egyptian-union parties) and soon to be first prime minister of Sudan, ruled out any redistribution of wealth and power. When the Sudanese nationalists took over administration in 1953 they spent heavily on education (a GGC priority), but also ruled out the possibility of redistributing wealth. The colonialist policy of concentrating development along the Nile valley and the central provinces was continued. Market forces were expected to correct the sharp regional and class divisions in the country: government intervention was restricted to land grants for a few wealthy clients of the elite[6].

Sudan's complex independence struggle is narrated in detail elsewhere[7]. Briefly, the GGC split into parties affiliated to the two patricians, and the rival colonial powers haggled over a post-war settlement. The Egyptians wanted to annex Sudan, including the south, into a united Nile valley, and al-Mirghani's party supported the Union. The British had long planned to annex the south to the more culturally congruent colonies of East Africa. They isolated the south from the north and gave Christian missionaries a monopoly over social services (to emphasise its cultural difference and also to save money). At the conclusion of the second world war, Britain's Sudan policy became a bargaining chip in negotiations with its condominium partner Egypt for access to the Suez Canal. The British reversed their southern policy as a concession to Egypt, and forced the under-developed south into the north on terms that greatly disadvantaged the south: a mutiny followed a few years later.

In 1953 Sudan held its first elections for a pre-independence legislature. Southerners won nine of the 97 seats. Darfur was scarcely more developed than the south, but it had a clearer connection with nationalist politics at the centre, because the Mahdists had been organising there since the 1920s. The Mahdist Umma party swept the vote there (for the next thirty years Darfur was to be a vote-bank for the Umma party).

However, Darfur and the south were not the deciders of the elections: the NUP won an absolute majority. Voters in the northern Nile valley wanted to forestall the monarchical ambitions of 'Abd al-Rahman al-Mahdi. At the last minute, he was reconciled to 'Ali al-Mirghani, and the resulting coalition opted for a republic independent of Egypt. The powers of the colonial state passed to an independent Sudan led by the native elites it had patronised.

The election was overshadowed by the Egypt question, and was won by patrician management of their rural vote-banks. Their common interests meant that ideology was secondary to factional conflict (a major complaint of Taha's first work)[8]. It set the stage for the next few decades in Sudan – patrician power linked to patrician money and religion, and the neglect of the big questions of inequality and diversity. In some respects, small urban parties like Taha's made more of an effort to think through Sudan's big questions. Their views were limited by their time and place, but their views were important for conceptualising possible future changes to the nature of the state. The following analysis of Sudanese parties in the 1940s looks only at the tiny pre-independence "modern forces", and tries to relate those political movements to the big constitutional questions raised above. In addition, the chapter will try to assess how those groups responded to economic and gender imbalances.

The Black Bloc

Some groups concerned themselves directly with problems such as ethnicity, poverty and the state. These groups were not always able to get a colonial license to operate as a political party, but their organisation was to some extent determined by experiences created by the colonial state – its migrations and armies, its ethnic categories, urban neighbourhoods and big enterprises. One such group was the Black Bloc, which arose out of neighbourhood clubs and co-operatives catering for ex-slaves and discharged soldiers in Omdurman. It called for "elimination of social distinctions between Sudanese citizens"[9]. The British estimated its strength at 3,000, and in 1948, two of its leaders were elected to the Legislative Assembly, even though the Bloc had no party license[10]. The Bloc had the cautious support of the Umma party in the assembly. Its constituency, however, did not extend to Southerners who had recently arrived in Khartoum, who sometimes barred Arabised and Islamised Southerners from their social clubs. This mistrust was reciprocated: Zayn al-'Abdin 'Abd al-Tam was a member of the Legislative Assembly from the Bloc, but he opposed concessions to the south: "if minority problems were created, the whole structure of the state might collapse", he told the assembly[11]. But northern parties were reluctant to give support to groups they saw as "racist", and the British eventually restricted the Bloc's activities to social affairs. The movement fell apart, although its members later were involved in parties formed in the mid-1950s representing non-Arabised groups such as the Nuba and the Beja[12].

Communists

People drawn into the colonial economy also had new methods of social organisation, through labour activism. Pay freezes and inflation during the war, and the political openness of the post-war years helped mobilise the labour force in large colonial enterprises. A wave of strikes in 1947 culminated in the establishment of the Sudan Workers Trade Union Federation in 1948, with the support of the Sudanese Movement for National Liberation (SMNL, later the Communist party). Sudanese students from Egyptian universities had secretly established the party in 1946.

Unlike the Republicans, who were hostile towards the GGC, the Communists initially sought to work with nationalists. They won seats on the GGC executive, and worked in the students union at Gordon College. A new leader in 1947 moved the SMNL away from elite politics to the struggle of the workers in the labour unrest of 1947–8. Republican pamphlets had to contend with Communist competition, and Communist graffiti specialists[13]. Their pamphlets began to attack bourgeois nationalists in language even more vehement than the Republicans':

> Down with the Criminal Imperialist Government. Long Live your struggle against oppression. Ask Azhari what he had achieved in Egypt. What are you going to do with a man who spends his time leisurely at the Continental [hotel]? ... Remove the traitors from Congress[14].

Like the Black Bloc, the Communists used social networks created by colonialism, and through their involvement in the trade union movement they won themselves a lasting constituency. Sudan's small industrial workforce sought their help in labour unrest, but they voted for patrician parties in general elections, even though the religious families jostling to control the state had no sympathy for their struggle – when Port Sudan dockers went on strike, Maryam al-Mirghani (one of Sudan's few female religious leaders) urged them to return to work[15]. Communist core support was among educated Northerners. They were able to address

Sudan's big questions through a Marxist analysis of the state as a creator of class divisions[16]. As early as 1954, Communists were talking about the state's complicity in creating ethnic divisions, calling for regional autonomy for south Sudan[17].

Muslim Brothers

Patrician legitimacy was based on religious institutions built around a holy family. Other groups, influenced by the Egyptian Muslim Brotherhood or Saudi Wahhabis, used the ideological resonance of *shari'a* to build their support[18]. The Islamic Liberation Movement (ILM) was one of the first of these *shari'a* pressure groups, established in Gordon College in 1949 by students from rural areas. Like Taha and Amin Siddig, they were uneasy with the lax morals of the town. The ILM drew heavily on the Egyptian Muslim Brotherhood; indeed after 1954 they took their name. They had a hostile admiration for Communist tactics, but were not able to expand as fast as their rivals[19]. They did not become a significant force outside educational institutions until the 1960s.

'Ali al-Mirghani, an old-style Islamist, mournfully remarked in 1948 that "there are no longer any true religious *tariqa*s, only politicians"[20]. Perhaps he sensed that the ILM, like the Republicans, were alienated by patrician involvement in colonial politics, and the deferential culture of Sudan's institutional religion. This sense of moral mission, says El-Affendi, distinguishes the ILM from patrician parties[21]. The ILM were also different in that they represented an educated sub-elite – their distance from patrician interests is clear from their early espousal of socialism[22]. But their answer to the constitutional question was the same as the patricians' – they wanted to rework an imagined Arab-Muslim past to impose an Arab-Muslim state on a highly diverse nation. Like the patricians, they were often obliged to ignore that diversity.

Republicans

Republican activities restarted after Taha's *khalwa* ended. At a party meeting in November 1951, Taha explained his ideas for a new Islam, an ideology that would balance informed individual freedom with the needs of society. Islam was the ideology that was lacking from Sudan's factional political conflict:

> There is no good government without Islam... If the Sudanese call
> for a struggle to exalt the word of God, they will have made true
> the struggle and purified their souls. If ... [the Legislative Assembly]

... succeeded in ousting the colonialists, we fear that this would lead
us to all out civil war ... for we are divided into two great sects with
a historic enmity between them. ... Our nationalist movement can
accomplish nothing if it does not gather up the fragments of groups
and sects and parties too, around the eternal idea which Islam has
brought[23].

My Way

In 1952, Taha published a second booklet, *qul hadhihi sabili* ("Say: this
is my way"). He did not talk about his *khalwa* mysteries, but proclaimed
a new Islamic civilisation of eastern spirituality and western material
development. Islam, he said, resolved the competing demands of absolute
human freedom and total social justice[24]. The booklet maintained Taha's
concern for nationalist activism, calling for civil disobedience to remove
the colonialists.

Freedom in this second booklet meant freedom from fear, ignorance
and poverty, involving just distribution of wealth and land owned by a
central government and managed co-operatively. Private ownership would
exist only in the home. Democracy was curiously mixed with educational
elitism – voting should be a right for the educated, he said, and in order
to extend the suffrage, the largest government ministry should be the
ministry of knowledge. It would organise a comprehensive educational
strategy for the country, teaching sport, chastity and self-reliance, as well
as medicine and astronomy[25]. Education would liberate the mind and
unite the individual's spiritual abilities and material needs. People would
maintain a constant spiritual alertness through following the *tariq* (path)
of Muhammad. The use of the word *tariq* here is significant – it suggests
a mystical Sufi path. Taha was thinking Islamically, but most Islamists
would prefer to revive the *sunna*, another "path" but one which had been
defined by centuries of jurisprudence rather than spiritual exercises. His
new civilisation would spread to the world, giving it spiritual unity, a
personal and global *tawhid*. This Arabic word means monotheism, literally
"coming together as one".

Qul hadhihi sabili differs from Taha's 1946 work in that he asserts
more stridently the need to redistribute wealth. Taha also changed his
analysis of the state. He still hoped that independent Sudan would
provide a golden age of goodness, as he had suggested in his first
manifesto. But *qul hadhihi sabili* had none of the references to "Arab
excellence". He no longer wanted an Arab-Muslim state for Sudan, but

he wanted Sudan to be a model for a coming world government, where Islamic values formed a framework for local diversity – indeed, he came to see Arab nationalism as racist[26]. Taha was thinking hard about Sudan's constitution, and the fruits of his reflections came out in a book in 1955, discussed in chapter nine.

The party

Many early members of the party left when they realised that Taha had turned from nationalist action to religion. Amin Siddig, Zanoon Gubara, Muhammad Fadul and 'Awad Lutfi were among the few who remained with Taha. However, Taha gathered a new following of young men of religious outlook. Among the first to join the new Republican party (in 1951) were Sa'id Shayib and Jalal al-Din al-Hadi, both secondary school students from Wad Medani[27]. The students, and a few older Republicans, attended discussions at Taha's office. Taha did not contribute much, but he introduced, moderated and summed up the discussion. He used the remarks of others to build up a case, so that each person felt a part of the conclusion: "In the end, you would think it was your own idea", said one participant[28].

Taha was making himself into a religious leader, but he was not the *shaykh* of a *tariqa*. Instead, he took the title of a Sudanese school teacher – *al-ustaz* Mahmud. The party was already centred around him, and he became the sole spokesman at meetings and lectures. Party men no longer roamed the cinemas and cafes dodging policemen. Instead, Taha wrote learned letters to the press. In 1953, he wrote against *shari'a* as a basis for the constitution, and for the need for a new kind of Islamic state of virtue[29]. But Taha's *khalwa* transformation was not apparent to British security, who still saw the Republicans as "a small party of fanatical reactionaries"[30]. They occasionally followed his lectures in clubs:

> [Taha] addressed the officials in their club at Wad Medani and the workers at the Workers Club urging them to stick to their Islamic Religious principles by means of which they could attain their national aspirations[31].

In 1954, the party started its own short-lived newspaper, *al-Jumhuriya*. One of the contributors was Sadig al-Mahdi, the grandson of 'Abd al-Rahman, who became a regular attender at Taha's salon in the 'Arabi market. He was a student at Comboni College at the time, like Taha's own children, but he left for university in England, from where he would write to Taha to ask for explanations of Islam[32]. Taha's own capacity to question religious and social norms and yet emerge full of certainty reassured these young men.

Small parties

Small urban parties had certain ideological and organisational similarities. The ILM, the SMNL, the Black Bloc and the Republicans all organised in the new clubs and unions. Graffiti, pamphlets and lectures were new forms of communication for Sudan, eagerly taken up by these aspiring, but relatively powerless, political actors.

Three parties shared a sense of unease about the direction of the state towards the interests of the Arab-Muslim elite. The Black Bloc was the only radical group which addressed the problem of ethnicity in Sudan. It failed to connect the ethnic interests of its urbanised constituency with the interests of the Sudanese periphery where they had originally come from, and in any case it was suppressed by elites who thought that mobilising around ethnic interest was a form of racism. Communists had a Marxist critique of the state, and that led them to recognise the state's alliance with narrow ethnic interests. The Republican understanding of diversity, in contrast, was expressed through Taha's monist spirituality: he conceived of an Islam that could work as a unifying force for the personality and the country, but rejected the imposition of the norms of the Arab-Muslim state.

Taha shared similarities with the ILM too. He spoke in mosques and preferred religion to economics. Muhammad Yusuf, a founder of the ILM, was aware of these similarities. Yusuf visited Taha in his Rufa'a *khalwa* to ask him to lead his student movement. El-Affendi says that "After a lengthy discussion he decided that Taha's views were too unorthodox for him to lead the [ILM]"[33]. Taha was not interested anyway. He did not like Muhammad Yusuf's idea that Islam could be taken off the shelf and made into a constitution. "They thought Islam was ready-made, it was just a matter of getting the people together. Taha thought that Islam needed new understanding," says Ibrahim Yusuf[34].

The ILM found it hard to recognise Sudan's diversity. They flirted with socialism when they began organising in Sudan, but their main fixation was to incorporate *shari'a* into state law. By aligning Sudanese society to past urban metropolitan societies of the Middle East, they believed that they were restoring a lost authenticity to Sudan[35]. This claim found a response in educated urban Sudan, which for over two centuries had seen the future in the urban Mediterranean. *Shari'a* was a way to "upgrade" Sudan from an African past to a prestigious Middle Eastern future.

Women and politics

Class and ethnicity played a significant role in determining Sudanese women's rights – women in small-scale subsistence economies had a role in production, but respectable urban women stayed at home, wore elegant but cumbersome clothing and did not go to the market. In the towns, poorer women could still work. As late as the 1950s, women could be seen in small-town market places, their uncovered hair proclaiming their former slave status[36]. Women members of the elite participated at the margins of power through the education they had shared with their brothers. The elite who led independent Sudan needed women in the workforce. But the work performed by tea-ladies and nurses was stigmatised as female and low-class (slave) work. Women were not granted the vote until 1965.

The Black Bloc has been little studied, and the position of women in its ranks cannot be assessed. However, Sudan's political parties created women's sections in the 1940s and 1950s. Women's groups run by the Muslim Brotherhood (as the ILM came to be known in 1954) and the Umma party gave a respectable route to political participation for educated women. The Communists had an early foothold in the Sudan Woman's Union (SWU), founded in 1952[37]. The literate women who joined were committed to the kind of educational reformism that was a feature of Taha's thinking. Taha's 1952 work devoted one of its four sections to women. He called for the abolition of the veil, but he defined women in terms of their family role. He was beginning to think about ways for women to express their femininity in his new civilisation, and that in itself would greatly influence the history of his movement.

Private life
Family tragedy

After 1951, the Republican party was much less prominent, indeed, some British security men wondered if it was still in existence[38]. While Taha nurtured his small following in Khartoum, calamity struck in Rufa'a. In 1953 or 1954, Amna Lutfi and the children were visiting. Muhammad, her son, was down at the river with the Rufa'a boys. They were all village boys who could swim, but he had been in Omdurman, playing in parks and going to cinemas. He went into the river anyway, and drowned. Taha was not with the family, but someone came and told Amna:

> An old lady came and sat with me. She brought some goat's milk, the best thing, she said, for this kind of tragedy. They searched for Muhammad, they never found him. They found someone else who had drowned, a clerk, drowned in his clothes and his watch. But that one was not found[39].

Amna lay on the bed and the old lady held her while her sisters ran to the river to look. The search lasted three days. Everyone noticed her patience, she did not cry, and she told the tearful: "Don't cry. God ordains patience. That's all"[40]. Taha came down on the train the next day. He did not show his emotion either. This inscrutable piety is a striking and sometimes alarming feature of some funerals of Muslim children, and one admired by the Lutfi women[41]. Taha only stayed in Rufa'a for three days and then went back to the city to carry on with his work. Amna stayed on with her daughter and her enormous patience.

Amna had another daughter that year, called Sumaya. But Taha was more and more often away, and eventually moved out of Omdurman. Amna went back to Rufa'a. Over the next ten years they saw little of each other. Many years later, he mentioned the death in passing to 'Abdullahi An-Na'im:

> We were talking about how children look up to parents. [Taha] said, "A child expects his father to be capable of everything. I used to have a son who once asked me, 'I want *khatim al-muna* [a fairy-tale ring that can grant every desire]' ... I am of course still trying to get it for him.

Kosti and Korea

Taha turned to party activity – meetings in his office building, lectures in clubs, occasional tracts on the political situation. He began to make trips to Sufi shrines, where he would test his new beliefs in prayer and dialogue. But he was also supporting Amna in Rufa'a and also his brother Mukhtar's children in Omdurman, and he went to where the money was. In 1955 he left Khartoum for Kosti, to work as an engineer on new agricultural pump schemes. Kosti is a provincial capital on the White Nile 200 miles south of the capital, at the southern tip of Aba Island, where 'Abd al-Rahman al-Mahdi had his estates. Named after a Greek trader, it symbolises in many ways capitalist Sudan.

The Korean war in 1950 sent cotton prices up. Sudanese with

access to information, land and cash were quick to employ them in cotton farms. With cotton at £E 50 a hundredweight, the pump schemes boomed – 185 were built in four years[42]. The pump schemes offered some of the best returns on investment in Sudan at the time. The colonial government's agricultural investment in the share-cropping schemes of central Sudan paid off: it covered administrative costs and left Sudan with a healthy £E 13 million surplus of revenue over expenditure in 1956[43]. Elites sponsored by the colonialists had invested their winnings mainly in private pump schemes, slightly more rapacious than the government schemes (which provided welfare services to tenant farmers and landless workers)[44]. On some private pump schemes the tenants' share of their crops was as low as 25%[45].

Private pump schemes along the White Nile, primarily for cotton production, proliferated in the 1950s, and Taha's engineering skills were at a premium[46]. He moved to the Kosti resthouse, a small hotel run by the railway department set in three or four acres of neglected garden. It was there that he saw Girgis Iskander, a doctor of Coptic origin whom he had first met at Gordon College. Girgis Iskander became a close friend, and his sympathetic but critical reminiscences of Taha shed a great deal of light on his character.

Dr Girgis Iskander

Girgis Iskander felt rather reserved when he first saw Taha again. He was a Christian, and Taha had a reputation as a starchy Muslim – he remembered his prayers at school, his conservative rebellion at Rufa'a, the way that he referred to the prophet as "the infallible [one]", a primly theological honorific used by the kind of Muslim hard-liners who would take Girgis Iskander's religion as a cause for offence. Reserve did not last long – Taha was charming, friendly and candid. Girgis Iskander did not recognise the severe and pious schoolboy he remembered, and he did not hear any crazy talk about religion.

Taha was still strange. Most of his friends were made through his work, but when he eventually rented a house, a little coterie of "not quite presentable people" would come round to his house for help[47]. They were often *maddah*s, poor hymn-singers[48]. Such men often attached themselves to Sufi *shaykh*s who provided food and hospitality for them, and many of them began to stay at Taha's house – sometimes they would help themselves to small valuables, but Taha would not mind[49]. They did not prevent Taha from keeping up relations with richer groups in Kosti.

He had friends among the cotton lords, judges, doctors and merchants of the town. One friend, 'Abd al-Rahman al-Nagar was a left-wing merchant whom Taha employed to distribute charitable gifts to poor people. Taha had a small survey staff too, who sometimes stayed in the house. It gradually became a small salon where members of a provincial elite with an interest in religion or politics came and talked. Taha was a great talker and listener, as Girgis Iskander explains:

> ... when he informed me of his global politics, and being medically trained, I diagnosed him as suffering from paranoia. As we proceeded to argue and discuss, I quickly revised my views, nay! I was infected with his 'BUG'. And being only human, I behaved like the privates in the Congolese army. When the Belgians were there, there was a Congolese army of privates and no generals. As the colonialists left, every individual in that army promoted himself into a general and there were no privates. So when I caught his bug, I made myself the General and Mahmoud became my prophet!!
>
> My brain and my whole being began to act in fantastic ways, ideas flowing smoothly and mystically to my great astonishment and dazzlement. Being still medical I applied my skills to understand myself. My diagnosis was that I was raving mad at that moment. Mahmoud was egging me not to be a coward and push on and on ... Mahmoud was like a terrific whirlwind blowing on my personality and brain. Ideas and self possession, life and death were uprooted and blew to where no one could predict yet it was all very pleasant and unique experience. Eventually I sobered up...[50]

Girgis Iskander still went along for a talk most days. More and more people came to meet this sympathetic listener with wild ideas and perfect manners. And Taha was rich and successful. He bought a Land Rover and he was making six times as much as Girgis Iskander, himself a busy doctor making ten to 30 Sudanese pounds ($£S$) a day – up to 120 times as much as a labourer[51]. Girgis Iskander heard people say that the promise of super-profits in agriculture had seduced Taha away from his religious life. But asceticism still lingered around him. He rented a shabby house in a middling area of Kosti, which he furnished sparsely and opened to odd, poor people. Girgis Iskander took to him:

> Personally I think he had sobered up and become an abnormal normal person ... on one level he had normal feeling and compassion like other humans and on the other level he still had his mega ideas ... after his sojourn in the land of the unknown and the unseen he emerged but he was still there[52].

Conclusion

In the early 1950s, Taha built up a small support base. His regular meetings in Khartoum were interrupted by his stay in Kosti, where he also had a small following. He gave the appearance of indifference to material comforts; he was now a rich man supporting a large extended family. Some of contemporaries say that Taha had left the railways in the 1940s because of his frustrated sympathies with workers' demands for rights. But now, in Kosti, his answer to the exploitation of migrant labour in plantation agriculture lay in education for a new civilisation. In some respects, his views tallied with the graduates in the government – their notion of state investment in development was to double the education budget, not to challenge the economic order. Taha was an educational reformist, like the intellectuals who had joined up with the patrician parties. Yet he held himself aloof from those parties – the Republicans, like other small urban parties, rejected the patrimonial structure of the state, and adopted policies for change drawn from European and Islamic traditions which they had encountered in their own education.

Taha's *khalwa* had changed him for good. The intimacy that he found in his cell in Kober overshadowed every other intimacy in his life. He and his wife used their religious faith to cope with their son's death. But the experience may have marked a change in the family, with Taha looking harder at his religion. His life now had a purpose which drew him away from the ordinary and into the absolute. This attracted many people to him – the professional men of Kosti discovered a man who listened to them intently, and spun out their thoughts wildly, and gave them a sense of their own extraordinariness. However, these were his friends – the people who committed themselves to his ideas tended to be younger men. When Taha began to travel around Sudan speaking and listening in clubs and Sufi shrines in the late 1950s, he was accompanied by men 20 years his junior. Much of the rest of his life was lived surrounded by young hopefuls.

Chapter 9

Independence for the elite

Independence, which came in 1956, was independence for the Arab-Muslim elite. They did not address the ethnic and economic imbalances which colonialists had helped to create. This chapter examines the years from 1953 to 1958, and Taha's writings about Sudan's big questions. It also looks at his expectation that Sudan and the world would be flipped over into perfection.

The challenge to the state
Parliamentary elections

An Anglo-Egyptian agreement on self-government in 1953 prepared the way for elections later that year, supervised by an international commission. Sectarian conflict led to street riots when the Umma party lost the elections in the face of a powerful, Egyptian-funded campaign for the NUP[1]. But the civil war Taha had predicted did not happen, thanks to an agreement reached by the two patricians in 1955. Sudan did not unite with Egypt: instead, it was divided between the two patricians. Radicals, and the people of Sudan's periphery were marginalised. The new order was seriously challenged twice in the six months between August 1955 and February 1956.

Torit – the first challenge

The independence struggle of the northern elites was also the beginning of a new phase of the nineteenth century conflict between the central state and the people of the south. In Bahr El Ghazal Province the Aliab, part of the Dinka tribe, who considered the 1953 elections to be merely a plot to gather the people together so that they might be killed or enslaved, refused to vote in three electoral divisions[2]. Southern distrust was not without justification: in 1954, Isma'il al-Azhari promised "the force of iron in dealing with any Southerner who dares to divide the nation" – that is, who resisted Britain's 1947 decision to unite the south with the north[3]. Southerners began to feel cheated when official posts promised to their own people were given to Northerners. In 1955, when Northerners replaced southern technicians at an Equatorian cotton scheme, six Southerners died in riots. The incident caught the southern mood: in August, resentment spilled over into armed resistance. When the soldiers of the Southern Equatorial Corps were ordered to Khartoum, without ammunition, they believed they were about to be massacred. They killed several hundred Northerners, including the officers sent to relieve them. Independence went ahead a few months later in January 1956, and the bloody challenge of the southern mutineers ended on the gallows – over 70 were hanged. Sudan's elite had won independence, and in the next few months, more people who challenged their idea of Sudan were to die.

Sudan's constitution

In 1955 Taha wrote down his idea of Sudan – "The fundamentals of Sudan's constitution" (*usus dastur al-sudan*). Taha's book calls for a devolution of power for all five regions of Sudan (the Legislative Assembly had struck down modest concessions for southern autonomy when it adopted the British-drafted constitution in 1952). Taha wanted a hierarchy of popular representation, five levels of autonomous councils from village to nation[4]. Taha's constitution even allowed for regional legislatures to dissolve the central legislature. The constitution envisaged its own development: the centre was to cede its power gradually to the regions[5].

Taha was prepared to dissolve the central Sudanese state, founded so bloodily in the nineteenth century. But his constitution accepted (albeit temporarily) the enormous inequalities that the nineteenth century had wrought. His constitution made one parliamentarian the representative of 200,000 Southerners or Westerners, while representation would be 1:50,000 in the developed centre of Sudan[6]. Taha's proposals for regional representation were even more imbalanced than those of the electoral commission (see table). However, Taha envisaged the cession of central power and eventual equal representation as people in under-developed regions became educated. Actual representation over the subsequent 30 years aggravated ethnic imbalances.

**Regional share of representation in 1953 and 1986 elections –
parliamentary representative: population[7]**

region / year	Upper Nile, Bahr al-Ghazal, Equatoria	Darfur and Kordofan	Central and eastern Sudan
1953 election/ 1956 census	1:126,500	1:134,391	1:84,403
1986 election/ 1983 census	1:146,416	1:143,883	1:69,571

Educating the south

In 1955, an "International Commission on Secondary Education" toured
Sudan. It was made up of British and Egyptian educators under an
Indian chairman. One member was 'Abd al-'Aziz al-Sayyad, an Egyptian
professor. He was scandalised by the Dinka lifestyle of rural Bahr al-
Ghazal (Dinka people in that time and place wore little in the way of
clothing). Dinkas had to be forced to fit in to the life of the rest of the
country, he said, and he refused to allow that the Dinka might be happy
as they were:

> if human beings are to be happy they have to live as other members
> of the human race ... if these people are too backwards to think for
> themselves ... it will be the duty of the Government to think for
> them[8].

Al-Sayyad's coercive version of development, and the role of education
in that development were not unusual for his time. They are sometimes
implied in Taha's constitution:

> [Province governors should] make it possible for pastoralists to settle,
> by providing water for them and their animals and by conserving their
> land ... before settling, there can be no education and no civilisation
> ... It goes without saying that education is the one method which will
> destroy differences and bring together customs and work towards the
> unity of the people through unity of language, killing or weakening
> local dialects[9].

Like al-Sayyad, Taha believed that education qualified people for
democracy, and his reluctance to grant the vote to the uneducated,
expressed in *qul hadhihi sabili*, finds some echoes in his constitution.
However, Taha rebutted the suggestion that "primitive" people need

educations in order to "deserve" sovereignty:

> This is used as an apology for absolute rule ... although people need
> education, absolute rule ... can only give them the education of
> slaves. Absolute rule will not prepare people for democracy, but for
> conformity and docility. We want to alert people to the devastating
> danger of this trend, and to assert that there is no way for educating
> any people except to put before them their problems, and help them
> understand them, and find ways to solve them by themselves[10].

Taha believed in modernity and Islam; he also believed in grassroots
action and individual self-expression. His modernising universalism
could however adopt a lethal attitude towards linguistic diversity. His
Islam was universalising force that standardised belief and culture, and
asserted a universal law. However, Taha's law, based on the Qur'an, was
not only the framework for the constitution: it was the law of the human
heart[11]. The purpose of the law was not to preserve the state, but to
abolish class distinction through communal ownership of the means of
production and narrow, fixed income differentials. The purpose of his
fierce educational policy was also to remove class from society:

> We develop all resources, animal, mineral, vegetable and industrial,
> in order to develop human resources, improving their kind and
> destroying their differences through intellectual cultivation and
> civilisation ... so that all classes can relate to each other, and in that
> way classes will be abolished[12].

Al-Sayyad saw little value in social and cultural diversity, but that is not
the lesson of Taha's book. Social uniformity was a means to the goals
of his constitution – he believed that the abolition of class differences
would allow individuals to develop their own talents independently, in
autonomous communities to which power was gradually devolved by an
educative state.

A constitutional committee
In 1956, the cabinet set up a committee to replace the 1952 constitution
with a permanent one. Three of its 46 members were Southerners, and
they left after the committee rejected autonomy for the south[13]. Taha, the
Republican party representative, only lasted a few months. He objected
to the fact that the committee was answerable to the government and
not the legislature. When he failed to persuade the committee to claim

its independence, he resigned[14]. The next month 'Ali al-Mirghani and 'Abd al-Rahman al-Mahdi announced that Sudan should be an Islamic parliamentary republic, a recommendation taken up by the committee, to southern dismay. In any case, a military coup in 1958 ended the discussion. Taha played no part in these decisions – he was an oppositionist, and he responded uneasily to his brief taste of official power.

Joda – the second challenge

Taha arrived in Kosti in mid-1955, the last year of British rule, and he stayed there for over ten years. He observed Sudan's independence from an economically dynamic vantage point. He discussed the Torit events with friends in Kosti. The convolutions of British policy in the south, and the bad faith of the northern politicians were, in his view, the main reason for the tragedy[15]. But Taha was now part of a Sudan integrated into the world economy, where Korean demand for cotton meant more to daily life than hinterland massacres. He was nearer to the second challenge to the regime, which happened in Joda, in February 1956, just after independence[16].

Joda was a privately owned pump scheme south of Kosti. Its 700 tenant farmers had not been paid for the 1955 harvest, and refused to deliver any more crops without payment. With support from Communist agitators, they also demanded increased profit shares and union recognition, and some of them were arrested. Rural Sudan was still largely governed by Native Administration, and a Baggara chief/judge dealt with the strikers. He found urban Kosti too restive for the case, and moved his court to the Joda home of the scheme owner. Demonstrations there led to several deaths. Over 300 farmers were arrested and taken to Kosti, and locked in a sealed-up barrackroom, 18 metres by six. All requests for water and ventilation were ignored. The next day, 189 of the prisoners were found dead, of heat exhaustion and carbon monoxide poisoning. They were buried in a secret mass grave. One hundred and eleven living prisoners were found stripped and chanting the Qur'an.

The Communists (at that time called the "Anti-Imperialist Front") roamed Kosti's streets calling for vengeance[17]. The Communist trade union leader al-Shafi' Ahmad al-Shaykh told Kosti demonstrators that the incident exposed the regime's hostility to "the working classes"[18]. Communists pointed out that the colonialists' Native Administration bore a significant part of the blame. In the capital, students went on strike, and lawyers marched to the prime minister's office demanding the government's resignation. The government replaced the out-classed Native Administration with emergency laws and civil judges who sat at dead of night. Small parties protested – the Muslim Brothers (formerly the ILM) denounced the prime minister, Isma'il al-Azhari; the Republicans called for the resignation of the interior minister "for neglecting the people in the twists of party competition for power"[19].

Girgis Iskander wrote an attack on Communist tactics in the press – he believed that the farmers had little idea where the Communists were leading them, and that the Communists ought to acknowledge their part in the tragedy, rather than attacking the state. He discussed the matter with Taha, who agreed that the Communists were exploiting the situation. However Taha sympathised with the workers demands:

> [Taha] was rather accepting [of] the idea that the Communists had to arouse the farmers to take action to gain more rights[20].

Al-Azhari's government lost al-Mirghani's support and fell in June 1956. Al-Mirghani's Khatmiya now supported the People's Democratic Party [PDP], who formed a government with their Mahdist rivals in the Umma party to ride out two years of fractious coalition and diminishing economic returns. The war in Korea was still more important. After it ended in 1953, cotton gradually slumped until it reached a quarter of the 1950 price. In 1958, the Umma prime minister 'Abdallah Khalil handed power over to a general, Ibrahim Abboud, as the sectarian coalition fell apart and the balance of payments plunged. Cotton still amounted to about two-thirds of the value of agricultural production[21]. Khalil and al-Azhari got pensions, and the Communist leader al-Shaykh got a five year sentence. Al-Mahdi and al-Mirghani blessed the new government; the Republicans, like many of Sudan's elite saw Abboud as the leader of a "benevolent military regime"[22]. Taha had little time for a parliamentary version of the Arab-Muslim state, and he was in any case spending his time trying to find out what he should do with his revelations.

From the shrine to the club
Wasil

Taha was a wealthy member of Sudan's modern economic sector, but he had not stopped roaming his imagination for answers to the world's questions. Although he now considered himself a socialist, he did not concern himself much with workers' rights – instead he looked for intellectually grand solutions for poverty, ignorance and fear. His *khalwa* experience made him believe that he had reached a watershed in understanding these problems.

Asma Mahmud, Taha's daughter, saw little of him, but she heard about his strange ideas. One day she asked him why he did not pray, and he told her to wait until she was older to understand[23]. Since the end of his *khalwa* he had ceased to pray the canonical prayers of Islam[24]. Taha believed he was a *wasil*, which translates as "someone who has arrived". He later described the state of *wusul* (arrival) in a letter to the American writer John Voll:

> To the great Sufi consciousness has two levels. One fundamental and supreme. It transcends time and space. It is well-nigh static. This level is the attribute of the Infinite, of the elect, of God.
>
> The other level of consciousness is dynamic, and evolutionary. It is the attribute of the finite. These two levels of consciousness have a difference of degree not of kind.
>
> Every Sufi tries, through his spiritual development, to work his way up the ladder of consciousness, from limitation to abundance, from Man's opportunity, to God's proximity.
>
> At a certain stage along that ladder discord gives place to harmony and the inner conflict cools down. The individual enjoys eternal bliss. This stage of progress is called wusul. The Arabic word "wusul" literally means arrival. The Sufi, in his spiritual development, is exemplified metaphorically, to the traveller who arrives at his destination after a weary and hazardous journey through the desert. That would be an oasis. It has its temptations ... Many spiritual mediocres forget their eternal journey and happily settle down.
>
> To the great Sufi the stage of wusul only marks the beginning of unity with God[25].

Taha made the claim of *wusul* or the analogous claim of *asala* to some of those around him in the mid-1950s. He explained to one friend that "in this state one arrives to his own *asala* (authenticity or self-attainment) and no longer needs to imitate anyone or follow the road of others, including that of the Prophet Muhammad"[26]. This idea was linked to that of *al-insan al-kamil*, often translated as "perfect man", a person whom Taha associated with Jesus and who was part of the speculations of early theosophical Sufis, like ibn al-'Arabi. Ibn al-'Arabi described the type:

... the highest type of Sufis "who keep their esoteric doctrine to
themselves and never divulge its mysteries to the public or even to
one another"[27].

Other Sudanese Sufis also abandoned canonical prayer in pursuit of
perfection, men like Muhammad 'Abd al-Sadig, Taha's flamboyant
forebear, or 'Abd al-Bagi al-Mukashfi who led a small Blue Nile *tariga*
in the nineteenth century. Taha's audience were familiar with this kind
of evasion of the rules, and like Ibn al-'Arabi , they associated it with
"the highest type of Sufi" – the *khawass*, the Sufi spiritual elite. Taha
could make his experience comprehensible by identifying himself with
this spiritual elite.

But Taha was not sure that the *khawass* should have it all. Ibn al-
'Arabi's belief in secret mysticism opposed Taha's democratic and
socialist instincts. Taha accepted the spiritual eminence of the *walis*, but
wanted to invite everyone to the mystical feast. His huge psychological
experience had given him a sense of mission, and the strength to return
to a new kind of life and leadership, but he still was unsure about the
knowledge he had received. Was it for everyone?

Visiting the dead

For Taha, the answer to this question lay not so much in the books read
by intellectual Sufis in Khartoum, but with Sudan's spiritual leaders. He
asked them whether his proposals for modernising Sufi Islam deserved
publicity. Throughout the 1950s he toured the *masid*s and *khalwa*s of
Sudan, seeking guidance from living and dead Sufi *shaykh*s. Three young
men accompanied the middle-aged Taha – Sa'id Shayib, Jalal al-Din al-
Hadi and 'Abd al-Latif 'Umar. The last had joined in 1955; he was from
the Shaygiya area of northern Sudan. He arrived in Khartoum in the early
1950s and worked as a water seller. After he became committed to the
Republican cause, he learned to read and write and became a newspaper
proofreader and one of the party's most prolific writers[28].

Taha and his friends tried to visit every Sufi centre in Sudan. Taha
explained his transformative ideas about Islam to the local *shaykh*s. His
controversial views sometimes sparked off fights[29]. If living *shaykh*s
rejected him, Taha could always pray for the support of their dead
forebears. According to Abdullahi An-Na'im, Taha was not proselytising
the *shaykh*s, but securing their blessing for his mission[30].

The shrine and the club

In the late 1960s, Taha wrote that:

> [The spiritual] heights used to be the habitat of the chosen few. The
> rank and file teemed at the bottom of the ladder, trying to work their
> way up ... This state of affairs will not be allowed to continue. Our
> present civilisation of collectivism and impersonal bigness is giving
> way to the age of small things – the individual, the man-in-the-street.
> Every individual is, authentically, an end in himself. He is not a means
> to any other end. He – even if he were an imbecile – is a "God" in the
> making, and must be given the full opportunity to develop as such[31].

Abdullahi An-Na'im says that Taha's conversations at the shrines helped
him conclude that the distinction between the *'awwam* and *khawass* should
end, and that the secret knowledge of self-realisation had to be shared by
an ever-growing circle of people[32].

Taha wanted to transfer the secret knowledge, hidden in the *khalwa*
experiences of Sudanese saints, to the people of modern Sudan. He
went from the shrine to the club, providing a continuity between the
old familiarities of northern Nile valley Muslim society and the new
familiarities of the city and town. In the clubs, he tried to persuade people
of the need to free society, and Islam, from fear. He seldom mentioned
his wilder Sufi ideas in these places, although he was already making
claims about the new Islam. A lecture in Wad Medani, for example, in the
late 1950s, took the title "Islamic *shari'a* is not eternal"[33].

Taha believed that his controversial new ideas needed to be
incarnated in an authentic individual who would bring authenticity to the
world, just as the fiery psychological experiences of Sudan's founding
Sufis had brought healing knowledge to small communities. Was he to
be that incarnation? Taha hoped so, but he thought that he needed to
convince people of the need to rework *shari'a* before he could move
them on to more esoteric knowledge. But legal reform was not Taha's
dearest wish. Although he was a middle-aged man, he was still looking
for the magic ring that would grant every desire, the *khatim al-muna* he
had promised his now-dead son. He thought he could find it by desiring
perfectly. He accepted that perfection was far off, but his spiritual
ambition was enormous, as Girgis Iskander recounts:

> He believed that he, Mahmoud, would be that Perfection which
> humanity is yearning for!!!!? And that he is actually 'God in the

making'. It would only be one step before that final quantum leap!? He had actually fixed the locality where that fantastic transformation would take place[34].

Taha the teacher

Taha believed that he, and everyone, was a God in the making. His newspaper articles and lectures tried to bring this belief to the people around him, but these methods effectively restricted his message to a chosen few – "chosen" by their presence in Sudan's modern sector. Its methods of social organisation were new, diverse and responsive to change. However, for Taha, individual self-realisation was for everyone. That was the purpose of the social and educational changes envisaged in his constitution for Sudan: they were intended to use Islam to liberate the individual, not to twist peripheral social groups into the logic of the state.

Taha desire to make the illiterate read was based on his belief in the transformative power of education, an education that would turn the '*awwam* all into *khawass*, or make them all Congolese generals, as Girgis Iskander would put it. Changing each individual heart was a long teaching endeavour. In the 1950s, Taha's views on the nature of social change led to an amicable parting from one of the Republican party's early members, Muhammad al-Mahdi al-Majdhub. He was a poet with a wide readership from a Sufi family based at al-Damer, one of the most prolific groups of Sudanese Sufi writers in Sudan[35]. When Taha emerged from the *khalwa*, he felt that the way to achieve change in Sudan was to go through this protracted period of education, but Muhammad al-Mahdi al-Majdhub said that this was too slow to be a solution. Taha responded that it was the only way, and any short-cut would turn out to be longer[36].

Taha turned decisively from political to educational activism. In 1958, Sudan's only teacher training institute recognised this, asking him to write proposals for a new curriculum (a concern of the Republicans' 1946 work, *al-sifr al-awwal*). Taha's proposals were utopian: schools should train people for work and in virtue. Exemplary teachers were needed, he said, not a course in religious studies. Rather, students should read the life stories of great men and women, both Muslim and non-Muslim:

> By focusing on the higher qualities of the great characters, Muslims and non-Muslims, we are going to inculcate in the minds of the pupils the glorified human experience[37].

Having chosen to walk a long road, Taha gave his time to people around him, inviting them in to his beliefs. However, he never demanded that people accept what he taught, and no-one was rejected for rejecting his ideas: they could be committed Republicans or they could be "friends". He was increasingly based in Kosti, but he maintained his office in Khartoum. About 20 people would attend his gatherings at his office there, and when the party met in Wad Medani, they could all fit into a small room[38].

Conclusion

It is hard to "place" Taha in the politics and culture of this period. This chapter has drawn parallels between him and the Sudanese political, Sufi and commercial elites, Communists and even a short-tempered Egyptian professor. Taha implicitly accepted cultural hierarchies in Sudan, and he remained detached from a particularly deadly outbreak of class conflict near his base in Kosti. In some ways, he could be viewed as someone who assented to many of the values of Sudan's rulers in his own contrary way, in spite of his theoretical support for workers' rights and his unpresentable friends. He did not seem to be able to turn his political concerns into action. Perhaps he was still concentrating on his immodest but still largely unspoken spiritual life.

In his *khalwa*, his reflection had made him shabby and incomprehensible. Now, he was attractive again – people wanted to be part of his life, and they hurried round for meals and chat. This attraction was to become his chief method of mobilising support. His experience in the constitutional convention suggests that he could not handle the strictures of government work, that he was an oppositionist at heart. But he believed in tolerance, and his organisation tried to avoid the exclusivity of the *tariqa*s – people could join, or they could be friends, or they could leave and still be friends. Taha threw away the kind of party disciplines that most groups use to maintain coherence and order – instead, he learnt to offer himself to those around him, drawing them in to his hospitality and imagination.

Chapter 10

Battle lines

In 1958, Sudan's squabbling parliamentary parties handed over the state to a general named Ibrahim Abboud. Abboud coped with Sudan's fluctuating economic fortunes, and his military regime was able to turn the ethnic and religious prejudices of the elite into decisive action. Taha initially welcomed the change, but for him military rule was the beginning of a confrontation with Sudan's Muslim establishment.

Abboud
Sudan's Muslim establishment
Taha's new ideas about Islam had not yet brought serious conflict with Sudan's Muslim establishment. He had published attacks on the political power of the patricians, but managed to keep up good relations with 'Ali al-Mirghani throughout his life. There had been some scuffles during his visits to Sufi centres, but he had friends amongst the Sufis too. As well as the two large sects and the smaller *tariqa*s, Sudan still had the colonialists' network of *shari'a* courts under a grand *qadi*, and a *shari'a* institute with branches around Sudan which taught Islamic studies in the traditions of the metropolitan Middle East, *al-ma'had al-'ilmi*, (the religious institute, later to become Omdurman Islamic University). *Shari'a* courts still played an important role in legitimating the state, but their jurisdiction remained restricted to family law. Sudan's statutory and customary courts dealt with all other matters. In spite of this restricted influence, Taha had already begun to propagandise against *shari'a* legists in his 1946 pamphlet on the *mufti*. The legists were a driving force behind the call for the incorporation of *shari'a* rules into Sudanese law.

The Turkiya brought *shari'a* legists to Sudan, the Mahdi expelled them, and the British rehabilitated them. British and Turkiya policy fostered authoritarian, Middle Eastern forms of Islam. Taha, and others, criticised legists for trying to revive anachronistic rules in modern Sudan. But in some respects, *shari'a* legists were the wave of the future, representing the sophistication of colonial cultural policy, and creating a privileged Islamised centre that dominated the rest of Sudan. Sudanese Muslim leaders, like the Mahdi, denounced this policy as inauthentic and self-serving, but for aspiring educated young men it had the glamour of power and the promise of textual rigour, more attractive than the spiritual decay they perceived in Sudan's factionalised nineteenth century religious institutions[1].

Theoretical religion

Direct confrontation between Taha and *shari'a* legists began in the late 1950s and did not finish until his death. In 1958, Taha got to know some of the students of the religious institute, and his ideas began to penetrate Sudan's small legist circle. One student, Ibrahim Yusuf, was from a Sufi family based near Wad Medani. He was a religious young man, and in his village felt the attracting power of textual metropolitan Islam, the "theoretical religion" that was lacking from his religious home[2]. He was disappointed:

> At that time it was the early fifties, the nationalist movement was on, speaking of freedom, socialism, women's rights. That wasn't part of our studies – our aspirations as citizens and as people. What was useful to me as a young man wasn't in the books. They were all about the past. We lost our hope in *fiqh* [*shari'a* jurisprudence]. And we were in a difficult position, because we thought that *fiqh* equalled religion. We might have left religion altogether were it not for one thing in our favour. We found al-Ghazali. [His book,] "The Revivification of the Religious Sciences". He was a legist and became a Sufi ... He found that *fiqh* is not religion[3].

Al-Ghazali rescued Ibrahim Yusuf's faith in Islam, but he did not answer his questions about contemporary Sudanese society. He was looking around for an answer when he walked into Taha's office with a couple of student friends.

> We went and greeted him. It was a warm greeting. He said, "Are you Republicans or friends?" We said, "We are Ghazalians". He said, "Ghazali stands over me as teacher"[4].

Taha invited them to his home for an evening meal. As the sun went down, they took the chairs out to the courtyard to sit in the evening breeze. Taha explained everything, straight from the Qur'an and the *sunna*. The teachers at the religious institute had told them that Taha was not an *'alim* (a recognised teacher, or *shari'a* legist). But, says Ibrahim Yusuf, Taha knew the books and had the answers, and he and his friends defied their teachers to become Republicans. Ibrahim Yusuf and Muhammad al-Khayr al-Mihaysi, another Republican, were both studying the university level course at the institute, where teachers debated with students, rather than using the rote-learning of the *khalwa*. Taha's views started to crop up in the religious institute's classrooms. His Islam got rid of many *shari'a* laws, including the traditional *shari'a* discriminations against women, and Ibrahim Yusuf defended women's rights to his teachers[5].

Becoming an infidel

The institute did not respond to the students' critique of *shari'a*. Instead, in January 1960, they launched an attack on Taha's prayer life. Taha believed that his spiritual station of *wusul* exempted him from the five daily canonical prayers of Islam – his followers were still required to pray as Muslims. Girgis Iskander, a Christian, had told him that he was good enough to be president of Sudan, if only he would stick to the rules of prayer, but Taha said he had to be true to himself[6]. Taha's antinomianism aligned him with past Sufis. In 'Abd al-Sadig's day, the Sufi mainstream could cheerfully challenge *shari'a* tradition by labelling it as foreign (see chapter two). In Taha's day, Sudanese Muslims ceded some authority to the colonially sponsored legist class, which was established specifically to delegitimise Sudan's old-time religion. *Shari'a* legists now had the power to label Taha a heretic, and they did.

According to *al-Ra'y al-'Amm* newspaper, Ibrahim Yusuf and his friends declared that Taha was above the common obligations of Islam, and was infallible[7]. One student, Muhammad al-Khayr al-Mihaysi reportedly said "Mahmud Muhammad Taha, if he prayed I wouldn't follow him"[8]. The students were expelled. Taha was sorry to have brought their educations to an end, and challenged the institute staff to a debate which would reinstate them if he won. He was refused. Instead, the institute and its supporters outside – former students who had jobs as *shari'a* judges and mosque preachers – began a campaign of sermons and petitions against him. They said he was an infidel, and could be killed with impunity[9]. Abboud's security forces promptly clamped down on Taha's activities, and he was no longer able to speak in public.

Clampdown

Taha had thought that Abboud would save Sudan from the fractious sectarian coalition that had brought it to independence. In the event, he was not the only one to feel it clamp down. Abboud's dictatorship maintained the connections between wealth, power and the Arabised Muslim elite that had been nurtured by the British.

Post-independence regimes faced challenges to the colonialist legacies they inherited, such as the Communists' criticism of Native Administration. Other colonialist legacies, however, were not challenged, and became part of the assumptions underlying the post-colonial state. The British used ethnic categories to analyse Sudan, and came up with a patchwork of tribes that were variously warlike, indolent, mercantile or whatever. The warlike tribe of the north was the Shaygiya, based on the bend of the Nile north of Khartoum. The Shaygiya consequently dominated the higher ranks of the army: Abboud and most of his staff were from this group. Most Shaygis followed the Khatmiya *tariqa*, and the Abboud regime had close links with 'Ali al-Mirghani and his supporters. The economic fortunes of the Khatmiya elite were tied in with Mediterranean markets, and the period saw closer ties with Egypt. The regime made some progress in addressing economic problems, liberalising cotton prices and modestly improving infrastructure. After a few years of stability, the trade balance fell again[10].

Both patricians welcomed Abboud, who did little to harm their interests. 'Ali al-Mirghani remained loyal, but when a Mahdist general was supplanted by two Khatmiya brigadiers in 1959, the Mahdists distanced themselves from the regime. However, leadership problems obstructed Mahdist opposition. 'Abd al-Rahman al-Mahdi died in 1959, and his son Siddig died two years later, whereupon Siddig's brother, al-Hadi, became leader of the Ansar, the sect behind the party. Siddig's son Sadig was now an Oxford graduate in his twenties. He tried to challenge his uncle for the political leadership of the Umma, starting a feud which ran until al-Hadi's death. Neither of the patrician parties posed an immediate threat to the regime, and opposition came from a different source – the regional and Communist movements. The latter led some vocal campaigns against military rule, and managed to co-opt and then ditch the Umma party. In 1963, a small group of Communists began to move towards armed struggle. The movement was short-lived – armed struggle was the preserve of regional groups in the hinterlands of Sudan, and not of the urban intellectuals.

Battle lines in the south

Military command of the state allowed the northern elite to impose more decisively its view of the country. But the Torit mutineers had not gone away. They did not turn into a rebel army overnight, but the realisation spread across the south that independence for Sudan would not promote southern interests. Rural areas of the south still had "bandits" – that is, the former soldiers and tribal groups who still resisted the new Northerner DCs[11]. They did not become an organised force until the early 1960s when Abboud's military regime followed a policy of assimilating the south to Arabised Muslim Sudan, which began in tactlessness and ended in brutality. Sunday and Christmas holidays were abolished; Christian missionaries (who provided most of the social services of the region) were expelled; mosques and branches of the religious institute were set up, and government posts were filled by Northerners. *Al-Ra'y al-'Amm* denounced Equatorian Christianity as a religion of "gross immorality"[12]. Educated Southerners began to organise resistance in the bush and in Congo and Uganda. In 1963, localised guerrilla groups began to attack the government, gradually forming themselves into a series of movements called Anyanya. The army responded with assassinations, massacres, and burnings of villages. The civil war eventually brought down the regime (see chapter 11).

Arab-Muslim

Taha had already begun to criticise the idea of an Arab-Muslim state, and in the 1950s he turned away from the idea that Arab ethnicity or culture bestowed privilege. The party had not been very active politically – its paper folded in 1954, and it now produced occasional topical pamphlets. But the question of ethnicity was often a theme. Taha disliked Arab nationalism, and began to characterise it as racist[13]. He denounced the Egyptian president Gamal 'Abdel Nasser for using Arab nationalism against the western world, and therefore in favour of international communism. Although Taha kept up relations with Sudanese Communists, the Republicans regarded the Soviets with greater alarm than the God-fearing west[14]. Taha believed that Arab nationalism was not just a tool of Soviet expansion, but a racist idea. Arabs should take pride in Islam, not their ethnicity

Taha critique of Arab superiority came out of his religious beliefs. He and his movement did not analyse the social construction of racism in Sudan, where culture, religion, language and skin colour were hierarchically ranked and prejudice against the culture and religion of non-Arabised groups had widespread economic consequences for subaltern groups. Taha defended the economic rights of the south in his first works. In the 1960s, he and the Christians and followers of Noble Spiritual Beliefs in the south were targets of the Muslim establishment. Taha's Sufism and his attachment to Jesus symbolism made him sympathetic to followers of other religions. By the late 1970s, Republicans were campaigning extensively for non-Muslim rights.

From his religious standpoint, Taha advanced the claim that Sudanese Arabism was racist. The Arabic word '*unsuriya*, racism, is seldom used to describe the belief that Arab language, culture and genes are better than the others on offer in Sudan. Indeed, Sudan's educated elite preferred to use the word to denigrate groups which advanced the interests of disadvantaged ethnic groups – even the Republicans used the word in this sense in a 1984 book[15]. Their universalism was uncomfortable with the regional particularism of groups like the Beja Congress, the Black Bloc, and southern parties which began to organise before independence. Those that existed in the Abboud period were repressed, although some began to organise illegally[16].

Al-islam

In the 1950s, Taha wrote a stream of press articles on the inapplicability of *shari'a* in the twentieth century and the need for a new civilisation built on Islam that would supersede communism and capitalism[17]. But he had not yet set out his beliefs in detail. Abboud's ban, and the strident attacks on him in the mosques pushed him to bring out a short book in 1960, *al-islam* ("Islam"). It was Taha's first book-length attempt to explain his new view of *shari'a*. Taha began with an account of the theory of relativity. Its identification of energy and matter is proof of the unity of God and the world, a unity that is written into the heart's desire. Religion attempts to express that desire for unity, in language whose precision increases as humanity develops[18]. Human society refines its laws towards a framework for individual freedom in God. Taha believed that humanity inevitably developed towards goodness, as defined by the Qur'an. The secret of the Qur'an, said Taha, was this teleological Islam. The Muslim scriptures had two messages. One fitted a harsh, rudimentary past that Taha constructed out of evolutionary theory; the other fitted a golden future where just society allowed the free development of the individual[19]. Some verses of the Qur'an expressed the first message, and others the second. The first message was nearer to the law of Moses, the second to the law of Jesus – but Islam was better than Christianity, he said, because Islam provided a "social regime and a governmental regime" wherein people could achieve self-realisation[20]. Taha gave a long account of how this regime would work – fixed income differentials to end class distinction and allow inter-marriage; collective (not state) ownership of capital to empower communities against the state; elections for local and national government and for the management of collective capital[21].

Taha also explained his prayer life – canonical prayer was a temporary injunction, and when someone became *asil* (authentic, the equivalent of *wasil*) he or she could leave off the imitation of Muhammad and learn from God. He quoted Qur'an 4:103 "Prayer is a timed prescription for the believers"[22]. The word "timed", *mawqutan*, is usually taken to mean that worshippers had to perform the prayer promptly[23]. Taha admits this, but goes on to expound the controversial secret meaning: for authentic believers "a time when [this prayer] will end has been fixed"[24]. His book ends with a testimony to his personal view of truth: "This account is true and faithful, for me, and I hope that it is true and faithful for God"[25].

Al-islam is a short work, but it is very hard to summarise – Taha's mind roams from Albert Einstein to the laws of prayer. This eclecticism is part of all of Taha's longer works (to be discussed in detail in chapter 12). They are a useful pointer to his audience too – his mix of physics and *fiqh* would only be taken up by yearning religious intellectuals. *Al-islam* set the direction for Taha's ideas, and he called it "the mother-book"[26].

A visit to a *shaykh*

Until the late 1950s, Taha spent his free time visiting dead and living *shaykh*s seeking their blessing for his endeavour. However, by 1960, he was much more confident about propounding his ideas. When his student followers were expelled for upholding Republican beliefs, he began to feel that his ideas were being distorted. Opponents fixed their aim on Taha's anomalous prayer life, and the grand *qadi* warned against discussion of his ideas. Taha wanted to explain his beliefs about *shari'a* before entering any discussions about Sufi theosophy. But the attack on his prayer life wrong-footed him, and in his first book on *shari'a* development – *al-islam* – he was obliged to include an excursus on prayer. Taha was no longer allowed to speak in clubs, and newspapers were quietly told not to publish his views[27]. The party was still small – about 100 members mostly in Wad Medani and Khartoum – and held meetings in private houses. Taha campaigned against his followers' expulsion in the press and also tried to explain himself to opinion formers in Sudan. Influential people were invited to presentations of his beliefs[28].

One of these meetings was at the home of 'Ali al-Mirghani, in 1962[29]. 'Ali al-Mirghani had met Taha in the 1940s and subsequently tried to spring Taha from jail. Although Republicans attacked his involvement in the patrician system, they respected his Sufi piety, contrasting it with the politicking and economic exploitation of the Mahdi family. Al-Mirghani's Khatmiya *tariqa* had its power base along the Nile valley, and supported parties that represented the interests of its commercial elite, while the Mahdist Umma was more involved in the west and with the big-time farmers. Taha and his followers were from the Nile valley, and this may have enhanced their respect for the ascetic power-broker. Al-Mirghani invited them to tea, but Sadig al-Mahdi, formerly on the fringes of the movement, was now making a bid for power and could not afford to dally with the idealists[30].

When they arrived, Al-Mirghani asked brightly, "Where's the Shaygi?" He was referring to Amin Siddig, the son of a Khatmiya *faki* who had refused to kiss al-Mirghani's hand at their meeting 17 years earlier, and who had the Shaygi *shillukh* on his cheek[31]. Al-Mirghani sat Taha next to him on his simple bed. Al-Mirghani's followers were taken aback by this presumption, but Taha explained his ideas and left a copy of *al-islam*. Al-Mirghani made no comment on Taha's ideas apart from nodding and saying "good, very good"[32]. He asked Taha one question: "Have you [God's] permission for this?" Taha said he did. Al-Mirghani died a few years later, without ever responding to *al-islam*.

A bed of roses

After 1955, when Taha was touring Sudan's Muslim shrines, writing to Egyptian leaders, lecturing on *shari'a*, becoming an infidel, dazzling his friends with his talk and charming them with his manners, his family were getting on with life in Rufa'a. Amna Lutfi, with her daughters Sumaya and Asma, along with al-Rabb Biyjud, did not see much of Taha.

Having a saint in your life can be as thorny as a bed of roses. Taha was not often home: he came for funerals, the most inescapable obligation in northern Sudanese society, but not for much else. When Asma saw him, there would be lots of Republicans there. She thought they were his friends, and that they were talking about politics[33]. Taha's absence was not unusual – many marriages in Sudan were lived apart because of labour migration. However, some observers decided that Taha's family had become a casualty to his spiritual ambitions. In the mid-1950s, a *shari'a* judge in Rufa'a told Muhammad Lutfi that he would grant Amna a divorce – a difficult thing for a Muslim woman to obtain in Sudan. Muhammad Lutfi said she did not want one, and Amna rejected the offer with an angry look. This talk came to Taha's attention, and he asked if Amna herself had requested the divorce: she had not[34]. He told Amna that he was away collecting her bridewealth. Amna understood that this bridewealth was mystical knowledge and perfect worship. Taha did not ask his daughters to understand what he was doing, but they eventually became his close collaborators.

Conclusion

During Sudan's military regime, battle lines were drawn in Sudan and in Taha's life. For Sudan, military rule meant that the ethnic and religious divisions of the country were translated into decisive military action. The civil war that resulted from this decisiveness eventually brought down Abboud's regime, as the next chapter shows.

As the state reasserted Arab and *shari'a* themes, Taha came under attack. His literate reworking of antinomian and latitudinarian themes, some of them culled from the Sufi mainstream of pre-modern Sudan, implied a rejection of *shari'a* laws. Taha's battle was not with the whole Muslim establishment – he had tacit support from senior figures – but he had an abiding antipathy for the *shari'a* legist class. This was amply reciprocated by the mosque-preachers and *shari'a* teachers who campaigned against him. Taha challenged their institutions, but he was also beginning to challenge *shari'a* laws, the building blocks of a hegemonic legal system. His opponents did not discuss this challenge, but instead directed their fire at his ideas about prayer. This tactic turned the debate into a struggle between the Sufi and *shari'a* tradition, and it became the standard form of attack against Taha. His strange claims to mystical importance were cast into open battle. Although these claims hampered his attempts to propagate new legislative proposals, he was not able to disavow them.

Chapter 11

Glorious October

Chapters 11 to 15 deal with the period from 1964 to 1983. Taha's optimistic philosophy of time will be discussed in the next chapter. Taha lived this optimism in his daily life too – he watched the changes in Sudan's government and waited for his fantastic moment of perfection. In October 1964, he watched a revolution in Sudan and thought it was glorious.

The October revolution
Professional Front

In 1964, Abboud's regime was seriously weakened by the southern rebels and was not delivering economic stability. Urban radicals in the north, who had been sidelined in the independence struggle, were now able to use their tactics of urban mobilisation against a flailing military regime. In October, their demonstrations brought down Abboud. Now it was the patricians' turn to be sidelined. The unelected cabinet of radicals and intellectuals who took control in 1964 proposed land reform and the ending of Native Administration, measures which would have seriously affected the rural power structures of patrician parties. In 1965, the Mahdist Ansar were sent out to demonstrate for parliamentary elections, which they knew would be won by the patricians with their rural vote-banks, and not by the Professional Front, the Communist-dominated cabinet. In the event, the radical parties only won seats in constituencies reserved for graduates. Groups representing marginalised areas – the Beja Congress and the Nuba Mountains Union – fared better than the intellectual movements. It was the first time that parties representing non-Arabised areas of northern Sudan had parliamentary representation.

Out with the old

Khartoum crowds chanted: *la za'ama lil-gudama'* (no leadership for the old)[1]. The revolution began with riots at Khartoum University – the former Gordon College. Even in Taha's day, Gordon College had been a centre of political agitation. In the run-up to independence, radical parties and Egyptian agents, seeking a foothold in the Sudanese political scene, paid court to youth there. In the 1950s, educational institutions were strongholds for small radical parties. After independence, Communists and Muslim Brothers traded control of the student union at Khartoum University. After October, the patrician-dominated parties realised the value of the trade, and established their first youth organisations in the colleges[2].

Colonialists feared their new educational institutions would foster political agitation, and they did. Graduates pressed the British to expand educational provision, which in turn forced the pace of the nationalist movement. Student numbers grew enormously after independence: in 1956, the total number of students from primary to university level was 232,539; in 1964, it was over 542,000. Those at higher secondary level and above were most likely to be politically active – in 1964, there were almost 30,000 of them, almost half in Khartoum and Gezira[3]. In Taha's day, there were less than 400.

The new generation of students was radicalised in the colleges and began to compete for control of the state with the older educated elite – which had been incorporated into Sudan's sectarian power structure.

How was it for Taha?

Taha was in El Obeid (the capital of Kordofan) in October. The Republicans, who now identified themselves as educators, not agitators, played no part in the revolution[4]. But Taha saw connections between Khartoum street politics and his dreams of spiritual liberation. He believed that October's model of non-violent change was the first stage of a revolution. In a 1972 work, *al-thawra al-thaqafiya* ("Cultural revolution"), he said that although October had been frustrated by the patrician parties, the revolution's "second stage" had yet to come. It would empower people with knowledge and make effectual changes[5].

Khartoum University had plenty of young intellectuals who were looking for the kind of religiously-tinged empowering knowledge that Taha offered. He, in turn, was looking for a young teaching vanguard to spread his secret knowledge. In 1965 or 1966 he moved back from Kosti to Omdurman, to a house by the river. Amna Lutfi and the children had stayed in Rufa'a for the past decade. Sumaya, Amna and al-Rabb Biyjud moved back to the capital, to be together – Asma was at school in Shendi. Taha rented a house in Bayt al-Mal, just a few yards from the river, where the children could play down by the water[6]. One of his brother's children had become an architect. He built Taha a house in Sawra, a residential area in Omdurman, in gratitude for Taha's support for his family[7].

Taha gave away his Land Rover, and concentrated on his message. He held meetings in his office in the 'Arabi market, with the words "Republican Party" over the door. Students came along to meet Taha. At 9pm, he caught the Omdurman bus, but the students, whose university accommodation was nearby, would hang around the office and talk. They could get a *ful* sandwich, city fast-food from a street stall, and wander back to campus[8].

Taha goes full time

Taha was free to lecture now that Abboud's security men had stopped watching, and in the late 1960s the party opened a centre in Morada, Omdurman. Taha produced four major books between 1966 and 1968. The movement was small enough for him to find time to write, and three full time party workers helped produce the books[9]. Some were short pamphlets, but several ran to 200 pages. These books appeared in shops, but most were sold by the party's colporteurs who were becoming a feature of the capital's streets and campuses. The income from booksales allowed Taha to support his family.

Taha's books from this period are examined in chapter 12 – they were the fruits of his *khalwa* reflections and his conversations with the dead saints. Now he believed he had their blessing to publish their elite knowledge and bring the techniques of Sufi self-realisation to the masses. In 1965 the party addressed a statement "to the followers of all *tariqa*s and all sects" which announced that the *tariqa*s, which had served a noble purpose, must now unite in the *tariq* (way) of Muhammad. (The Mahdi had made a similar call)[10].

Taha's decision to begin his mission had been pre-empted by the campaign against his ideas at the religious institute. That campaign attacked his personal prayer life, and not his ideas about *shari'a*. Taha felt that he could not explain his spirituality without first explaining his reworked *shari'a*, but he was obliged to come up with *risalat al-salat* ("On prayer") in 1966, before producing his main work on *shari'a* – *al-risala al-*

thania min al-islam ("The Second Message of Islam") – in 1967. In these works, Taha argues for an Islamic connection between personal and global development. People develop towards a perfect religion; although their first efforts are crude, they are refined by human development. Modern lessons supersede and abrogate ancient ones, and the *shari'a* and Sufi traditions give way to personal and global worship.

The prophet and the constitution

The 1965 elections brought to power the Umma party, divided between Sadig al-Mahdi and his uncle al-Hadi. The Muslim Brothers fought the election under the banner of the Islamic Charter Front (ICF). They won two seats in the new parliament, and the Communists won 11. The ICF had two main strategies: first, to subvert their Communist rivals; and secondly, to galvanise the traditional parties into adopting an Islamic constitution. The traditional parties were acutely aware of how Communists had outflanked them in October, and gratefully supported the ICF campaign against the leftists. Usefully, a young Syrian Communist publicly defamed the prophet in November 1965, and the party was eventually banned, in defiance of the constitution. The ICF were astonished by the success of their anti-Communist campaign, and began to press for an Islamic constitution. They and their fellow-travellers in the patrician parties and the *shari'a* court system set up a committee to include *shari'a* in Sudan's British-drafted 1951 constitution.

Al-Hadi al-Mahdi, the leader of the Mahdist Ansar sect, energetically supported the Islamic constitution, threatening to impose it by force[11]. Other senior members of the patrician parties were more equivocal: Muhammad Abu Rannat (Taha's judge in 1946, now a chief justice with Khatmiya links) and 'Abd al-Rahman 'Abdun, (an Umma member of the collective presidency that had replaced the dictator) told British diplomats that:

> it was wrong to talk about an Islamic constitution. The Sudan was not an Islamic country because of the two million non-Moslems in the South. If there was no way of avoiding some reference to Islam the right solution might be to have a paragraph in the constitution saying that it should be drawn up in the spirit of Islam but they both obviously hoped that even this could be avoided[12].

However, neither *shari'a* nor western civil law applied to most Sudanese: as late as 1968, customary law governed 80% of the people[13]. Powerful parties controlled rural patrimonies by working the colonial Native Administration system, but their reliance on Islamic forms of legitimacy made it necessary for them to support the ICF campaign. In private, they saw no need for an Islamic constitution, but they told the British ambassador that they could not imagine a Sudan without Native Administration[14]. Some Umma modernisers were committed to ending Native Administration, but they caved in to the opposition of tribal leaders in 1969[15]. In contrast, Sudanese leftists, and some impatient rural people demanded that the despotic powers of tribal leaders be removed[16]. Only then could they begin the process of distributing wealth and power away from the ethnic and centre/periphery divisions that were a legacy of colonial rule. The first Muslim Brotherhood organisation had toyed with socialist slogans in the 1940s, and the ICF made half-hearted attempts to organise labour support, but their successes came in working the patrician system. They and their fellow-travellers denounced socialism as an attempt to "stir up class war"[17].

Taha the oppositionist aligned himself with radical secularists, and he gained prominence as a result. When the *shari'a* courts issued a statement telling the hapless Syrian Communist, now in an asylum, that defamers of the prophet had three days to repent or die, Taha wrote a blistering attack on their "malice" in *al-Maydan*, the Communist newspaper[18]. "Anyone who closes the door of [God's] mercy in the name of religion has no right to talk of religion"[19]. According to the southern politician Bona Malwal, Taha joined him on a secret committee formed to combat the anti-Communist campaign[20]. (However, Fatma Ibrahim, a Communist member of parliament [MP] at the time recalls little Republican involvement in the committee)[21]. The call for free expression dominated Republican lectures, newspaper articles and leaflets. Sadig feels that the campaign "helped greatly in publicizing the Republican and Communist thoughts. It is during this period that the Republican party started to influence a large number of university students and graduates"[22].

Communists tried to widen their bases in marginalised rural areas, but they only had real success at the centre of power. They set up links with radical army officers who modelled themselves on the "Free Officers" of the 1952 Egyptian revolution[23]. This alliance eventually was to bring them briefly into government. The Muslim Brothers had been urged to do the same by their Egyptian colleagues in the 1950s, and had a peripheral role in minor coup attempts of the 1950s and 1960s. When they eventually penetrated the army in the 1970s and 1980s, they were able to establish a durable hold on power[24].

Centre and regions

Many political histories of the period – including Republican ones – concentrate on the dogfight between 13 ICF and Communist parliamentarians. In hindsight, the most significant change in the 1965 elections was the 17 MPs from the Nuba Union and Beja Congress. These groups continued the politics of ethnicity, pioneered by the Black Bloc in the 1940s. Sadig al-Mahdi told the radio in 1965 that he regarded them as a danger equal to Communism – they represented the first attempt by marginalised non-Arabised groups to challenge the constitutional order, at a time when the war in the south was in full swing[25]. In the 1960s they were joined by non-parliamentary groups from Darfur[26]. Their views were uncompromising:

> O people of Kordofan, the Nubia Mountains, the Darfur, the Suni Organization appeals to you to unite against the Norther bloodsucking imperialism which has sucked your blood in the name of religion, the religion which has absolved them ... We in the Free Suni Organization implore and caution you against the northern imperialists who have killed your brothers in the south ... murdering nearly two million – African Suni Organization [sic][27].

Darfur radicals successfully scared the local northern elite, but the Umma party, which dominated the political scene in western Sudan, eventually co-opted Darfur's activists, prolonging their hold on the province[28]. In the south, it was a different story. The Anyanya's war there had helped topple Abboud. In 1965 the October revolutionaries in Khartoum tried to conciliate Southerners with a round-table conference that promised political autonomy and economic development – originally proposed by the Communists in 1954. The conference was one of the few times that northern and southern leaders met on equal terms, and Northerners were shocked by the extent of southern bitterness towards the north[29]. The south had after all only had links with the north since 1947, and had been at war with the north for part of those two decades. It was remote, understood through simplistic and generally hostile prejudice. The October radicals might have been able to reorient southern policy, but they were not given the chance: they were swept away by the patrician parties in the 1965 elections, and those parties decided to deal with the south through military confrontation and Islamisation. The war spread.

War and religion

The African Suni Organization and the southern rebels were wearily familiar with the themes of war, ethnicity and religion. Taha was also thinking of those themes, but like many Khartoum intellectuals, he was disconnected from events in Sudan's periphery. In 1967, he started talking about Israel. He chose the six-day war between Israel and her Arab neighbours as his topic for a lecture in Kosti. Taha had rejected Arab nationalism as racist; and believed that Gamal 'Abdel Nasser, its Egyptian leader, was a demagogue and the Soviet doorman in the Middle East. He wrote in 1968 that Islam did not hold favours for particular ethnic groups – it was instead the purpose for everything. The Arabs' enemy was not Israel, but themselves, and they should recognise the Jewish state[30]. On the first day of the war he gave a lecture saying that the Arabs would lose to Israeli technology. Muslim Brothers waited outside, yelling "Mahmud is a Zionist agent", but Taha ignored police advice not to walk past them. The next day, Egyptian forces collapsed and the Republicans hired a taxi to go round Kosti announcing that Taha would speak on the Middle East crisis. He got a full house[31].

Taha's forceful, capricious intervention on the questions of war and peace, Islam and Arabness in 1960s Sudan did not discuss the south. His book on the Middle Eastern problem, published in 1968, was all about the Arabs, the Jews, the Soviets and the west[32]. Like many urban Sudanese, Taha lived in a different world from that of the African Suni Organisation. When he heard God speaking, God spoke about the Arab catastrophe, not the southern massacres[33]. His audience listened to the same God, and wanted to hear about war in Sinai.

Asala

Taha had wandered Sudan for guidance, but now he took to the road with a handful of followers to spread the message whose time had come. He had a striking command of classical Arabic, but he used plenty of Sudanese idioms in his speeches: he wanted comprehension not admiration. He was an attractive speaker who could fill a cinema with people[34]. In the late 1960s, Republican party membership was around 300, and they began to organise outside Khartoum[35]. Taha, formerly the sole spokesperson of the movement, began to invite others to contribute to his lectures and debates. Most contributors were from the generation which joined in the 1950s, who were eventually given leadership positions. Around 1966, the party faced a challenge from one of its most loyal members[36]. Muhammad al-Khayr Mihaysi was the student expelled from the religious institute for his belief in Taha's authentic prayer life (*asala*). Mihaysi declared that he too had found *asala*, an immediate and authentic relation with God.

The movement could not accept the direction of two separate *asil*s. Taha told Al-Mihaysi told that an *asil* must work alone, and generate his own following. He was expelled from the movement[37]. Al-Mihaysi's departure underlined the importance of Taha's spiritual claims to the party's structure. Taha believed that *asala* was for all people, that it was only a stage on the way to the transformative perfection he sought for himself. But Republicans felt that the movement's spiritual hierarchy could not be challenged if the movement was to survive.

An apostasy trial

Taha's other-worldliness did not prevent him from entering into Khartoum's political fray. The Muslim Brothers and their fellow-travellers did not rule the country, but they dominated political discourse with their committee for an Islamic constitution and their anti-Communist attacks. Taha's tactical support for the Communists won him new supporters in Khartoum University: his attack on the proposed Islamic constitution was to do the same. In 1968, Taha responded to the campaign for an Islamic constitution with a book and lectures entitled *al-dastur al-islami, na'm ... wa la* ("The Islamic constitution: yes ... and no"). He gave prominence to a question raised by Philip Ghaboush, an Episcopalian priest and leader of the Nuba Union, who asked the Muslim Brothers how a non-Muslim could hold high office in a Muslim state[38]. For Taha, the constitutional committee evaded *shari'a* discriminations towards non-Muslims, and could not produce a constitution for a multi-religious country. He asked Sudan's Islamists (*du'a' al-islam*) to consider the Republican idea that Islam should provide a framework of values for co-operation, rather than a set of immutable rules drawn from the past[39]. Taha's informed but non-conformist attack on the idea of an Islamic constitution made him a good target for another ICF campaign against free speech – this time, it was an apostasy trial.

The trial

In November 1968, two lecturers from the Islamic institute petitioned a *shari'a* court to declare Taha an apostate, divorce him from his wife, dissolve his party, and sack Republicans from government jobs. Although the *shari'a* courts had declared the Syrian communist an apostate, they had jurisdiction only in Muslim family law, and no jurisdiction in apostasy cases.

In spite of legal nullity, all the protagonists in the almost-mock trial invested it with great significance. Republicans believe that the trial was fixed in advance, and this seems to be borne out in the trial reports which the Islamic institute men themselves produced after the trial. The lecturers published letters of support from Sudan's collective presidency, and contacted the trial judge and the grand *qadi* (the senior judge in the *shari'a* court system) to see if they would hear an non-constitutional case[40].

The trial was a brief affair. Taha's first accuser, Amin Da'ud, was a Gordon College contemporary of Taha's, and later an author of a book against him. He gave a hostile and sometimes distorted record of Taha's views: that Islam discriminates against women, that believers should share all surplus capital, and not the fixed percentage of capital mandated by the Qur'anic *zakat*, or alms tax. Taha, he added, believed that prayer was unnecessary, did not fast Ramadan, and like past Sufis, he made the pilgrimage to his own heart, not Mecca[41]. Taha's second accuser, Husayn Zaki, began with a Qur'anic verse on hellfire and unbelief. Zaki quoted Taha's "Second Message of Islam", which says that perfected human beings could "live God's life, know God's knowledge, will God's will ... and be God"[42]. This was blasphemy, said Zaki. Taha also attempted to recast the Muslim doctrine of hell as purgatory, quoting a 1968 passsage of Taha's:

> It is the greatest falsehood to think that the torments of the fire will never end; it makes evil a fundamental principle of Being... When torment is eternal it is the revenge of an envious soul[43].

This passage, said Zaki, accused God of envy. Taha's rejection of *jihad* denied "almighty God's lack of love for unbelievers and sinners"[44].

Other Muslim Brothers testified to Taha's bizarre beliefs, including 'Ali Taliballah, the Muslim Brother who had heard Taha claim in Kober prison in 1948 that he was Jesus the son of Mary:

> The accused informed him [Taliballah] when they were together in prison in 1948 that he – that is Mahmud – had been made accountable for Islamic *shari'a*, and that all the *shari'a* that had gone before was abrogated, and that anyone who died not believing this died an infidel[45].

Taliballah was now, like the grand *qadi*, on the committee for an Islamic constitution.

After three hours of evidence, the judge retired for 20 minutes to consider his verdict. (This haste led Republicans to conclude that the judgement had been prepared in advance)[46]. He found Taha guilty and gave three days to recant. Taha's views on prayer proved the case, said the judge – Taha was a Sufi rebel against *shari'a*. His judgement quoted Ibn 'Abdin, an Ottoman legist:

> Ibn 'Abidin said in his chapter on apostasy: "a Muslim should not be judged an infidel if his words can be construed in a good sense". [However] the defendant persists in his beliefs and acts to publicise this doctrine in the name of the Islamic religion, and this action is one of those which the noble *shari'a* declares to be false, such as his belief and declaration that he is relieved of [the duty of] prayer[47].

The judges in this secondary jurisdiction were paid less than their civil colleagues and spent most of their lives listening to unhappy families, often from the poorest section of society, who were seeking divorces[48]. Taha and his *effendi* friends did not have much time for their brand of religion – Amin Siddig, one of the party's oldest members, had left the *shari'a* section of Gordon College because of its obsequiousness, and Taha had traded accusations with them for several years. Taha saw Sudan's *shari'a* court system as reactionary and compromised by foreign imperialism, against his progressive Sudanese faith. He refused to attend the trial. Instead, he and his followers stood in the courthouse corridors distributing their books[49]. Amin Siddig, one of the party's oldest members, feared things might get out of hand. He came up from Wad Medani with a revolver and three rifles in case of trouble, but Taha forbade him to use them – it was better to die than be a killer, he said[50]. Taha fired off some words instead: in a pamphlet published that day he attacked the links between *shari'a* judges and the colonial state

> I was the first and the most stubborn opponent of colonialist terrorism in this country ... I did this when the *shari'a* judges were licking the boots of the English"[51].

There is no record of the responses of the litigants caught up in the bitterness of broken endogamous marriages to Taha and his eager tractarians. But the grand *qadi* 'Abd al-Majid Abu Gusaysa was infuriated by Taha's vitriol. Abu Gusaysa rounded on Taliballah's self-appointed messiah.

Mister Mahmud ... you have claimed you have no father, because
you are Jesus the son of Mary. Are you sure ... that Mary the chaste
virgin came to Daym Graydab? Or that Gabriel, peace be upon him,
descended there?[52].

The significance of the trial

In the 1960s, Sudanese urban politics was dominated by arguments
between secular and Islamist radicals over the nature of the state and
the law. Taha's trial showed his tactical alliance with the secularists and
the left, and this publicity brought him new converts. The trial also
encouraged the patrician-dominated parties to support the Muslim
Brothers' constitution – six days after the trial, president al-Azhari told
Abu Gusaysa that he believed the *shari'a* judges should have seniority
over the civil judges[53].

Taha challenged the Muslim establishment's notion that the official
book-Islam of the Muslim heartlands could provide the laws for a
peripheral, partially-Islamised, multi-cultural state. Instead of using
the Qur'an to generate legislation, Taha wanted to use it to generate
constitutional values. Both sides, however, ignored the important legal
fact that most Sudanese, subject to customary law, were little affected by
changes in either *shari'a* or civil law. Islamists in some "post-Ottoman"
Middle Eastern states were trying to reconcile remodelled Ottoman
versions of *shari'a* laws and institutions with colonial and civil laws. But
Sudan's historical experience of *shari'a* was much more limited, and *shari'a*
there was one of a number of modernising, divisive forces.

The Republicans flitted between a secularist rejection of the Islamic
constitution and an Islamist acceptance of the importance of religion
to state and society. Their concern with legal theory allowed them to
ignore the legal facts of Sudan – a state dominated by one culture still
needed a pluralist legal system to rule its vast periphery. When Taha and
his followers tried to conceptualise that diversity of law and culture, they
were forced to use the Islamic terminology of Ottoman cities – there
was no mention of Sudan's Noble Spiritual Beliefs.

Calling these courts "*shari'a* courts" misleads and deceives people [into
thinking] that *shari'a* is in force. The correct term for these courts is
"confessional courts" [*mahakim milliya*, an Ottoman term for minority
religious jurisdictions]. The secular colonialist government, when it
occupied the country, designated courts for each confession of the
people of this country, Muslims, Christians and Jews, so that personal

law cases could be judged according to their religions. Worse than this, no judgement of what we call a *shari'a* court was ever carried out except by the English district commissioner, because executive authority was in his hands and not in the hands of the "*shari'a* judges"[54].

Taha's focus was on relatively unimportant family law courts in the towns: he did not mention the much more widespread and powerful Native Administration judicial system.

Sufis and the *shari'a* tradition

A second significance of Taha's trial was the explicit references it made to pre-modern conflicts between the Sufi and *shari'a* tradition. To some extent, Taha accepted these terms of debate. His appeal to the Qur'an and the faith gave purpose and legitimacy to the polemical, religious and sometimes exasperatingly intellectual life led by men like Zaki and Da'ud. The latter identified themselves with the *shari'a* tradition, with its transcendent God and pragmatic understanding of the political and legal potential of Islam. Taha was not unwilling to represent ancient Sufis, and their experiential knowledge of an immanent God.

A Sufi could coherently make Taha's claim that worshippers could "be God", meaning they could cede their personal uniqueness, veiled in flesh, to the extravagant uniqueness of God, in spirit. But legists emphasise the incongruity of God and flesh. Zaki, the hellfire man, responded pugnaciously to Taha's claim:

> Lifting the veil between God and his servant will in no circumstances happen in this world. That is what the almighty declares: "It belongs not to any mortal that God should speak to him, except by revelation, or from behind a veil" [42:51]. The veil will be lifted on the day when Mahmud Muhammad Taha and his people know the truth about themselves, the day when God's promise comes: "We have now removed from thee thy covering, and so thy sight today is piercing" [50:22] ... How many heretics and atheists has God shattered before they have damaged Islam even a little: the heretics' and atheists' words remain in the books, which find no audience amongst Muslims up to today[55].

The legists needed a textual and historical context to try a thought-crime. They trawled Middle Eastern religious history to find parallels between Taha and Muslim heretics – messiahs, incarnationists and Baha'is[56]. (Taha had access to Baha'i literature from Girgis Iskander, but Taha's search for mystical union with the divine is not part of Baha'i teaching)[57].

There may be more tangible motives for the awakening of Sufi-legist tensions at the trial. One of the long term aims of Sudanese Muslim Brothers was to supplant the Islamic legitimacy inherited by Sufi holy families whose patrimonial systems held the voting allegiance of most of Sudan in its grip. Replacing that structure of legitimacy with one where urban-educated intellectuals with little rural organisation could hold the loyalty of the masses requires an invocation of the power of the book[58]. The Muslim Brothers needed a tactical monopoly over the interpretation of the book. By this reading, the Taha-problem, then, was not his Sufism, but his fluent use of "their" texts. Taha was a competitor in the tight market for urban intellectualised Islam in Sudan, and he had to be put out of business.

After the trial

Taha's conviction encouraged people to support his movement. Mansur Khalid (then a journalist, but subsequently one of very few northern leftists who joined the southern rebellion) published an attack on supine *shari'a* judges[59]. Newspaper secularists pointed out that the courts had no rights to hear such a case, that free thinkers had a raw deal, and that Taha was a nationalist hero[60]. The publicity brought the movement many converts in the next few years, and Khartoum University became a centre for Republican activity[61]. Taha was in his late fifties, but he could appeal to much younger people, and students could relate his ideas about spiritual development to their own experience in a socially dynamic educational institution.

Taha gave up his engineering work and devoted himself to the party. Most members were professionals from the northern Nile valley, the developed core of Sudan. Some got jobs in the regions, and the party began to have a presence in Darfur and the east. They would all join together at the end of Ramadan and the feast of sacrifices (*'id al-adha*, also called the great Bairam) for a party congress[62]. His daughter Asma had finished school and was now at the University of Khartoum studying law. She chose law because it was her father's favourite subject. She admired his commitment to women's rights, and he encouraged her independence.

> [Taha] always wanted you to experiment, he didn't give you direct guidance ... I am one of the people closest to him, and he didn't intervene in my freedom. For an oriental Muslim man it's unusual. They treat their daughters strictly, they create lots of barriers. The *ustaz* didn't. He had me go out alone and ride the bus alone ... he said

these are things you must practice because they make your personality mature[63].

The hero of a dream

Khartoum University had all sorts of opinions on offer – Communists and Muslim Brothers competed with Nasserists, Ba'thists and Democratic Socialists. There were also southern students, who had separate political affiliations (a few joined the Communist party). Students, many from relatively rich families, had state-subsidised educations, so they could spend four years enjoying themselves. Although the university was unquestionably part of modern Sudan, one Sudanese student leader of the 1970s chose to dwell on the traditionalism of his contemporaries:

> Hero-worship is deeply rooted in Sudanese society. It is reflected in the saint cult, in the glorification of witch-doctors and fekis, in the popularity of football players, singers and film stars ... Even the Sudanese Communists are traditionalists. Once they have accepted Marx or Lenin, they reject any other Communist philosophy, such as Mao or Marcuse[64].

Taha was a hero. One of the law students who was friendly with Republicans was al-Nayl Abu Gurun. He was the son of a Sufi *shaykh*, but his fine singing voice had led him away from religion, and he was viewed as something of a scapegrace. In 1969, Abu Gurun had a dream, seeing himself in a huge gathering of people with Taha up above them[65]. Taha was told about Abu Gurun's dream. Taha was very interested in dreams. He asked about people's dreams in the morning, like a psychoanalyst. He often asked a strange question: "Has anyone see me die in a vision?"[66] Dreams offer Sufis a compelling internal reality, a way into the spiritual world, which Taha sometimes described as a collective unconscious:

> This long story [of all life] grew up in the unconscious, made of such stuff as dreams. From this same matter was made the Qur'an[67].

Abu Gurun did not understand his dream, but it came true all the same, as chapter 16 will reveal.

Conclusion

In the late 1960s, Sudanese political actors realised the importance of the country's educational institutions, after educated radicals overtook the patrician parties in those institutions for the first time. The patrician parties and the Republicans began to organise in Khartoum University:

for the Republicans this decision was to prove very successful. Taha's complex ideas were responsive to the intellectual hopes of the students. His implied tactical alliance with the left and his religious worldview made him attractive to students from pious northern backgrounds who were not going to join the Communists, but wanted something different from the patricians and were repelled by the likes of the ICF. The wide publicity that his trial brought him helped attract more of them.

The late 1960s were also a time when regional problems became politically prominent in the capital. Political groups began to articulate Sudan's big ethnic questions. However, in the late 1960s, the parliamentary regime was discussing *shari'a*, the key Muslim Brother demand, and ignoring federalism, the key southern demand, echoed by groups in the east and west. These groups were marginalised from the Arab-Muslim state system. The Muslim Brothers, in contrast, understood that the Arab-Muslim state was the way to hold on to power in Sudan and knew that the patricians had to welcome their calls for *shari'a* in order to maintain their Islamic legitimacy. Their campaigns against Communists and Republicans kept attention fixed on the *shari'a*/civil law question of the centre, rather than the big question of the relationship between the centre and the regions, partially expressed in the customary/civil law distinction.

Taha benefited from the trial – his movement began to grow rapidly – but the trial itself kept attention focused on the Muslim Brothers' agenda for Sudan. In the late 1960s and 1970s, most Middle Eastern countries were trying to unify their dual *shari'a*/civil law jurisdictions, and a few African countries were trying to reconstruct their legal system away from the power-relations of colonialism[68]. Sudanese Muslim Brothers imagined a more-papist-than-the-pope Arab-Muslim state system, at a time when Arab Muslim states were moving towards civil law. They were articulating the aspirations of northern Nile valley elites for the prestige and dignity they saw in Middle Eastern culture.

Scottish memories

In 1968, a draft Islamic constitution reached parliament just before the government fell. The pro-Khatmiya PDP merged with the NUP which it had broken with in 1956, to form the Democratic Unionist party (DUP) in 1967. New northern elections brought a coalition of the DUP and an Umma faction to power, and they sent the draft to a committee. The supreme court vindicated the Communists in their appeal against parliamentary expulsion. However, parliament persisted in its ban, and the chief justice resigned to join the Communist politicians and radical officers and talk about a coup. The war in the south worsened[69].

In the summer of 1969 Taha went off on another speaking tour of Sudan, followed occasionally by irate Islamists. In May he predicted the fall of the patrician coalition in El Obeid. The next day, Sudanese people woke up to Scottish military marches on the radio. The army had taken over.

The Republicans who accompanied Taha to El Obeid were dismayed at the end of democracy. But Taha told them not to worry, that the parliamentary sham of the past four years was better off ended. Perhaps he believed that the time for change, the missed October, had arrived. Taha's relationship with the new regime is examined in chapters 13 to 17. The next chapter looks at some of the books he wrote in the 1960s.

Chapter 12

Pyramids

Taha's *khalwa* led him to conclude that he could construct a comprehensive new ideology for Sudan and the world from Islam. He produced several books in the 1960s and early 1970s: *risalat al-salat* ("On prayer", 1966), *al-risala al-thania min al-islam* (1967, translated in 1987 as "The Second Message of Islam"), *al-marksiya fil-mizan* ("Marxism in the balance", 1968) and *tatwir shari'at al-ahwal al-shakhsiya* ("The evolution of personal status *shari'a*", 1971). More inspirational than analytical, these works set out an unprecedented approach to the textual sources of *shari'a*. This chapter briefly summarises the history of *shari'a* in Sunni and Sufi traditions and then presents Taha's views in detail.

History of *shari'a*
Muhammad and empire

Muhammad was a merchant from Mecca, an Arabian town developing towards the markets of the Mediterranean. After a period of meditation, he began to hear promises and threats from God, and stories about past prophets. He called his fellow-citizens to accept his revelations, and take up a moral contract with his personal God, in return for paradise. Muhammad called for a system which alleviated Mecca's poverty through the *zakat* alms tax[1]. His moral message aroused hostility in Mecca, and he fled to nearby Medina. Medinans accepted his message and the preacher became a political actor. His revelations became more legal than homiletic. Muhammad's laws created a tax-system and army, and his sensitive understanding of the lineage system fortified alliances between citizens of Arabian towns and the nomads who ran their trade routes.

Within a few decades Arabian armies over-ran most of the empires of Byzantium and Persia. The Arabian lineage system which kept the armies together could not cope with highly stratified imperial towns. Nor could the (meagre) legal material of the Qur'an be used to govern – Muslims tried to incorporate it into legal structures, but they often had to rely on local precedents. Circles of pious legists began to criticise the luxury and legal syncretism of the new empire, inspiring a revolution by the Abbasids in 750. The Abbasids were the prophet's kin, and they allied themselves with non-Arab Muslims, whose social advancement was obstructed by the Arab lineage system. Legist condemnation of imperial luxury became part of the ideology of the Abbasids, who gratefully patronised the law schools.

These schools legislated from the Qur'an the *sunna*, which was recorded as *hadith* and became a fundamental source for law. There was initial reluctance to countenance any textual authority other than the Qur'an, but when the legislative needs of the state demanded new texts, too many texts appeared, and the *hadith* became a vast body of disputed material. Collecting *hadith* was an important way of influencing the content of legislation, but some schools depended more on legists' opinion, or on deduction by analogy, to legislate from the sources. Other schools objected to the idea that legists could overrule judgements ascribed to Muhammad.

Abrogation and tradition

Disputes about the source texts of the law became a problem for the Muslim state. Muhammad Idris al-Shafi'i (d 820) came up with a methodological coup to rid the law of inconsistency. He made *hadith* an infallible, fundamental source of law. Al-Shafi'i's creation of a new corpus of infallibility long after the end of revelation was problematic. To solve the problem, he modified an existing doctrine of abrogation, based on a Qur'anic verse (2:102) that states that later passages of the Qur'an are better than earlier ones. Later verses of the Qur'an abrogated earlier ones, he said, and later *hadith*s abrogated earlier *hadith*s, but the subordinate *hadith* could not abrogate Qur'an, nor vice-versa[2]. Where once it had played a pivotal role in synthesising sources into law, human agency in legislation was largely restricted to dating and authenticating *hadith*. Conflicts between *hadith* and Qur'an still needed the effort of human reasoning (*ijtihad*), but by the tenth century, the sources had been synthesised into *shari'a* texts and institutions, and *ijtihad* was deemed redundant.

Tradition (*taqlid*) supplanted *ijtihad*. Republicans saw this shift as a defeat for creativity: "the jurisprudents ... ossified religion"[3]. But *taqlid* met legal needs. It allowed the justice system to operate consistently, if not creatively, when consistency was needed[4]. Legists had functioned as important ideological critics of the state, but they became increasingly bureaucratised.

Taqlid could be used as an ideological bulwark of the state, and in political crises, its custodians could assume leadership[5]. However, the dominance of the *shari'a* tradition was such that many challenges to the state were articulated as attempts to purify or extend *shari'a*. Reformers who challenged existing states, or created new larger-order communities from smaller groups, often claimed the right to practice *ijtihad*, to enhance their control over *shari'a* ideology.

Bureaucratic *shari'a* served the needs of the Ottoman empire, one of the most enduring Muslim states, but it could not cope with the needs of European capital, which began to penetrate the empire in the nineteenth century. *Shari'a* commercial laws were displaced by laws that could respond to capitalist investment. *Shari'a* schools and courts survived, but often dealt with a new set of rules. The displacement of *shari'a* as law caused much heart-searching amongst *shari'a*-minded Muslims. They asked themselves whether foreign institutions and ideas should be assimilated into Muslim society; and how the unified authority of the Ottoman empire, with its religious legitimacy, could be transferred to the colonial state and then to the nation state. In addition, European rule granted power to the new groups it organised: urban industrial classes and educated sub-elites who could grasp quickly the uses of new technologies. European-inspired Ottoman liberalism promised enhanced rights to previously subordinate groups: non-Muslim minorities, women and slaves[6].

Muslims negotiated the new political and legal changes in differing ways. Revivalists wanted to return to a rigorist *shari'a*. Modernists sought to mediate between Islamic traditions and modernity, and secularists wanted to relegate Islam and its laws to the periphery of the state's power. Feminists and other modernisers in the twentieth century took a slightly different tack. They could not argue for equal rights for women on the basis of *shari'a*, and made appeal instead to Islam's "ethical vision"[7]. Fadel notes:

> Many Muslim feminists have argued that at the core of Islam lies a gender-neutral belief system that has been obscured by a centuries-

long tradition of male-dominated interpretation. Although this gender-
neutral system of belief had been almost entirely suppressed by the
ruling Islamic discourses, according to Leila Ahmed, marginalized
discourses such as Sufism ... were able to preserve Islam's message of
the ethical equality of men and women[8].

In the twentieth century, speculation about the need for change in *shari'a*
became a pervasive part of intellectual culture in Muslim societies.

Analysing law

Shari'a has a number of different functions including: a set of laws to
organise society; an ideological weapon to support reform or the status
quo; and a theological metaphor for people whose view of spirituality
stresses obedience. In the Islamic tradition, there are controversies about
the historical development of laws that organise society; different views
about the relationship of the law to the state; and different views about
the purpose of law. Taha played on all these differences, and he did so in a
legally plural society where *shari'a* was seen by some groups as a problem
and others as a solution. The following section tries to introduce those
differences from Taha's historical perspective.

1. Enforced law and privileged rights

In eighteenth and nineteenth century Sudan, *shari'a* was used to
introduce Middle Eastern urban mores, commoditise land, and justify
the social stratifications implied by landlessness and slavery (see chapter
two). Sudanese Muslim reformers saw *shari'a* as a means of "purifying"
a corrupt society but also as a means of "upgrading" a traditional one.
Many writers detect Islam's dynamic, modernising force in its earliest
history – it stimulated commerce and was a template for building larger-
order communities from smaller ones, cities and states[9]. For Ahmed,
writing from a feminist perspective, Muhammad's marriage laws explicitly
affiliated his system to the imperial cities of Persia – their individuated
property rights required female chastity in order to safeguard inheritance.
Muhammad mandated their patrilineal marriage forms[10].

Islam adapted quickly to the social and commercial structures of
those cities. Muslim social scientists in the second Muslim century could
identify different urban classes: rulers, bureaucrats, merchants, educated
middle ranks, and the "vanishing scum" of the lower class[11]. But Islam
did not, as AlSayyad points out, impose an urban form on society[12].
Many subjects of Muslim states lived in rural subsistence economies.

Muslim states created or expanded a cash sector, which allowed for the ownership of the means of production and the development of wage labour. *Shari'a* commercial law fixed class relations in Muslim towns early on, and the wealth they produced drew primitive-communal societies into their system[13].

Shari'a laws assigned privileged rights to males, Muslims, owners of slaves and capital. The success of these laws can be seen in the fact that they were maintained over a wide range of times and places. Where they did not meet needs, privileged groups could invent loopholes. "Loopholes" (*hiyal*) became a special branch of *shari'a* commercial law – they allowed the cash sector of the economy to buy and sell credit in spite of a prohibition against usury[14]. (For example, a merchant may buy a worthless item from another at one hundred currency units and then sell it back at one hundred and fifty, payable in twelve months: the first merchant has thus disguised a loan at 50% interest as a sale).

People without legislative power found other strategies to manipulate the law. Women slaves used for sexual services could get special rights by bearing male children to their masters. Tribal groups whose social organisation was threatened by *shari'a* inheritance laws could marry their daughters to their nephews, and keep the patrimony in the family.

Shari'a law was predictable, durable, but also capable of compromise. Some laws were quietly abandoned where they did not work. Republicans repeatedly pointed out that the Qur'an (eg 4:89) obliged Muslims to kill, enslave or punitively tax people who opposed or even disagreed with the new faith. The Qur'an admits that this intolerance is difficult: "Fighting is prescribed for you, though it is hateful to you" (2:216), and toleration is a characteristic of many Muslim societies, and the verse scarcely has a legal meaning. In al-Shafi'i's synthesis these later verses stand: they abrogate earlier verses of toleration.

2. Law and ideology

Shari'a was a central part of Sudan's violent route to modernity in the nineteenth century[15]. But the belief in its immubality was pervasive, as Amna bint Ahmed found out. She was a slave woman in Kordofan who ran away from her master in 1932. Her owner found her and took away her children (his property) and a local *shari'a* court affirmed that he had acted within *shari'a* norms. The British governor of Kordofan did not intervene: "as long as the *Shari'a* was immutable, there was very little he could do"[16]. This view of *shari'a* as an eternally valid ideal was a powerful ideological weapon for scholars, reformers and state authoritarians, even if they happened to be Christian colonialists.

The scholars who supported the Abbasids successfully used the text against the state. Opposing an idealised *shari'a* to "inauthentic" authority became a commonplace of Muslim reform movements. The Ottomans incorporated the *shari'a* system into their bureaucracy in response[17] . At the rural margins of the Ottoman empire, reform movements could mobilise social groups not integrated into the state, with the appeal to *shari'a*. In Arabia, tribal coalitions were given ideological direction by Muhammad ibn 'Abd al-Wahhab (d 1792), and reformed central authority in Arabia. Sometimes reformers appealed to *shari'a* to defend practices which were scarcely Islamic. One nineteenth century Hijazi leader called for a *jihad* to defend the right to own slaves (no more than a peripheral part of *shari'a*), after the Ottomans had begun to outlaw the practice[18].

The power of textual tradition was not only used against the state. Reformers used *shari'a* criticism of folk religious practices to revolutionise and control popular culture. The Mahdi's "liturgical centralism" weakened Sufi tariqas but gave Sudan a coherent Arab-Muslim identity. West African reformers used *shari'a* schools to penetrate rural culture, and used *shari'a* standards to decide whether the people of a tribe were infidels who could be enslaved (see chapter two).

These interpretations of *shari'a* made one person free and another his or her slave. They could challenge the state, but more often were appropriated by the state, which could use them to construct a social hierarchy. As well as providing laws and an ideological focus for society, it created a prestigious kind of theological reflection. This "*shari'ah* minded" piety had the dignity of the text behind it, and could grant or withhold that dignity to all other forms of Islam[19].

3. Law and theology

In his "Second Message of Islam", Taha promised people that they could "become God"[20]. In contrast, his prosecutor Zaki wanted a veil between God and humanity (see chapter 11). Their antagonism reprised past battles of Sufis and legists, but also expressed different approaches to life. Legist spirituality drew on themes such as obedience and clear direction, and disliked theological speculation.

Theologians close to the *shari'a* tradition established a deterministic and indisputably objective notion of revelation which frustrated the desire of the human subject to comprehend the content of revelation.

Theological determinism attempted to "safeguard" God's distance. The same urge for "coveted objectivity" and fear of over-reaching knowledge is found in the legists' idea that law is independent of the human subject[21]. Scholars hoped to make the truth truer by lifting it out of human experience. Their prestigious, obedient spirituality was often state-controlled, but it was not always successful in winning converts, especially converts outside Muslim territories. Sufi missions, which drew on other traditions, were more successful in winning marginal groups for the faith.

Sufism originated in ascetic rejections of the sumptuous Muslim empire. Ascetics paid particular attention to the ethical and religious doctrines of the Qur'an, at the same time that the scholar circles scrutinised the law. Sufi ethical purists were open to mystical ideas from non-Muslim traditions, and looked for different modes of perception, ultimate unities and inner meanings. Theosophical Sufis identified God as a lover – sometimes they believed their own personality was dissolved in God's and sometimes tried to speak in the divine voice that had taken over their own. *Shari'a* legists executed al-Hallaj (d 922) for making remarks like "I am the Truth".

This strange Sufi gnosis and disconcerting monism opposed the inaccessibly objectified knowledge and stark moral dualism of the *shari'a* tradition. One important compromise between the theosophists and the legists came in the ninth century. Influential Sufis distanced themselves from the wilder reaches of the Sufi imagination[22]. Around the same time, legists like Abu Hamid al-Ghazali (d 1111) looked for a more accessible God[23]. Instead of trying to identify with God, Sufis began to identify with Muhammad. For them, he was not so much a legislator as a pre-existent symbol of God's creativity. Sufi spiritual writers and celebrities translated this idea into hymns and songs, which attracted many people at the social and geographical peripheries of the Muslim world to Islam (see chapter two)[24]. Sufi spirituality facilitated widespread conversions to Islam.

Sufis challenged the spiritual and ideological functions of *shari'a*, but, with a few exceptions, they did not challenge the legal detail. Only the *malamatiya*, an international Sufi school which had a vogue in Sudan, challenged enforceable *shari'a* laws. Men like Muhammad 'Abd al-Sadig al-Hamim deliberately committed illicit acts to train themselves in contempt for the world's blame (and by extension, praise). Their flamboyant ironies did not amount to a proposal for reform of *shari'a*. However, Taha used the Sufi tradition to mount an unprecedented reform of *shari'a* spirituality, ideology, laws and rights. This attack is discussed below.

Taha and *shari'a*

Taha wanted to rework *shari'a* as a nationalist and also as a Sufi mystic. As a Sufi, Taha was looking for a version of *shari'a* that dynamically linked the present to a utopian future. As a nationalist, he was seeking a comprehensive ideology for a country whose social and political systems excluded many citizens. Challenging this social and political system – the Arab-Muslim state – meant challenging a political ideology and an associated spirituality which drew on themes like obedience to immutable laws. It also meant challenging the laws themselves. Sudan's divisions, as Taha saw them, were between women and men, rich and poor, Muslim and non-Muslim. His reworking of *shari'a* was not based, however, on an analysis of social relations in Sudan – instead, he based his reforms on a sometimes sketchy use of Islamic legal reasoning, linked to his reading of evolutionary versions of history from the Enlightenment tradition.

Abrogation

In the 1950s, Taha distinguished between *shari'a*, that could no longer be used as legislation, and Qur'anic ethics, that should form the basis of constitutional law[25]. In a work published in 1960, he made this distinction clearer: he said that there were two messages in Islam, appropriate to different historical periods[26]. The second message, the second period, was to be more egalitarian than the first. Like other modernisers, Taha wanted to do away with legist historical "accretions" to the "ethical core" of Islam. However, many contemporary Muslim reformers identify that core with the Qur'an and *sunna*, and the accretions with later legists[27]. Taha identified the ethical core within the Qur'an and *sunna* themselves. In his 1960 work, he said that "greater" verses of the Qur'an should replace "lesser" ones[28].

In 1967, Taha published his best known work, "The Second Message of Islam". Here, Taha explicitly said that there are two classes of texts in the Qur'an. The first class of texts have an eternally valid message which calls all humanity to moral purity and to faith in the oneness of God and of creation. The ethical standards of these texts proved too high for the people of Arabia to meet, and accordingly a set of concessive standards appeared. The second class of texts was revealed in response to the dictates of Muhammad's time and contained legal standards that were enforced by Muslim authorities. These two classes of texts correspond approximately to the revelations at Mecca and Medina. In Mecca the prophet invited a hostile polytheist audience to believe in one God and to recognise that acts had moral consequences, and had a handful of followers who were prepared to make personal sacrifices for the sake of his message. However, in Medina the prophet addressed a group of people who accepted his authority but were unable or unwilling to make similar sacrifices.

Taha employed a similar approach when he dealt with the *sunna*. He contrasted *shari'a*, "that degree of religion addressed to ordinary people in accordance with their level of understanding"; and *sunna*, which is the higher standard by which the prophet lived[29]. Muhammad performed certain supererogatory practices, and enjoyed certain legal privileges, which legists claimed were inapplicable to ordinary Muslims. In contrast, Taha claimed Muhammad's *sunna*, or higher standards, were *tariqa* (*tariga*), the Sufi way[30].

Taha thus extracted from the Islamic sources two opposed sets of standards: a later, concessive set, which he called the first message of Islam, and an earlier, absolute set, which he called the second message. The second message was revealed first, however, in order to demonstrate that the people who lived at the time of the revelation could not live by ethical standards, and to show them that they had chosen to be controlled by lower laws. In 1967, Taha used his new abrogation theory to make the shift. He said that the second message was abrogated, while the first message ran its course, until society had acquired the capability to enact it. When the first message no longer applied, the second message returned to abrogate the first.

Abrogation was a technique used since the time of Muhammad to harmonise conflicting verses of the Qur'an[31]. Al-Shafi'i felt that abrogation was being used too loosely – he used it to centralise legislative authority and retard localised development of the law. Abrogation gave the interpreter enormous powers over the powerful text, and subsequent Muslim scholars tried to minimise its application and keep its power in the distant past[32]. But Taha used abrogation as the starting point for a set of reflections on the mutability of rules and the growth of spiritual knowledge.

New rules and rights

From early times, Sufis had challenged *shari'a*'s claim to provide ideological and spiritual frameworks for society. Taha could go further – by reinventing the old theory of abrogation, he could recast the hierarchy of rights that *shari'a* institutes, and overturn its laws. Taha got rid of privileged rights assigned to Muslims, slave-owners, property owners, males, and to the Muslim state. Instead, the second message of Islam accords freedom to slaves, and legal and moral equality to women. Here is a summary of the major legislative changes proposed by Taha.

Women

Shari'a, drawing on Medinan passages in the Qur'an, assigns subordinate rights to women. Men are their guardians, with rights to beat them (Qur'an 4:34)[33]. Women can only marry one man, while a man can marry several women (4:3)[34]. A woman's testimony (2:282) and inheritance (4:11) is worth half that of a man. The Medinan Qur'an deals with divorce from a male perspective (2:226f), and *shari'a* impedes women's rights to divorce[35]. The Qur'anic obligation to pay bridewealth (4:4) could be taken to suggest that a wife is the purchase of a husband[36]. Taha's theory abrogates all these subordinations with Meccan verses that assign equal moral responsibility to all humans (eg 74:68).

Capital

The Qur'an allows for ownership of capital: accumulation is only impeded by a two and a half percent alms tax called *zakat* (eg 9:103). However, Taha takes 2:219, "They will ask you what they should disburse. Tell them [to disburse] the surplus", as a higher injunction to share all surplus. One *hadith* commends an Arabian tribe which had no private ownership, says Taha[37]. Socialism, the sharing of surplus, is thus the second message of Islam.

Jihad

When Muhammad was at Mecca, he was no more than a persuader (88:21). At Medina, says Taha, he was obliged to resort to warfare or *jihad* to prevent non-believers from abusing their freedom (eg 2:190). This violence has no place in the second message, says Taha: the original technique of persuasion abrogates *jihad*[38].

Slavery

The Qur'an accepts the institution of slavery (eg 30:28). Taha sees this permission as a consequence of *jihad*, to force resisters to accept Islam or lose their freedom. Islam assigned limited rights to slaves, but they are due full rights in the second message, where they are enabled to cope with the uncertainties of freedom[39].

Democracy

The Qur'an only expects Muslim leaders to consult their subjects (42:38), so Muslim subjects have no rights to self-determination, says Taha. A Meccan verse (88:21) which says that Muhammad has no dominion over people is taken to mean that in the second message of Islam, Muslims can participate in democracy. Muhammad and his successors were only granted a temporary guardianship over his followers, who could not face up to moral responsibility themselves[40].

The next section evaluates the consistency of Taha's legal theory.

Imprecision

Taha had to show that the Qur'an could be clearly divided into two classes of text, and he needed to find Qur'anic authorisation to shift from one to the other and then back again. By doing so, he could turn al-Shafi's methodological coup on its head. The following section shows that Taha's version of Qur'anic authorisation is plausible but somewhat perfunctory and his division of the Qur'an is vague.

1a. Qur'anic authorisation

Taha seeks authorisation in a variant reading of the proof text for all abrogation theory, 2:106.

> And for whatever verse We abrogate or cast into oblivion, We bring a better or the like of it: knowest thou not that God is powerful over everything?[41]

The word translated by "cast into oblivion" is *nunsiha*, "we cause it to be forgotten", but Taha chooses an established variant, *nunsi'uha*, "we postpone it". He interprets the verse as follows:

> The phrase "Whenever we abrogate any verse" means cancel or repeal it, and the phrase "or postpone it" means to delay its action or implementation. The phrase "We bring a better verse" means bringing one that is closer to the understanding of the people and more relevant to their time than the postponed verse; "or a similar one" means reinstating the same verse when the time comes for its implementation ... The dictates of the time in the seventh century were for the subsidiary verses. For the twentieth century they are the primary verses[42].

1b. Perfunctory reworking of abrogation

Lichtenthaler points out that verse 2:106 is crucial to Taha's attempt to conceptualise a higher ethical core Islam which can be used to overturn the laws of the lower concessive Islam[43]. But Taha does not acknowledge that he is using a variant reading, and even the variant used, *nunsi'uha*, is not the same as that used by most authorities, *nunsa'uha*[44]. His whole exegesis of the verse only runs to one paragraph.

Al-Shafi'i's abrogation theory stipulated that Qur'an only abrogates Qur'an, and *hadith* only *hadith*. In contrast, Taha is willing to abrogate Qur'an with *hadith*. He wanted to end the Qur'anic practice (4:3) of paying bridewealth, because he believed that it suggested that brides were bought by their husbands. Taha refers to an alternative practice in *hadith*: the prophet permitted the marriage of a penniless man who could only offer his wife the Qur'anic verses he had memorised. These verses, says Taha, are a spiritual bridewealth to replace the monetary one[45]. However, he does not acknowledge the significance of his jurisprudential innovation.

2a. Two classes of texts or two classes of message?

Exegetes of the *shari'a* tradition acknowledge the distinction between Meccan and Medinan texts. Many editions of the Qur'an classify the texts in the rubric of each *sura* (chapter). Muslim exegetes used the recollections of Muhammad and his companions to date *sura*s[46]. Western exegetes prefer to use linguistic evidence – certain themes, rhythms or phrases are associated with earlier revelations. Taha prefers linguistic evidence. Medinan passages, he says, can be distinguished by the fact that some verses are addressed to believers, they mention *jihad*, and they criticise the hypocrites who were beginning to appear in the new religion of the town Muhammad ruled. Meccan passages can be distinguished by the fact that some verses are addressed to humankind, they refer to prostration, and the *sura*s are prefaced by mystical letters. But, says Taha, there are exceptions to these rules, because there are overlapping stages between the two messages.

> The Meccan and the Medinese texts differ, not because of the time
> and place of their revelation, but essentially because of the audience
> to whom they are addressed[47].

Taha establishes two classes of text (Meccan and Medinan) and two classes of message (first and second) and he does not clearly define the relation between them. Meccan verses are defined by certain categories, such as the mention of prostration, for example. Exceptions to these categories are then listed – *sura*s two and three mention prostration, but are Medinan. Taha's defining and excepting categories do not fit accepted Qur'anic chronologies – for example, 48:29 is an accepted Medinan verse that mentions prostration. It is not clear if Taha is proposing a new Qur'an chronology. Nor is it clear if Taha's exceptions relate to the classes of text or the classes of message:

> any chapter which uses the phrases: "O, mankind," or "O, children of Adam" is Meccan, with the exception of *surat al-Baqara* [*sura* 2] and *al-Nisa'* [*sura* 3][48].

Taha says *sura* two is an "exception": is it excepted from meeting the linguistic definition of the Medinan Qur'an; or is it excepted from the Medinan first message? Taha does not say, but he sometimes assigns Medinan verses to the second message.

2b. Taha says Medinan verses can abrogate other Medinan verses

Taha's abrogation theory states that Meccan verses were abrogated and postponed in the first message of Islam and then re-instated in the second. However, the theory is difficult to evaluate because of the looseness of his definitions. He does not always produce an abrogating verse, and sometimes produces a Medinan verse. For example, Taha cites a Medinan verse to promise equal rights to women in the second message: "Women have such honourable rights as obligations" (2:228) to establish the rights of women in the second message[49]. 2:219, the verse which abrogates alms tax and makes surplus shared, is Medinan[50]. However, this confusing use of abrogating Medinan verses may be explained by the "overlap" mentioned in 2a.

2c. For Taha, jihad defines a verse as Medinan, but there is a Meccan jihad verse

For Taha, the mention of *jihad* establishes that a text is Medinan, and therefore subsidiary. There is, however, at least one Meccan *jihad* verse, 25:52, "Obey not the unbelievers but struggle with them (*jahidhum*)". Taha does not mention this, nor an awkward *hadith* which says that "*jihad* shall remain valid to the day of resurrection"[51]

Evading precision

Taha's second message invites people to look beyond the complex world which needed Muhammad's pragmatic but authoritarian laws, to a world where all people lived as one. By keeping his readers' attention fixed on a golden future, Taha can evade the demands of legal precision. For example, although Taha sought to grant divorce rights to women, he envisaged a time when people would no longer need divorce, when all marriages are made in heaven[52]. The Qur'anic verse he uses to abrogate all divorce laws (41:53) is a strange one:

> We shall show them Our signs in the material world, and within themselves, until it becomes clear to them that He is the Truth[53].

What has this to do with divorce? Taha believes that a wife is a total "sign", a marker of male self-recognition, the means by which God reveals man to himself. This compelling abstraction means that Taha avoids the need to find more specific Meccan legislation against divorce.

An example of legal argument

Taha's imprecision and abstraction might suggest that he was more interested in mysticism than in law. However, there are reasons to avoid that conclusion. First, Taha's reworking of abrogation was an unprecedented Sufi assault on *shari'a* as a system of laws which instituted a hierarchy of rights for different classes of people. Sufis who attacked the *shari'a* edifice had never made such a systematic attempt to criticise *shari'a* laws. Secondly, documents and reminiscences from the 1970s show that Taha and the Republicans seriously engaged with the *shari'a* tradition.

In 1971, the Republicans produced a pamphlet entitled, *khutwa nahw al-zawaj fil-islam* ("A step towards marriage in Islam")[54]. The pamphlet proposed a means of extending rights to brides without overstepping *shari'a* limits. It used an existing provision in one of the *shari'a* schools of law, the Hanifiya: a pre-nuptial contract conceding rights to the wife. In the Republican version of the contract, the man conceded that the marriage would be monogamous and granted the unilateral right of divorce to the wife. The contract reduced the bridewealth to a nominal £S 1. Republicans publicised the contract, which met all the requirements of *shari'a*, in the streets and even on the television and radio[55]. Taha was prepared to use Hanafi jurisprudence to assign equal marital rights to women with the consent of their husbands, without directly challenging the *shari'a* edifice.

The debate that led up to the publication of this contract shows how seriously Republicans engaged with *shari'a*. Republican leadership was hierarchical, but Taha encouraged diversity of opinion, and his discussions involved some of the cleverer legal minds in Sudan. The party line was determined at debates, where Taha would moderate the discussion, using different opinions to build consensus. A visiting Catholic priest described his meetings in 1973 (they were open to outsiders):

> During meetings, he takes his place at the door of the room, on a seat like any of the others, putting himself out to bring a chair or cushion for those who come late. Far from ... monopolising the conversation, he never resorts to speaking in public gatherings, except to bring the discussion back to the point at issue or to promote dialogue and research[56].

The Republican debate on marriage contract examined the question of slavery. The Hanafi contract replaced the right assigned to the woman's legal guardian to prevent an undesirable marriage, with a duty assigned to the woman to marry within her social class. This principle of social parity, *kafa'a*, was adopted from the pre-Islamic practices of urban Persia, and was one of the ways in which *shari'a* was used to reinforce urban social stratification[57]. *Kafa'a* does not allow slaves or those of slave ancestry to marry the free-born. Abdullahi An-Na'im explains:

> We had a very divisive debate about this. We [were] a group of radical, anti-slavery, [young members], even any reference to slavery in Islamic history we were ashamed of. We maintained that this should not be an issue in Sudanese society ... Taha was not open to that; he said "it is not an irrelevant factor because you cannot impose your choices on society. Slave ancestry is still a social issue, and ... you cannot pretend it's not an issue". And he said that in intimate family relations, when a man is becoming part of the family by marrying into the family, it is reasonable for the father to object to this man on the grounds of slave ancestry. But he would qualify that by saying "but if the woman wishes to go her own way, she can still do that, but she will be over-riding an objection, not that there is no objection"[58].

Slaves and liberation

Slave ancestry was and still is the major class marker in northern Sudanese villages, and according to Republicans, few people from the northern Nile valley, not even Communists, then questioned why people of slave ancestry should not marry outside their class[59]. A 1968 study of Khartoum University student attitudes found that people of slave ancestry still carried the drink-and-prostitution tag which British and Sudanese elites used against them[60]. People of slave ancestry had heterogeneous experiences, however: some urban groups attained a higher status than the members of the peripheral societies from which their ancestors were stolen[61]. In 1973, a young woman who intended to marry an educated man of slave origin had to take her father to the *shari'a* high court to establish her right to marry her fiancé. The court, which used Hanafi law, acknowledged the couple's social parity and ruled that Sudanese slavery, based on kidnap and sale, had been practised in defiance of the *shari'a*[62]. In 1971, however, Taha was not able to rule against the aftermath of slavery so neatly.

Taha and his audience

The needs which Taha's ideas met were not the needs of the people who would stand to benefit from their implementation; they were the needs of the modernist educated elite of Sudan who followed him. What they wanted was a way to live out their Islamic identity in a country emotionally attached to Sufi Islam, yet not see that identity used to oppress marginalised groups. One of Taha's followers, Abdullahi An-Na'im, says strongly in a later work:

> It is morally repugnant, in my view, to subject women and non-Muslims to the indignities and humiliation of *Shari'a* today. I believe the public law of *Shari'a* was fully justified and consistent with its own historical context ... [but] these aspects of the public law of *Shari'a* are no longer politically tenable[63].

Taha's audience was not the poor and the non-Muslims likely to benefit from his new rights. Women later became central to his movement, but in the 1960s, they were still peripheral. In any case Taha's written style in the 1960s did not aim at widespread comprehension. He used a language that was sometimes bafflingly obscure.

The obscurity of Sufi language might spring from its eternally frustrated desire to express the inexpressible. It might also be a way of isolating Sufi speculation from mainstream religion, or encoding otherwise censored criticism of the law[64]. But Taha used the ancient vocabulary for publicity, not secrecy. Abdullahi An-Na'im says that Taha fully accepted the author's responsibility to explain as against the audience's duty to understand[65]. Yet his choice of idiom reflected a choice of audience. His new ideology was directed to a small, urban, Arabised audience familiar with relatively inaccessible Islamic sources. In one book, he addressed the reader as follows:

> You are in the city of Omdurman, where the rule of law prevails and security men are vigilant – there is no virtue in your walking the streets with a weapon ... but what is a virtue in Omdurman is not a virtue in the desert of the Kababish, or the Red Sea hills, or the southern jungles[66].

Taha satisfied his audience with this choice of idiom. Erudite and spiritual rather than forensic, Taha's books use non-legal discourses to subvert *shari'a* and to re-construct a tolerant and eirenic Muslim identity for a place where Islam had been used as a war ideology. He also opened up for educated women a means of expressing their loyalty both to their Islamic faith and to their new western education.

Making the case for the second message with non-legal discourses

The pyramid is one of the most frequently used metaphors in the "Second Message". Taha's fondness for the metaphor, which he sometimes uses with impenetrable complexity, seems to lie in the fact that the pyramid is both ecumenical and teleological: that is, it has a broad base which encompasses the multiplicity of creation, and a fine summit which expresses soaring aspiration. Usefully, it has a top and a bottom, so it can be employed to bring opposed dualities into unexpected unities, or to use Taha's terminology, to say that all differences are difference of degree, not kind. Taha uses the pyramid metaphor to give a positive interpretation of evolution, from gases through solids to the human, which would have satisfied most Darwinists. The metaphor also serves to unite opposites such as God's irresistible "will" and perfect "desire". The thorny theological problems of predestination and theodicy are given surprisingly convincing pyramid treatments. Taha's pyramids can be taken to unite two historical schemas: the first is the *shari'a* tradition's view where a brief moment of authentic revelation towers over an inauthentic past and future; and the second a slow evolution towards perfection, that has its counterpart in the Sufi spiritual quest. The pyramid is an expressive metaphor for the ecumenical, teleological and monist themes of Sufism.

Taha deals dextrously with these Sufi themes, but he also flatters his audience's western educations. He uses Sufism to explain and develop western ideas about evolutionary biology, sociology and anthropology.

Sufi biology

Taha's account of evolution is given in a long introduction to *risalat al-salat*, which sees "all living things as links of one connected chain"[67]. The secrets of evolution and the physics of creation are hidden in the Qur'an, for example: "Then He lifted Himself to heaven when it was smoke and said to it and the earth, 'Come willingly, or unwillingly!' They said, 'We come willingly'" (41:11), which Taha interprets as follows:

> Smoke means water, in a state of vapour, and heaven and earth were a cloud of water vapour, all held together: they were torn apart, and diversity appeared out of this unity. The human seed was not absent then, it was a drop of that water vapour[68].

Poetic verses like this one teased the minds of Sufis like Suhrawardi (d 1234)[69]. Like them, Taha used them to give a positive account of human development. Life moved from one-cell organisms to *bashar*, people, who have yet to evolve into *insan*, human beings[70]. God created many morally sentient Adams before the Adam of the Qur'an and Bible appeared. The prophet Adam came later, after the extinction of many failed Adams "of the lineage of mud"[71].

The first two stages of evolution are inorganic and organic matter, which Taha calls *al-islam al-'amm*, general Islam. General Islam expresses the irresistible divine will (*irada*) to which all is submitted. The third stage is the creation of mind, which inaugurates *al-islam al-khass*, special Islam. Special Islam offers humanity the chance to follow God's perfect desire (*rida*) instead of involuntary submission to his will (*irada*). God's desire leads humanity to the highest stage of evolution, perfection. Early Muslim social scientists used the cognate terms *khawass* and *'awwam* (elites and masses) to make class distinctions. Sufis used the same term to describe spiritual hierarchies. Taha turns this distinction around: instead of having elect groups, he has an elect stage of Islam for everyone.

Sufi pre-capitalist economic formations

The long introduction to *tatwir shari'at al-ahwal al-shakhsiya* deals with human pre-history, using themes from anthropology, sociology, and Islamic and Marxist thought. Taha's 1968 lecture gave a thoughtful and positive account of Marx's evolutionary thinking and his economic analysis[72]. He accepted too, Marx's search for material explanations for the mystery of human society: his work presents history as a record of class struggle culminating in the commercial frenzy of European colonialism[73].

Taha's pre-history is a very legal one. Humanity's first laws regulated sex and property, two areas that need to be protected for society to come into existence. Early societies had to reconcile the individual's need for personal freedom with society's need for collective justice. At first, this reconciliation was effected through the bloody law of the jungle, with the excessive use of the death penalty, but present day efforts refine the means of reconciliation. Taha claims that the first message of Islam, the *shari'a* laws which marginalised women, slaves and non-Muslims, were appropriate for their time. Much of his work tries to vindicate these laws as necessary for the cruel past he constructs from Marx's history of class struggle and the Islamic picture of the *jahiliya* (the barbarous ignorance before Muhammad's revelation). *Shari'a* is only a modified form of the law of the jungle, an attempt to regulate the excesses of the *jahiliya* with the coercive power of the state. The claim that *shari'a* improved the pre-existing legal situation is a commonplace of Muslim apologetics. But it is careless to use that claim in Sudan, where the laws that operated in Sudanese jungles were not necessarily as harsh as those in the Islamised town: people in the Nuba mountains dealt with homicide through compensation before slaving, Islamising states encroached on their non-state society, and some described the death penalty as a policy of "two graves" – the loss of two lives instead of one[74].

Law and ethics

Comparisons between the *shari'a* tradition and Taha's laws are problematic, because he often redefines legal terminology. In 1952, Taha used *qanun wad'i* to mean positive law, but while most Muslim legists define *qanun wad'i* in contradistinction to *shari'a*, Taha defines it in contradistinction to ethics, or "heavenly law"[75] – that is, that the *shari'a* edifice has a positive law content that is temporary and an ethical one that is eternal.

Taha's attempt to distinguish between the legal and the ethical owed much to Sufi antinomianism. However, he also drew on the *shari'a* tradition's own attempt to acknowledge that laws and ethics can be different. In Islamised states, only part of the *shari'a* corpus is enforced law: the *mu'amalat*, or transactions, which cover everything from divorce to sales; and the *hudud*, the flogging, stoning, crucifixion and amputation for specified offences stipulated in the Qur'an. These Qur'anic punishments are considered to be the irrevocable rights of God, whereas all other laws are the rights of humanity. For Taha, the *hudud* are an expression of the golden rule of reciprocity, do as you would be done by. When people respond to freedom by choosing the good, they are rewarded with more freedom; when they choose the bad, that freedom is taken away. Law is a means of teaching freedom, it is an "educational programme"[76].

Taha's proposals overturn part of the positive law content of *shari'a*, the laws of transactions (*mu'amalat*). For Taha, the rest of *shari'a* is ethical: the rules of worship, and the *hudud*, the rights of God[77]. But even the *hudud* eventually disappear when "the self shall appear in all its glory"[78]. (Taha wrote the works discussed here at a time when the *hudud* were not part of Sudan's legal system: when they were incorporated into Sudanese law in 1983, he opposed their implementation on the grounds that they were inappropriate to Sudan's economic conditions).

For Taha, positive law withers away through God's grace. *Shari'a* is a progressive programme, which aims for a human ethic, *shari'at al-insan*. Human law will be the outcome and the reward for all this struggle, a perfect balance of social and individual needs. Finally, human law is recast as self-expression, as will be seen in the next section.

Sufi pyramids

For Taha, the outcome of struggle is predestined to goodness. Drawing on an account of creation first given by ibn al-'Arabi , Taha says that all creatures obey the creative decree (*al-amr al-takwini*) of God in order to come into existence[79]. God does not desire involuntary submission to his will (*irada*), so he draws people into his perfect desire (*rida*) through a rudimentary form of law, collective *shari'a* (*shari'a jami'iya*). Lower, collective *shari'a* restricted freedom by creating a powerful, paternalist state, so in order for humanity to be invited into God's desire, God provides them with a higher, individual *shari'a* (*shari'a fardiya*). For Taha, this invitation to goodness is greater than creation, it is the legislative decree of God (*al-amr al-tashri'i*). The law of each individual gives him or her the liberating choice to do good, which for Taha is absolute freedom. Thus the law is the same as creative self-expression, in the way that God's self-expression is regular and creative.

The law, then, is not a means for expressing power relationships at all, but a means for expressing the self. The individual chooses good or evil, but when evil is chosen, it is through God's permissive will (*irada*). God uses the law to coax believers into doing the good because they love it, so that they may enjoy the goodness of goodness. As the worshipper becomes more engaged with God, prohibitory laws have less and less meaning. And eventually, on earth or in hell, people will learn to choose goodness and thereby enter paradise. Thus all creatures, all religions, all laws lead inexorably to God. God accepted the law of the jungle, that is, the law that might makes right. He revealed traditional *shari'a* to curtail the excesses of jungle law. However traditional *shari'a* is not perfect, or at least its perfection:

> consists precisely in the ability to evolve, assimilate the capabilities of individuals and society, and guide such life up the ladder of continuous development ... It is in fact those who are perfect who evolve and develop[80].

Taha's pyramids draw the lesser up to the level of the greater, they include complexity in unity. That is to say that they express the ethical and monist themes in Sufism. The summit of law is not about prohibition or permission, but self-expression. Is Taha speaking here in earth or in heaven? He does not say.

Taha's accuser Husayn Zaki repeatedly criticises Taha's attempt to conceptualise absolute individual freedom – for him, life without enforceable *shari'a*, or positive law, is unimaginable[81]. But Taha's legal scepticism is bound up with the idea of *haqiqa* (ultimate reality, the aspiration of Sufism). The movement from collective law to individual law is the same as that from *shari'a* to *haqiqa*, and similar to the move from traditional *shari'a* to ethics. These grand upward movements are like a pyramid that leads from earth to heaven.

Taha's pyramid symbolism is nuanced and suggestive, but does not make for clear law. Rather he is calling for a new form for human unity – the unities of the law, the state and doctrine are all in fact causes of strife, but humanity can unite around *'ilm* (mystical knowledge, equivalent to ultimate reality). "The miracle of the second message is the 'mysticality' (*'ilmiya*) of the Qur'an", to which might be added, the "mysticality" of the law[82].

Time for a change

Different actors on the Islamic scene have different periodisations of history, and they use these periodisations for political purposes. The *shari'a* tradition's periodisation runs as follows: creation, barbarous and cruel period before revelation, short infallible period of revelation, period after revelation, and the end of time. But Taha spent his prison *khalwa* in a different time, an eternal present where golden past and future met. He did not see the present as a hiatus between the thunderous voice of revelation and the cataclysm of judgement, but saw the whole of history through the optimistic monist chronology of Sufism, which unites God, the world and time in a progressive upward movement.

Taha's pyramidal vision swerves perspective and allows these two conflicting chronologies to slide into unity. The *shari'a* revelation is not the centre of linear time, it is half-way up a pyramid to perfection. Beneath *shari'a* lies jungle law, above it, perfect unity. But all laws have their own time and purpose, and every form of human understanding leads to God. "It is wrong to reject anything in human heritage by judging it as absolutely vain", he said[83]. Religion did not descend from on high; it grew on earth and was purified by heaven as it rose upward. Taha says that God even willed atheism and polytheism[84].

Taha has to explain why the time is now ripe to enact this higher human law, which assigns equal rights to all humans. What allows Taha to switch from one chronology to another? In *tatwir shari'at al-ahwal al-shakhsiya* he settles for a familiar answer: changes in the modes and relations of production imply legal and social changes. The time has now come to change because, "by God's grace, technology has come to take on work instead of slaves, and production is abundant"[85]. Equally, women can expect rights because changing relations of production – including women in the highest professions – mean that they are capable of the highest responsibility[86].

But Taha believed strongly in the relation between the global and the personal, and the new introduction to the 1971 edition of his "Second Message" hints that the change will come about through a man whose stature compares with the prophet Muhammad's. Taha says that while Muhammad was the last prophet (*nabi*), there were still messengers (*rasuls*) to come. Both terms are titles of Muhammad, but Taha was trying to suggest that the change to the new society would come about through the perfection of one, "who knows the Qur'an, and is authorised to speak"[87]. In the 1970s and early 1980s, Taha began to make more explicit references to the place of this perfect man in his new order, as chapter 15 will show.

Conclusion
Domestic violence

Taha reworked *shari'a* into an allusive and persuasive Sufi version of history embellished with Marxism and evolutionary theory that made it attractive to a young modern audience. He used classical Sufi themes to articulate a widespread Islamic-modernist distinction between an ethical kernel and a legal husk to the Qur'anic message. Taha's contribution was definitive partly because he gave the whole effort the satisfying methodological clunkiness of al-Shafi'i's abrogation theory. He correctly identified the fact that al-Shafi'i's theory was a weakness rather than a strength of the *shari'a* edifice and used that insight to twist the whole edifice around. That was important for his followers. Abdullahi An-Na'im says that no other Muslim reformer can satisfactorily account for changing the legislative content of the Qur'an, which permits wife-beating:

> The Muslim who says "I will never strike my wife" has no response to the Muslim who does, and who has a legal right to do so. It is becoming rarer and rarer in urbanised middle-class communities ... [A] middle class professional career man is increasingly unlikely to hit his wife – but the legal right [to do so] remains under *shari'a*[88].

Taha may have used abrogation theory carelessly but that does not diminish his contribution. He was able to turn immutable *shari'a* into something malleable and open to discussion. Al-Shafi'i used abrogation to end the uncertainties of revelation, and create a legal and ideological product that could be more easily handled by a centralising state. Taha used it in a completely different way – to express the dynamism and responsiveness of Islam to changing society, and to point Islam towards a Sufi utopia.

Sufi law

Taha's use of Sufi themes was psychologically necessary – his ideas about *shari'a* were born in his intense moment of reflection which lasted from 1946 to 1951. His legal theory was bound up in his own self realisation, and that self-realisation was bound up with Sudan's Sufi heritage. He had the courage and breadth of imagination to mount an explicit challenge to *shari'a*, but those virtues were so closely tied to his religious experience that he could not untie them, even if it prevented his message being understood by people outside his tradition – the Muslim Brothers and the *shari'a* legists who prosecuted him, the followers of other religions, the uneducated women whom he wanted to liberate.

Finally, Taha's use of Sufi idioms to express his legal scepticism makes sense, because Sufi antinomianism has long implied a critique of *shari'a*. In the past, Sufis could criticise *shari'a* as a theological metaphor, or as an ideological tool of the state, through their flamboyant encounters with God and their dissident retreats. Apart from the crazy ironies of the *malamatiya*, they had never attempted to subvert *shari'a* laws. Other Muslims had manipulated the rules with commercial loopholes, and slaves and tribes had adopted strategies to extract concessions from *shari'a*. Taha had the self-confidence to rework the sources systematically. He took the existing legal scepticism of Sufism and used it to deconstruct the rights instituted by *shari'a* laws, turning Sufi theosophy into an activist political platform and not just a justification for pious dissent. Sudanese Sufi leaderships were familiar with Sufi antinomianism. But their attachment to the highest Islam, *haqiqa*, was private – they used *shari'a* to deal with the common herd. They were never able to use Sufism to challenge the increasing use of *shari'a* as a form of state legitimacy in the nineteenth and twentieth centuries, and that is why the Sufi patricians were vulnerable to the *shari'a* claims of the Muslim Brothers and their fellow travellers. Taha's contribution was not a small one, then: he used Sufism not merely to resist the law, as other Sufis had done in the past, but to legitimise a comprehensive reconstruction of the law.

Chapter 13

Modern Sufi

This chapter looks at Taha and his movement between 1969 and 1973. It shows how Taha used traditional methods to create a modern urban organisation, and suggests how that influenced the cultural identity of himself, his followers and Sudan. During this period, he set up a movement for women, which developed its own identity over the coming years, and the chapter follows Taha's Republican sisters into the mid-1970s.

Nimeiri

In May 1969, Colonel Jaafar Nimeiri's coup established a government led by military officers and radicals affiliated to the Communist and Arab nationalist parties. It was significantly different from the last coup, where patricians and their supporters had done a deal with the military high command. This time, small radical parties joined junior officers for a revolution. However, the parties were soon to be marginalised by alliances between the military and the south.

The May regime canvassed for support in rural Sudan and began abolishing Native Administration in the north. Nimeiri and his military supporters then proceeded to liquidate rival political forces. The leader of the Mahdist Ansar, al-Hadi al-Mahdi, was killed with several thousand supporters in a bombing raid on his Aba Island home after resisting the regime. Mahdist assets were confiscated in a sweeping but short-lived campaign of nationalisation. Communists manoeuvred for control of the revolution, but when a Communist major attempted a coup in 1971, the party was ferociously repressed. With Nimeiri's rivals destroyed, his May regime looked south for new allies. The war was going well for southern militias, now under a unified command, and the regime was able to broker a deal. A 1972 peace accord led to a permanent constitution for

Sudan in 1973, which gave approximate parity to African Noble Spiritual Beliefs, Islam and Christianity[1]. The widely-acclaimed accord attracted foreign capital and some able technocrats to the regime[2].

Country boy

Taha did not mourn the passing of the ICF and the sectarian parties, and he voluntarily dissolved his own party. The Republican offices in Morada closed and Taha's house in Sawra became the busy centre of the new Republican Brotherhood, as the party came to be called. Over the subsequent few years, Republicans passively supported Nimeiri. Taha saw him as a simple but straightforward country boy, *wad al-balad*, and he did not criticise the regime's violent suppression of the Mahdists and Communists, although he had defended Communist rights in 1965. He felt that their armed challenges to the state justified a severe response[3]. Nevertheless, he kept his distance from the regime, and Republicans refused to join Nimeiri's corporatist Sudan Socialist Union (SSU), which had a network of popular councils and party committees extending from village to nation. The council system was similar in some respects to Taha's 1955 constitutional proposal – single party democracy was seen in Africa at the time as a means to avoid configuring party structures around ethnic or other divisions[4].

Modern Sufi
Oh happy man

The ban on party activity gave the Republicans time to consolidate. They spent the next few years talking and discussing, occasionally producing books and supporting pamphlets which would be accompanied by a series of lectures or debates led by Taha. Since the late 1960s, Republicans had held meetings at the end of Ramadan and *'id al-adha* (a feast recalling Abraham's sacrifice of his son). These feasts are family occasions, but Republicans preferred Taha and the brotherhood to the company of their relatives. The Republicans began to function as a social group rather than as Taha's coterie. Two hundred Republicans celebrated the Ramadan feast at the 'Arakiya shrine at Abu Haraz in 1970, on the invitation of the *shaykh*[5]. Taha sent letters to the shrines of 'Araki *wali*s he visited. One read:

> If you know of any lack of guidance or sincerity in us, we hope you
> will turn with us to the blessed and exalted God that he might meet
> our needs by the blessing of our visit to you[6].

The letters were placed in the tombs of the *walis*: a worshipper who later visited the shrine heard in a dream a voice calling from one of the shrines "Oh happy man! Come and get the answer to your letter"[7].

The next year, the Republicans visited the Sadigab at Mundara, the Butana shrine of Taha's tribal forebear, Muhammad 'Abd al-Sadig al-Hamim. Taha and his followers chanted *zikr* (repetition of the name of God) from sunrise to forenoon, when they returned to Omdurman, with hearts "overflowing with joy, faces aglow with the light they had gained from that auspicious visit"[8].

Social movements

Taha used a repertoire of Sufi organisational techniques to create a new social movement. Communal *zikr*, hospitality, asceticism, charisma and charitable works: all established continuities with the religious experiences of his followers, many of whom were raised in the small-scale *tariqa* environment of the northern Nile valley. Taha had the sympathetic authority of a Sufi *shaykh*, but he used it to attract educated people. Probably he viewed the intellectual project of reform, and the personal development of his followers as more important than institution building. Taha did not want to use his spiritual celebrity like a miracle-worker – he sought intellectual conviction from his followers[9]. Nevertheless the movement had the authoritarian structure of a *tariqa*. Taha appointed deputies based on his appreciation of their spiritual merit. One exclusivity that may have helped group cohesion was a Republican ban on prayer in mosques – Republicans would only be led in prayer by one of their number. They did not go on pilgrimage, preferring to spend the money on the movement's propaganda. These Republican obligations separated people from the religious lives of their families and built loyalty to the movement. The Republicans had many of the characteristics of social movements in Sudan – they offered an urban identity and a new set of relationships, outside the ties of the family, market or state.

Many Republicans were linked to what was then Sudan's only university, producing about 600 graduates a year in the early 1970s[10]. The students held public debates on campus, introducing political, cultural, social or religious topics and then opening them up for discussion. These debates eventually were held on street corners, squares and roundabouts. Republicans came to see these "free forums" as the means to challenge the popular loyalties to patrician elites which thwarted Sudan's democratisation, and to challenge the "imported" ideologies of the Communists and Muslim Brothers (the ICF had reverted to its old name)[11]. The Republicans believed that they empowered people to decide their own futures.

Debate became a central part of the Republican movement's internal and external structure[12]. Chapter 12's account of the debate on marriage and slavery indicates how divisive these debates could be. Younger, more "rationalist" Republicans had a radical approach to social questions, which Taha sometimes opposed. The significance of the marriage-slavery debate was not only legal – it highlighted a division in the movement which began to be obvious in the late 1960s, between Republican rationalists and mystics. Abdullahi An-Na'im was from a secularist background, and identified with other young rationalist Republicans. These Republicans were young, clever activists who wanted a persuasive ideology for the Republican free forums. Other Republicans put more faith in a higher power.

Against the young rationalist Republicans were a group called the *waqtajiya*, or those awaiting the time (*waqt*) of transformation. They worked just as hard in the street discussions, but they did not have the modernising approach of some university men. The movement was not broad enough to include Muhammad al-Khayr al-Mihaysi, who left because he claimed the same spiritual rank as Taha, but it was broad enough to include radically different approaches to life and politics, mediated by Taha's personality.

Fatin Hamama and football clubs

After Taha wrote about new marriage laws, an Egyptian film called *urid hallan* ("I want a dis/solution") was in the cinemas, and Taha urged everyone to watch it. Fatin Hamama (one of Taha's favourite actors) topped the bill: she played a woman married to a tormentor, who was looking for a divorce.

Taha wanted Republicans to study *shari'a* with a beautiful Egyptian at the cinema, and he taught *shari'a* in football clubs. Mosque preachers, under the influence of the Muslim Brothers and their fellow travellers, refused Taha a hearing, so he would go and speak in the clubs set up by neighbourhood football teams. Football had been used by the British to reform leisure and to act as a political bromide but it had been eagerly taken up by the Sudanese. It was not just a sport – it offered local people a means of setting up small-scale social movements outside the control of the state or religion, and these autonomous spaces were perfect for Taha's purposes[13].

Other aspiring political groups used these autonomous spaces – the Muslim Brothers and the Ansar al-Sunna, a group following the radical, anti-Sufi Islam of the Arabian preacher ibn 'Abd al-Wahhab. Clubs also invited experts to talk about medicine or science. Television was underdeveloped at the time and clubs were still a place for informing and explaining[14]. Taha was better at it than most: he could draw 200-400 people, spilling out on to the street. He could manage an entertaining and complex religious and cultural argument in half an hour. He would hang around after the talk, and walk people home rather than disappearing into a car. Some of his lectures have been preserved, on tape or in print, and they are often more accessible and compelling than his longer works. Instead of Sufi obscurities, he would draw examples from stories in the papers, quote sonorously from the Qur'an, or make precise little analogies with popular science and culture[15]. "When he spoke, you couldn't leave until he finished", says Yusuf Hasan, then a philosophy student and now a senior official in the Ansar, whom Taha never persuaded[16].

Al-Ghazali tunes

Taha used group religious activities to create group cohesion, including a distinctive *zikr* – the Republicans would only repeat the word Allah, and not use the divine epithets chanted by the *tariqa*s. It was noted in chapter six that Taha was fond of the *maddah*s, hymn singers who would sing for their supper at family celebrations and Sufi centres. The Republicans did not use their *madih*, or hymns, but improvised a new form of religious music which they called *inshad*, songs. They had popular and recognisably secular melodies and style. Across Africa, new economic and social distinctions, and urbanisation gave rise to new musics to cope with the explosion of new identities[17]. This secular music was appropriated by Taha's young intellectuals.

Republican poets put the melodies were to words and Republican musicians sang them[18]. They also used Middle Eastern Sufi poets like al-Ghazali, sending away to Baghdad for particularly obscure classical writers who dealt with Sufi themes of love for God[19]. It was noted in chapter two how some Sudanese Sufis distinguish between older demotic poetry in praise of local *shaykh*s, and newer material about the prophet and God which was deemed more literate and theologically respectable. Republican songs were about God and the prophet, but they would also sing in honour of Sufi *shaykh*s, like Hasan al-Mirghani.

The songs had one or a number of lead singers with a congregational response at the end of each verse. Solemn and impassioned, they were sometimes introduced with long explanations which borrowed eclectically from the Qur'an, *hadith*, Arabic gospels, and Sufi poets. Often the congregation was led by a woman singer, a sound as strange as the female Republican muezzins[20]. Nile valley women may have sung *madih* within the family or at women-only occasions, but they did not sing for common worship[21]. But these women would put on a professional performance of mystical praise, every dawn, with the cocks crowing in the background.

Indigestion

In other ways, Taha appropriated traditional and modern themes from his own background. In his early twenties, he was still one of Mr Souper's students at Gordon College, and the young people who later surrounded him were going through a similar experience, living a lengthening gap between parental home and marriage. It was an increasingly common experience for the young men of the nascent middle class in Sudan, to leave a village home and share a small cheap house with other students or professionals. In the mid-1980s, Hanan Bulabula, the Sudanese singer, summed up the experience in a song that is a beguiling invitation to marriage:

> Indigestion, indigestion, that's bachelorhood
> You eat *ful* and lentils in bachelorhood

Many young men, eating urban fast-foods and waiting for marriage, turned to Taha, and it was decided that they should have a house together near Taha's. He did not like the usual term *bayt al-'azaba* (bachelors' house) and decided it should be called *bayt al-akhwan*, the brothers' house. In 1973 there were three of the houses in Khartoum, and their monastic arrangements drew the approval of a visiting Jesuit priest, Henri Coudray:

> Men and women live there for a period of ... detachment from the world to consecrate themselves to God, which means in particular sexual continence. They live in quarters segregated ... In these communities, they receive training to live out the virtues of the "Second Message of Islam": personal and communal prayer, especially in the "last third of the night", in accordance with Sufi and Brotherhood practice; sharing of goods by making communal a part of their salaries for the community's needs; militant action and teaching; organising retreats;

debates and the distribution of the works of Mahmud Taha in the streets[22].

The Republican houses spread around the major towns of Sudan, and each one had a leader appointed by Taha. There were 20-40 men in each house, sharing the cooking and cleaning. Not everyone was committed to the movement – some people stayed with Republican family members, but the movement had the fuzzy borders that allowed for their presence.

Republican sisters
Republican daughters

Since 1946, Taha had written on the question of women's rights. Like many intellectuals of his generation, he accepted the idea that women had the right to be involved in society. However, there were no Republican women's groups analogous to the Communist-leaning Women's Union or the women's sections of the Umma and Islamic Charter Front. In the late 1960s, a few women had begun to attend the party headquarters in Omdurman. They were all junior relatives of senior Republicans – the daughters of Taha, Muhammad Fadul, Zanoon Gubara, and Taha's niece Batoul Mukhtar[23]. In the 1970s, more middle class women went to university – almost 500 attended tertiary education institutes in the capital in 1973, and the movement began to recruit them[24].

As the movement spread through colleges and universities, it got bigger and younger. Women began to join up in greater numbers in the mid-1970s. Women's education had gained increasing acceptance in northern Sudanese Muslim society, but the expectation that women should live with a male relative and guardian was almost universal. This was not a social norm that Taha could lightly ignore, and it was decided that Republican sisters, as they were called, could stay with his family – his wife, daughters and niece. His sister Umm Kulsum stayed there too, as did al-Rabb Biyjud. The sisters became an important part of the movement: although most of them were related to Republican men, they developed their own identity. Eventually, they began to participate in Republican street debates. Although Taha had called for the abolition of the veil in his "Second Message of Islam", sisters chose to wear the elegant Sudanese *tob* (a sari-like wrap) out of sensitivity for local custom. They wore white *tob*s, because white was the colour of working women's tobs, and they believed that their missions were work. The brotherhood offered women religious equality and a chance to engage in communal worship which was denied them by most other Islamic groups in Sudan.

Life stories

Women's religion in Muslim Sudan is more eclectic as a result of women's exclusion from collective worship. Women and people of slave ancestry dominate the spirit possession cults. In some areas, women use some Christian rituals – a grandmother may mark the heads of sick children with a watery cross, in a ritual reminiscent of baptism. However, educated women with access to textual religion found these practices unsatisfying or associated them with heterodoxy, poverty, and illiterate culture. For example, Asma Gizouli, a Rufa'a woman, wanted to express her religious devotion, and she turned to the Tijaniya, a Moroccan *tariqa* which spread across west Africa and Sudan in the nineteenth century[25]. She followed the *tariqa* for 17 years, but she never once saw her fellow worshippers – they would drop books and rosaries through her door and expect her to get on with her devotion alone. She knew Taha – she had watched him praying by the river during his *khalwa*, and eventually she became a Republican. Her daughter, who joined up in 1974, attributes her mother's decision to the lack of pastoral care in the Tijaniya. Republican sisters had the attention and guidance of Taha and the leadership, which included women[26].

'Awatif 'Abd al-Gadir joined the next year. She was a school student from a religious Kosti family, and she had a strong sense of the discrimination that she and other women faced. She got hold of one of Taha's books from her brother (two of her brothers were Republicans). It was the first time that she had read that women and men were equal. When she visited Omdurman that summer, she went to visit Taha's house. She stayed the whole summer, and there she met women professionals, women judges, older women who could express their commitment to a prestigious, textual Islam, without having to adopt the practices she believed were oppressive. "In my mind, a woman could not be zealously religious unless she was stupid – because it gives her nothing," she said, but when she saw the respect that Taha accorded to her and heard more of his views, she joined up. Taha made a point of praising women who spoke up in large meetings for the first time[27]. Some of her family opposed her, but her father was glad to see that Taha had provided her with answers: "He thought that the *ustaz* had taken a big burden from him. He shut me up!"[28]

Nineteen seventy-five was the United Nations' International Year of Women, and the Republicans took up the cause. Taha decided that the sisters should join in the movement's activities, and he sent them out on the streets to preach. He had been accompanied by women followers before, and taken them into the clubs where he spoke. Sudanese women were excluded from urban mosques and market places in the Nile valley, and it was strange to see them in a club. Whatever Taha's topic, the first question was always: "Why are those girls here?"[29] Taha's decision to have sisters preaching on the street was even more of a challenge to the picture of respectable feminine invisibility that had been promoted alongside the *shari'a* tradition in Sudanese towns for a couple of centuries. One sister, Fatma Abbas, did not read or write but learned to make public speeches on the need for a new Islamic jurisprudence – Taha called her "*burhan al-fikra* (the proof of [Republican] ideology)"[30]. Howard notes:

> The women often endured insults while speaking or trying to distribute Republican literature on the streets of Khartoum. Because the members considered their efforts to raise the status of women the hallmark of the movement's progressive philosophy, the sisters bore the double burden of acting as symbols while trying to understand the changing order[31].

In 1974, Taha began a series of talks for women, with a few fathers present to ensure propriety. He told them that they were the equal of men, and ran through his ideas about the second message, the fallacies of *fiqh*, the difference between the Meccan and Medinan Qur'an. Taha used broad Sudanese dialect to phrase this dauntingly intellectual message, and then published his lectures in colloquial Arabic, a language seldom written down. By 1975, the movement was producing a large volume of pamphlets on the rights of women, the veil, women's spirituality, polygamy and the Sudanese Women's Union. Batoul Mukhtar and Asma Mahmud were the first to take to the streets, and they were later joined by others. They joined in the delegations which travelled around Sudan. Republican sisters could choose to stay in Taha's own home – they participated fully in the long round of activity from before dawn to late at night. Al-Rabb Biyjud lived there too, now an elderly woman and a Republican sister, accorded the deference due to Taha's mother by the educated young women in the house[32]. She died there, in the early 1980s, and Taha buried her in Omdurman.

Love and poverty

Taha's spiritual children now were taking up more time, and his devotion to the cause had led him deeper into asceticism. In the late 1960s he had given up engineering and exchanged his pith helmet for a turban. He ate sparely, with the women and children – who, according to the custom of the northern Nile valley, usually had the leftovers of men's meals[33]. He became a vegetarian, a highly unusual step in Sudan, and began to wonder about animal rights. Since the 1950s, Muslim Brothers and Communists had looked for friends in the army – Taha was still asking Buddhist questions:

What's the difference between Pif-Paf and a machine gun?[34]

Pif-Paf is a domestic insecticide spray. Taha would not kill mosquitoes, flies or scorpions. He liked going to the zoo, and all the local cats knew to come around at mealtimes. The cats might have done well, but Taha's intense morality meant that his family was getting poorer, and the food at home was getting less presentable. He travelled fourth class ("Because there is no fifth class" he said, quoting Gandhi, to anyone who asked why he was slumming it). He gave up his office and kept his possessions in a suitcase. The family also lived like this. Amna Lutfi had only one *tob* (wrap), and her only shoes had a hole. One day she was visiting her neighbour and cut her foot. She was crying, because she was the daughter of a school inspector who did not even have proper shoes. And one of her guests turned up her nose at the thin *mulah* stews she produced for her vegetarian husband. Taha would tell her that valuing your own humanity meant that you did not own much. Amna took some time to be convinced, but Taha's daughters, and his niece Batoul Mukhtar, were eager to hear about Taha's ideas.

Voluntary poverty

Taha expected some asceticism of his followers. By the mid-1970s, both Asma and her cousin Batoul Mukhtar had got jobs in government service, and they took responsibility for Taha and his wife. Amna was not well and finding life at home hard going, and she bought a house nearby, so that she could retreat at night from the incessant activity of Taha's house. Amna and Sumaya commuted between the two houses, but Batoul Mukhtar, their cousin, stayed with Taha. She paid his way for him, and Asma supported her mother[35]. Taha never touched money again. The brotherhood's funds came from voluntary contributions from the members and the sale of books.

Taha was "obsessed" with self-reliance, and he depended for funds on a group of young professionals, mainly teachers and students, plus the pennies that they charged for their pamphlets produced on a roneo[36]. The movement did not seek riches, and its outgoings were small too. Taha distributed his own household money, and the movement's funds, to people from disadvantaged groups. The Republicans were not involved in collective social action, organising poor people for change, but Taha had a function analogous to that of a small *tariga shaykh*, providing needy people with cash and access to a network of people with up-market professional services[37]. The kind of people who asked were mendicant dervishes and hymn singers, people from Heglig, his home town, and local poor people. Taha could get them the services of a Republican lawyer or doctor, or pay for a prescription. However, unlike rural *tariga shaykhs*, Taha did not encourage these people to join the movement, or even to acknowledge his religious claims – the movement was dominated by the educated[38].

Involuntary poverty

The brotherhood had no grass-roots social programme that would have mobilised marginal groups, and its theoretical preoccupations were unlikely to entice people whose time to think was taken up with toiling for subsistence. Republicans are keen to dispel the idea that theirs was a purely intellectual movement. Taha himself used to say that Republican recruitment was based not on texts or speeches, but on *lisan al-hal,* communicating spirituality[39]. Taha's spontaneous and unorganised response to poverty in Sudan was part of that attempt to communicate spirituality, and not an attempt to reconstruct economic power. Other political groups organised the economic interests of urban workers or professionals, but Taha's extempore charity was not aimed at mobilising a following. Taha believed that his charity, and contempt for wealth, was a means to his goal of perfecting self-expression through becoming a perfect expression of God. That perfection, he believed, was more dynamically effective than economic and social action.

Marriage

By the late 1970s, there were over 200 sisters in the movement, most of them from Republican families[40]. Taha paid special attention to their needs, he would say: "my work is my female disciples"[41].

Republican youth were encouraged to marry each other, under the spartan conditions of the Republican marriage contract, where the bridewealth paid by the man was only one Sudanese pound, and there were no extravagant wedding parties. Girgis Iskander, who no longer saw much of Taha, but still kept in touch, criticised him for condemning young people to bleakly ascetic marriages, where commitment to Republican ideas outweighed passion. But the young Republicans, he believes, were content with their lot: Taha was giving them the keys to life's mystery, promising a future of messianic gold, as well as some interesting travel for the present[42]. In addition, Taha played on psychological links between asceticism and romantic ardour: for him, a wife is "a sister of your soul, an emanation of your soul"[43].

Republicans do not recall their life with Taha as bleak – they often contrast his clean-shaven and quietly humorous demeanour with the scowling, bearded solemnity they associate with most religious leaders. Taha's sentimentality, fortunately, sometimes got in the way of his asceticism. Asma Mahmud, Taha's elder daughter, was a lawyer in the attorney-general's chambers. But she had no bed or pillow, and slept on a crowded floor. One day, a poor woman who was to marry a *darwish*, or religious mendicant, came to ask Taha for help with some tight finances. Taha told Asma and Batoul Mukhtar, his niece, "She's a bride. Go and get her some clothes". The two young professionals went out to the market to buy her a suitcase-full for her wedding[44].

Authenticity and poverty

Taha's movement was ascetic, intellectual and mystical, but it also tried to celebrate Sudan and Sudanese simplicity. Fourth class rail travel and thin *mulah*s were prized for their Sudaneseness, but Taha's plain meals followed the elaborate rules of northern Sudanese hospitality[45]. He washed the hands of guests and arranged their dishes[46]. Dirar's history of African foods notes how colonialists tended to promote the use of European wheat breads against sorghum pancakes. This prejudice was taken up by the Sudanese elite, who have spent huge sums since independence subsidising wheat, and downgrading sorghum. Wheat was explicitly associated with progress, and sorghum was labelled a "killer food" by a senior politician in the late 1960s[47]. According to Dirar, food was one of a number of markers for culture and identity, in a country conventionally bifurcated into Arab and African. This shorthand does little justice to Sudan's diversity, and to the fact that someone like Taha wanted to identify with the Sudanese or the African even when he had a fluent and appreciative understanding of Middle Eastern culture and religion[48].

Taha's Sudaneseness was his attempt to place his revolutionary ideas in the personal and the local – his revolution was to come about through the perfection of a perfect man. In a 1974 work on religion and social development, Taha wrote that Sudan was the heart of Africa, and Africa was the first home of humanity and the place where it would find freedom. Technology and mysticism (the word *'ilm* covers both) would be able to unite its dazzling diversity into a unity that would revolutionise the world[49]. The Republicans' Sudan romanticism was for a while to dominate their propaganda effort, and bring to Taha's middle class, Nile valley Muslims a taste of the hugely diverse country in which they lived. A government ban helped them make the decision to widen their preaching.

A ban

Nimeiri effectively out-manoeuvred Sudan's political forces, liquidating the Mahdist and Communist opposition to the May regime and cowing everyone else. He turned political attention to a new range of forces – the south and the marginalised regions. However, he needed political support in Sudan's developed core. He could not use the Mahdi and Mirghani family power bases, but many of his ministerial technocrats had links to the small-scale *tariqa*s of the Nile valley. In 1974, he set up a ministry of religious affairs, which drew these *tariqa*s into the structure of his ssu[50]. The Muslim Brothers used this ministry to penetrate the government.

Taha continued public lectures, which increasingly became the targets of protests from Muslim Brothers and their allies. Meetings often ended in a breach of the peace, and the police were called in, although prosecutions were never pursued with much vigour[51]. The Republicans could be just as litigious: in 1973 they raised a suit against Kosti preachers who were defaming Taha, one of a number in the 1970s[52]. The State Security Organ (sso) began to see Taha's lectures as a liability, and in 1972, Taha's prosecutors at his 1968 apostasy trial persuaded the Research Council of Cairo's al-Azhar University to denounce Taha. The Azhar legists complained to the ministry of religious affairs that Taha's writings were *kufr*, the capital crime of unbelief, because he had divided Muhammad's message into "fundamental" and "subsidiary" messages. They petitioned the ministry to stop his "destructive activities"[53]. In 1973, the National Security Council banned Taha from public speaking[54]. Republicans take the ban to be an example of collusion between Muslim

Brothers and their allies in the ministry that Nimeiri had just set up, and the security forces, tired of policing troublesome lectures[55]. But the ban was a loose one: in 1974 he lectured to students of the Islamic University, the former religious institute which had expelled Republican students 14 years before[56]. In 1975, al-Fatih ʿAli Mukhtar invited him on his Thursday night radio show, describing him as "the great Islamic thinker"[57]. The Republicans had little access to the state controlled media, and this made them depend on tracts and street discussions – the regime tolerated this activity, and Taha could rest from speaking, which was now increasingly the responsibility of his followers[58].

Conclusion

Taha's movement began to take off after the publicity of his trial. In the early 1970s, he began to use his leadership skills to build a new kind of social movement, which had similarities with Sudanese small-scale *tariqa*s and modern social organisations. One of his most lasting innovations was to include women at the centre of his movement – he attracted over 200 to his cause over the next few years.

Republicans sacrificed time and money to join Taha's movement. Young women had to swap elegance for plain frocks and white office tobs, and young men had to give up tobacco, alcohol and substitute the camaraderie of their young friends for the prayer fellowship of the Republican houses[59]. Taha's views were idiosyncratically progressive, but young members warmed to them. In part, this was because Taha's ideas answered questions about their personal religious experience and allowed them to make sense of modern education and social ambitions. However, Taha's warm introspection, indefatigable activism, and personal generosity were significant attracting forces. The next chapter shows how his followers appropriated his insights and tried to disseminate them around the country.

Chapter 14

Romancing Sudan

Sudan is placed in Africa in the place of the heart, and its shape is like a heart. (Taha, *al-din wal-tanmiya al-ijtima'iya* 1974:19)

The first Republican *wafd*s, or delegations, had toured Sudanese cities in the 1960s, with Taha leading and speaking. In the 1970s, Taha was banned from public speaking and he directed a new kind of delegation from his home. Republicans, from a fairly narrow ethnic and class group, tried to engage with unfamiliar people and societies on the margins of Sudan.

After the ban
Full-time teacher of law and mystery
In 1973, Taha could shrug off the sso ban on free expression. Rather than turn against Nimeiri, he began to move from passive to active support – he still believed that Nimeiri's centralised secularism was better than the sectarianism it replaced[1]. Taha did not condemn Nimeiri when he bombed the Ansar, nor when he repressed the Communist movement that they had both worked to defend a few years earlier.

Taha's movement was growing, and the Republican houses provided a spiritual formation to his young followers. He concentrated on their spiritual training, and become a full-time teacher of law and mystery. He produced spiritual self-help books, with titles like "Learn how to pray" (*ta'allamu kayfa tasallun*), and encouraged his followers to seek to express their authentic selves through scrupulous imitation of the prophet, just as he had done in Kober prison[2]. His self-help books mixed Sufi and psychoanalytic terms for the unconscious. He said that prayer was like a psychotherapy session, "a chance ... to engage in dialogue with psychological complexes repressed in the layers of the inner self"[3].

Since the late 1960s, Taha had delegated speaking authority to his followers, at first asking them to answer questions in public meetings, then letting them speak themselves. This devolution of power led to a greater stress on internal dialogue. The movement would debate an issue, and then appoint a group to write up the party line, which would then be distributed and discussed in their street meetings. When Taha was banned, he had a large cadre of trained and enthusiastic young people to speak for him. They no longer limited themselves to urban streets, but took off to the distant corners of Sudan, to spread the Republican message. Nimeiri's ban was Taha's opportunity:

> From the mid-1970s, the movement took off. His house was totally open, he had no privacy day or night ... You could go at six o'clock or five o'clock in the morning and people would be in his room. You could leave at 1am and people would be there[4].

Umm Kulsum and prayer

The houses of the young brothers and sisters were full of people at prayer. Taha encouraged the supererogatory prayer in the last third of the night, a time when the prophet prayed. In the hours before dawn, there were so many worshippers that it was hard to find a place to kneel. Taha, the *asil*, did not pray the canonical prayers. In the evening, the Republicans joined together for *zikr*, and as the call to prayer drifted across the evening sky, he would send the brothers and sisters off to pray together. Then he would retire to his room and listen to the news from the BBC, or to the long Egyptian love songs of Umm Kulsum, the most popular singer of the Arabic speaking world[5].

The book campaigns and street corner debates were part of Republican spiritual formation too. Taha believed that his own period of retreat was making his life whole, so that everything in his life would relate to everything else. This was his template for the unity of his followers, of Sudan and the world. Republican spirituality emphasised connections between prayer and propaganda. Young people prayed arduous night prayers, and in the morning rose for more, sang together, held a discussion on the day's activity, and joined in *zikr*. There would be more *zikr*, prayer and discussion of the day's mission at night. Opposition on the streets and fasting were part of spiritual formation[6].

Mixing with the natives

During summer holidays the students, and some older members, would travel in delegations of ten or more to spread the second message of Islam. They went as far as Darfur in the west and Juba near the Ugandan border. When they arrived in a town, they organised sales of Republican literature in the streets in the morning, a discussion corner at noon, more book sales at dusk then a lecture in the club at night. They sometimes organised exhibitions. The group would split up and go to outlying villages, and seek out a *shaykh*, a teacher or a student, anyone likely to know of their cause, and ask them to introduce them to the people[7].

In the mid-1970s, most Republicans were from fairly privileged Nile valley backgrounds. Their identity drew on Arabic language, the Sufi Islam of the Khatmiya or the small *tariqa*s, and their city educations. Some of them had travelled outside the Nile valley to the poorer regions of Sudan, but they usually travelled without really leaving home – they would stay with relatives from the northern Nile Valley working in regional cities who held important posts, and they would not mix with the "natives", non-Arabised, poor agricultural workers, non-professionals[8]. But the delegations changed all that – they were a chance for these graduates to find out about Sudan. They would travel by camel, bus, or walk between villages, sleep rough or in village *khalwa*s, and try to meet people who were different from themselves. Perhaps the encounter gave a social rationale to the movement's ascetic tendencies. Republicans belonged to a middle-class, urban movement which forsook material wealth for spiritual attainment, but now their voluntary poverty was used to identify with people from poorer, traditional communities.

Communion wafers and long beards

There was so much to see that their own class of people did not normally see. Muhammad 'Ali Malik, for example, remembers El Obeid's cathedral, the communion wafer that he wanted to taste, the cushioned prie-dieu, which compared favourably with the Islamic prayer mat[9]. Asma Mahmud remembers the scratchy woven palm mats she sat on, as she tried to shake obedient village wives and the local Muslim Brother with her brand of feminism, and being moved in turn by their kindness, anger or submissiveness[10]. Al-Baqir Mukhtar recalls the disruptions of the Muslim Brothers and their fellow travellers. The villagers, he says, welcomed his literate Sufi retorts to the Muslim Brothers, who opposed the villagers' introspective and miraculous rural Islam. Khalid Muhammad al-Hasan remembers turning up in a northern village at sunset, with no food or place to stay. He and his companions went to the village shop to buy dates and biscuits to eat, when a man with a long beard – the sign of a Muslim Brother – came in. Sudanese hospitality got the better of theological controversy: the Muslim Brother would not hear of them eating dates in the open, and took them home to eat and sleep there[11]. Elnour Hamad remembers how easy it was to beat a Muslim Brother in debate, and how Taha warned him against feeling good about it – that kind of debate, said Taha, just reduced personal potential, it was a necessary tool to be used against the Muslim Brothers, but no more[12].

Muslim missionaries in the south

The unlikeliest Republican missionaries were the ones who went south, in the late 1970s. By that time, Nimeiri had allied with the Muslim Brothers, and tensions between south and north were resurfacing. The Republicans were preaching in an area where Islamic missions have never enjoyed wide success. They accepted that Southerners had bitter associations with Islam – slavery, coercive conversion, wars and massacres. According to Al-Baqir Mukhtar, they went south to preach Sudan, rather than religion:

> In the south, they would preach a reformist understanding of Sudan
> and the project for a new Sudan, that nobody is to be barred from any
> office for religious reasons[13].

The delegation spoke at Juba University and to people in the streets and markets. Most of the people who listened were educated – the Republicans spoke English and Arabic, not African languages. As the era of peace in the south was drawing to a close, these missionaries wandered around Juba, preaching the unity of Sudan and the world in English, and selling their book, *The Southern Sudan: the Problem and the Solution*[14].

Sons of bitches

Another unlikely Republican mission came in 1975. Ibrahim Yusuf, who joined in the late 1950s led a delegation to Cairo, and tried to distribute Republican books among the cultural elite there. They did not have much success, although Al-Ahram newspaper later published an attack on their ideas, based on some literature picked up by one of their correspondents[15]. Ibrahim Yusuf and his friends met Tawfiq al-Hakim, the novelist, who was not taken with their ideas but greatly enjoyed one of their books, *al-din wa rijal al-din 'abr al-qurun* ("Religion and men of religion through the centuries"). The book was an engaging rant against lickspittle Egyptian clerics and flat-earther Saudi legists and part of an increasingly strident Republican campaign against the Muslim Brothers, in the wake of the 1972 Azhar condemnation and a subsequent attack by a Saudi organisation. According to Muhammad 'Ali Malik, al-Hakim spent an evening with the Republicans complaining of the "sons of bitches" of Cairo's al-Azhar University[16].

Opening up to the countryside

The Republican movement into the countryside was linked to Nimeiri's own policy of opening out to rural Sudan, which was first mooted in 1970. Communist cadres had in the past tried to build support in the Nuba mountains and among the tenants and workers of the agricultural schemes[17]. But the political and cultural mobilisation of rural northern Sudan was usually left to the rural ruling class and local religious leaders, who gave the Mahdi and Mirghani patricians their support in return for representation at the centre of the state. Like many African leaders of the 1970s, Nimeiri proposed to reconfigure the urban-rural link by creating a single party, overcoming patrician control of rural Sudan and avoiding ethnic fragmentation. Taha applauded Nimeiri's authoritarian centralism as the only way to overcome patrician dominance of the countryside[18]. Some people who enjoyed Republican debates nonetheless found their vocal support of the May regime exasperating. The Republicans believed Nimeiri protected the country from the sectarians and the Muslim Brothers, and would not criticise the arrests of Communists and Democratic Unionists that were happening at the time[19].

Conversion and self-realisation

The Republicans had daily campaigns in the streets and exhibitions which they held in an marquee which could travel from town to town. Delegations also visited rural areas. Every evening the day's activities would be reviewed in a session at Taha's home. When delegations returned, they would provide a report, lasting up to three hours, of their activities[20]. Republicans worked feverishly to produce religious material and instant comment on events in Sudan and in the world. They distributed two million books and pamphlets, the vast majority of them during the May regime (1969–1985).

Books and pamphlets published by the Republicans[21]

subject of books date	1945-57	1958-69	1970-83	TOTAL
Republican thought	3	6	43	52
Anti-fundamentalism		4	48	52
On women's question			31	31
Other	1	4	70	75
TOTAL	4	14	192	210

Taha always wanted detailed accounts of public responses to his mission teams. He encouraged the teams to evaluate their exchanges with people, to find the best method of getting the message across. But although Taha expected Republicans to give their all to the message, and was always concerned about its intelligibility, he acknowledged that the main purpose of the whole system was the spiritual development of the Republicans. Taha's mission was to inspire his followers to express their own sense of self with confidence, rather than generate a mass following[22].

Taha thought conviction was important, but he was reluctant to express his own certainties. He preferred to talk in the subjunctive, hoping that his truth was God's truth, that his worship would be acceptable, that he might reach a higher spiritual station[23]. He wanted Republicans to be able to communicate certainty. Taha told people he was not sure about himself, but he wanted other people to be sure[24]. Being sure about goodness was freedom:

> The aim of the Republican party is to bring about the free individual: we
> believe that this is the individual who thinks as he wishes, speaks as he
> thinks, acts as he speaks – and from all this produces only goodness[25].

Narrow social group

Taha's preoccupation with self-realisation and his baffling Sufi idioms may have made it difficult to recruit people outside the group that best understood his Nile valley Sufism, with its obscure borrowings from older Middle Eastern literatures. Until the late 1970s, most Republicans shared Taha's religious culture: "They were mostly from small *tariqa*s. They did not belong to the *tariqa*s, but they were respectful [of them], maybe someone in the family would belong"[26]. However, when the movement reached its peak, Republicans managed to recruit people from Mahdist backgrounds. There was still some tension between Mahdism and Nile valley Sufism. Taha, like many Nile valley Sufis, believed that the Mahdiya was a period of chaos, and that the Mahdi family had fewer political scruples than their Khatmiya rivals[27].

Sadig undertook a sociological study of Republicans in 1987, after the movement had folded. He interviewed 84 members, out of a total estimated at 1,000. (Others estimate two or three times as many). The vast majority belonged to the professional classes (86%), were aged under 40 (86%), and were from central Sudan (75%)[28]. University graduates made up 37.5% of the Republicans, and 54·5% had some form of education: only eight percent were illiterate. "It is safe to maintain that many of them belong to the middle or lower middle classes of Sudanese society", concludes Sadig[29].

Why were the Republicans such a narrow group? Many Republicans feel that a modern education was needed for people to understand Taha's views. His fondness for the warmly introspective Sufism of the village may have excluded people from the more militant Mahdist tradition. Republicans were expected to be committed to legal and social change, having gone through a demanding period of political and religious education. Most of the members understood that it was difficult for uneducated people to affiliate to their strange ideas.

Another trial

The delegations, and the street debates and exhibitions, could be rowdy affairs. 'Abdelwahab El-Affendi recalls one fiery Muslim Brother who would go along to university debates where Republicans would provoke him until he lashed out, and then the Republicans would raise complaints against him[30]. Others recall the verbal and sexual harassment faced by Republican sisters on the streets. Sometimes, sympathetic passers-by would intervene heavy-handedly to protect the sisters from the taunts of Muslim Brothers and their allies, but some sisters scolded anyone who resorted to violence to protect pacifists.

Republicans gratefully used opposition for publicity purposes. In 1975 a judge, Ibrahim Jaddallah, from the Port Sudan personal status courts complained to the police about a Republican exhibition in his local club which displayed Taha's opinions about *shari'a* judges. "And as for your declaration of my apostasy from Islam, well you have declared nothing except your ugly ignorance of Islam", said one of Taha's posters addressed to *shari'a* judges[31]. The police brought a case against Taha and the Republican delegation. To win the case, they had to prove that ugly ignorance was no slander against Jaddallah, so they subjected him to a quiz show about Islam and world politics. Jaddallah had no chance with Taha and his clever young men – when they got to the question about the North Atlantic Treaty the poor plaintiff cried: "God, is this an exam?

Is it a politics exam? I don't remember, but I read something about it once, but I don't remember"[32].

Taha's examination turned to a Hanafi rule that acquits husbands of their duty to maintain a wife when she is not available for his sexual gratification. He sneaked out of Jaddallah the admission that a man who did not maintain his sick wife was contravening his religion but not contravening *shari'a*. Having set up his legal/ethical distinction, he worked the theme, drawing attention to an unpalatable law which legists prefer to overlook. In his Kosti days, Taha was friendly with a *shari'a* judge who had been forced to find in favour of a husband who refused to meet the costs of his wife's birth because of the law. Taha wrote to the grand *qadi* asking him to change the ruling, because it was "not in the spirit of religion". The grand *qadi* replied "We agree with what you are saying, but we are under the text"[33]. Jaddallah was not the man to defend this ruling – he conceded to Taha, "I think that jurisprudence has developed and maybe that sort of talk was justified in its day"[34].

The Port Sudan case was followed eagerly in the town. One story which attached itself to Taha's name wryly alluded to wild sayings of al-Hallaj (the tenth century Sufi executed for his incautiously phrased claims of union with God). Taha was said to have been asked his name with the third person Sudanese formality *ism al-karim?* (what is the name of the noble gentleman?) and he answered "Allah". The judge was taken aback at the blasphemy, until the question was repeated and he realised that Taha's reply was scrupulously orthodox – *al-karim* is one of the ninety-nine names of God, and strictly should not be applied to a human. The story is probably apocryphal – in fact, the question asked in court is *al-ism bil-kamil?* (your full name?). However, Taha's audience in the town were playing with their perceptions of Taha's Sufism, his learning and pedantry, and the fact that he had out-foxed the Muslim establishment with his verbal skills[35].

In the end Jaddallah withdrew the suit. The Republicans taped the trial, and rushed out a triumphant transcript a few weeks later.

Evaluating the *wafd*s

Girgis Iskander criticised Taha's confrontational tactics and his relentless opposition to the *shari'a* system in Sudan, in a letter that Taha never replied to[36]. Fatma Ibrahim, who has worked in the leaderships of the Communist party and the Sudan Women's Union, also criticises Republican missions. She has experience of similar community education work in Sudanese villages, and believes that Taha's attempt to bring theosophy to the masses was doomed[37]. Republicans themselves have different views of their activities. Asma Mahmud, who went on some women-only delegations, does not describe herself as a theosophist, but a feminist challenging the new discriminations that *shari'a* -minded customs brought to rural Sudan. She opposes this to a slightly romanticised view of Sudanese customs:

> Customary law had a big influence in gender relations. People still had innocence and purity. There were ordinary relations between men and women. But as soon as *shari'a* entered, there was all this affectation, that people had to separate ... In the village, men and women would walk together, shake hands, meet at wedding dances. There were many non-*shari'a* practices. When you go to areas with *shari'a*, you find this burdensome separation between men and women[38].

Other participants mention religious rather than social lessons of the delegations. Taha and his followers cultivated and sometimes attained a dazzling and impatient sense of certainty, that was useful in debate, but may have hampered dialogue. The period they spent immersed in rural Sudan transformed their lives. The motive for this self-transformation was not so much to learn from the societies they encountered, as to teach those societies the Republican version of the truth, which they kept intact throughout the transformation. Omer El Garrai used the experience of explaining a means to deepen his convictions:

> When I debated, I would become more committed ... Republican ideology is comprehensive. The theory is true and cannot be changed. Dialogue is not the goal[39].

Elnour Hamad is not so sure: he wonders why he wanted to convert people, instead of helping them to grow the way they are. And Abdullahi An-Na'im is hesitantly critical:

> It was seen as – I'm guessing here – not an openness to have our ways of thinking or lifestyle transformed by the people we interact with, but rather to influence them in their lifestyle, their ideas, by the ideas we thought would make all the difference in their lives ... In retrospect I see it as negative. I see it as colonial. It's just being Muslim and believing that Islam is the answer to everything and that we have the key to understanding Islam. Now, ten or 15 years later, I'd be more open to a two-way exchange[40].

Conclusion

Public debates and literature sales made the Republican brothers and sisters a feature of city street life in the 1970s, and Republican delegations were a novel response to Nimeiri's policy of opening up to the regions. They began at a time when Taha faced relatively little pressure from his opponents, and the delegations show that he wanted to engage with Sudan's diversity, as he had done in his 1955 constitutional proposals.

Republican missions were often rowdy, and the Republicans often matched the polemical aggression of their opponents. Yet Taha did not feel that this activity was an end in itself: he wanted his young followers to develop themselves. His commitment to personal self-realisation meant that he allowed his followers to draw their own lessons from their experiences of travelling around Sudan and speaking to people on the street. But he saw Republican missions as an opportunity to prepare Sudanese audiences for his strange ideas. First, they would be taught his new view of *shari'a* and then they would be invited to consider that his perfect society could only come about through the dynamic perfection of an individual. This search for a perfect man might end in himself, thought Taha. While the movement's external purpose was to explain new rules and rights cast in Islamic terms, its internal purpose was different:

> The movement was an attempt to create an environment whereby the candidacy of *ustaz* Mahmud to become the perfect man [messiah] was successful[41].

Chapter 15

Perfect stranger

This chapter has two concerns: first, the Republican response to the rise of the Muslim Brothers between 1977 and 1983. Secondly, it examines how Taha, who believed that his missionaries had successfully explained his novel ideas about *shari'a* to a wide range of people, began to turn to even more spiritual topics.

National reconciliation

It was noted in chapter 12 that SSO restrictions on Taha's freedom of expression made him a keener supporter of the regime. Why? The title of a 1975 pamphlet, *al-ta'ifiya tata'amir 'ala al-sha'b* ("Sectarianism conspires against the people") gives a clue: Nimeiri's modernisation was going through rough times, and the traditional parties were once again to figure in Sudanese politics. In 1975, a group of Kordofan soldiers staged an unsuccessful coup attempt. Nimeiri's policy of opening up to the regions was not working. The south had won considerable autonomy, but the less rebellious west (Muslim but largely not Arabised) had little to show for itself. Nimeiri dismissed the coup as "racist" and hastily granted himself more emergency powers[1]. In 1976, Sadig al-Mahdi staged another coup attempt from exile, using some of the survivors of the 1970 Aba island massacre, now training in Libya. The Ansar-led group (many of them with links to Darfur) occupied Omdurman for a few hours but they were beaten back and some of Sadig al-Mahdi's supporters were hanged. The attack succeeded however in forcing Nimeiri's attention on to the politics of Sudan's centre, and he moved to conciliate the sectarian parties. In 1977, he concluded a pact of national reconciliation with the Umma party and other parties of the centre.

When restless regions and world oil price rises threatened political and economic stability, Nimeiri brought the Mahdi family and the Muslim Brothers into the cabinet. Republicans welcomed the news cautiously. A 1977 booklet contained the text of a letter to Nimeiri warning him of sectarian misdeeds, and asking him to include the Communist party in the reconciliation (he did not)[2]. The Muslim Brothers, used to subverting government for specific political ends, deftly infiltrated the May regime. In contrast, Sadig al-Mahdi's Umma party was marginalised. As in 1964, modern forces with urban power bases proved more adept at influencing a military regime.

Religion and cash

Money and religion were entwined throughout twentieth century Sudan. The Mahdi's oath of allegiance demanded renunciation of worldly goods, and his pillars of the faith included abstinence as well as war[3]. However, his son 'Abd al-Rahman reconfigured his father's support, appropriating the labour of his Darfuri supporters on farms granted to him by the British authorities, telling them that his wealth was for the cause of God[4]. The move from asceticism to accumulation was part of the process of institution building, and it occurred in many smaller Sufi *tariqa*s[5].

The Muslim Brothers initially had a socialist orientation. But they built their constituency around educated professionals; middle ranking army men; and urban merchants who did not have the same access to capital as the big patricians, and they had the sense to articulate the economic interests of their constituency. From the mid-1970s, Sudan's Muslim Brothers became the force of the future in Sudanese politics – part of this achievement is linked to the financial maturity they achieved in this period.

The ministry of religious affairs, which the May regime set up in order to co-opt minor Islamic institutions, encouraged those institutions to raise funds in the Arabian peninsula. El Hassan (1993) argues that these funds empowered rural religious leaderships, just as the rural political elite (the Native Administration) lost authority to new SSU structures. (Rural political and religious elites were often members of the same kinship group). The cultural agenda of Sudan's Arabian donors was to re-orient Sudanese Islam to their rigorist, textualist and anti-Sufi Wahhabi form of Islam. Saudi cash and ideology exacerbated existing disjunctions between wealthy Sufi elites, who understood the textualist call, and poor rural followers, who still wanted miracles and dancing[6].

Saudi money, and its ideological riders, were influencing Sudanese

Sufism and transforming Sudanese politics. The Muslim Brothers, whose accountancy was as deft as their politics, understood this. They were closely involved in the development in 1977 of Islamic banks – financial institutions which deal in profit-shares or options rather than the interest bearing loans which are forbidden by *shari'a*[7]. The banks were set up with Saudi funds, granted exceptional tax exemptions and by 1981, some were making over 100% returns on share capital. Faisal Islamic Bank alone controlled 30% of all Sudan's commercial capital[8].

Taha did not have the same appreciation of Saudi money or religion. In 1973, Republicans had met the Saudi cultural attaché and a delegation of Saudi *shari'a* legists. They wanted to discuss their strange ideas with the Saudis, but according to the Republican account, the meeting did not last long – one of the Saudis saw the word "socialism" on a poster that the Republicans had displayed, cried "*a'udhu billahi*", a phrase used to ward off the devil, and insisted that the meeting stop[9]. In 1975, the Muslim World League in Mecca condemned Taha as a would-be messiah and called for his execution for apostasy[10]. Republicans fought back. In 1976, they tried to make their case in mosques, but the ministry of religious affairs banned them from speaking there. A pamphlet that year, *ismuhum al-wahhabiya, wa laysa ismahum ansar al-sunna* ("They are Wahhabis, not Ansar al-Sunna") attacked Saudi Islam, Saudi princes and Saudi intervention in Sudanese Islam (the Ansar al-Sunna are a small Sudanese Wahhabi group)[11]. The May regime was trying hard to attract Arab capital, and the Republican attack on the Saudi ruling class did not help. Taha and eight other Republicans were detained for a few weeks in January 1977, as a gesture to the Saudi royals.

The detention did not affect Republican support for the regime, but it was a marker of the increasing influence of Arabian culture and finance in Sudan's political scene. After 1977, the Republicans became increasingly embroiled in a conflict with the Muslim Brothers and their allies. In 1977 a committee was set up to bring Sudan's laws into line with the *shari'a*; in 1978 Hasan al-Turabi, the leader of the Muslim Brothers, became attorney general. Republican attacks on *shari'a* became more strident, and the party began to publish detailed legal arguments against the legislative content of *shari'a*, which showed a familiarity with many of the source texts used by *shari'a* legists. Republican legal writing from this period was increasingly concerned with non-Muslims' rights, and it defended those rights without the grand allusiveness or curvaceous mystical logic of Taha's works of the 1960s[12].

Redivision

Nimeiri had removed some ethnic disparities in political structures by centralising state power, and jeopardised the Arab-Muslim state by addressing the interests of Sudan's non-Arabised majority. In the late 1970s, the politics of the Arab-Muslim state returned to Sudan with the Muslim Brothers and the patrician parties. Muslim Brothers, who began to dominate the regime with their coherent but divisive programme, wanted to impose a re-invented Arab-Muslim state on the diverse nation which had managed to find a measure of self-expression in Nimeiri's 1973 constitution.

Southern political forces were major allies of Nimeiri, but for the Arab-Muslim state to succeed, they had to be marginalised. From 1980, the May regime used ethnicity to undermine southern political institutions set up after the 1972 peace accord. Nimeiri played on tensions between Dinka groups (the largest group in the south) and the many small tribes of Equatoria. Some Equatorians, sponsored by Nimeiri, wanted to redivide the south. This policy was formally proposed in 1981. Nimeiri tribalised the schools (the scene of fighting between Equatorians and other tribes), imposed military rule, and jailed supporters of a unified south. Localised conflicts, which had been managed through local political structures, could no longer be contained, and the south headed towards war.

Republicans fight back

Republicans told Nimeiri in their 1977 letter that they wanted a "human constitution" for the republic[13]. Now Sudan was moving towards the Islamic constitution they had for so long opposed. Around 1982, they abandoned their delegations to the regions, and the sisters stopped speaking on the streets, as they concentrated their efforts on their opposition to the Muslim Brothers' programme for Sudan[14]. Republicans maintained their legal and theological attack on the Muslim Brothers, publishing a long study on Faisal Islamic Bank in 1983 which attacked its shaky understanding of *shari'a* commercial law and its funding of Muslim Brother expansion[15].

But the tiny Republican movement was no match for the powerful and organised Muslim Brothers. The latter penetrated the SSU; organised co-operatives that distributed rationed food; organised demonstrations to celebrate Khomeini's revolution in Iran; built up a network of social clubs and scouting camps; sponsored mosque preachers; spoke on the television and radio; gained ground in the military by teaching their ideology to officers; set up exhibitions and then arranged, through the education ministry, to bring schools to see them[16]. Perhaps their most important activity was banking. Islamic banks funded Muslim Brother activities, provided soft personal loans to government figures and access to capital for Sudan's growing small merchant class. Patrician dominance of Sudan's cash economy had been weakened by Nimeiri's nationalisations in the early 1970s: in the late 1970s it was challenged by an ambitious middle class able to attract Arabian capital through ideological persuasion, and to use it in a host of get-rich schemes. The petty municipal classes mocked in British police dossiers had found powerful suitors.

The new capital movements did not prevent rapid economic deterioration – the banks were helping to pay for an import boom that was bankrupting the country and bringing it under the tutelage of the International Monetary Fund (IMF)[17]. IMF structural adjustments increased pressure on the urban poor, whose street demonstrations helped maintain food subsidies in the towns. However, in the early 1980s when drought in the west and war in the south resulted in widespread famine, the regime was not so quick to respond to rural desperation.

In war and famine, Taha still refused to criticise Nimeiri. He believed that Nimeiri (already in hock to the Muslim Brothers) was the only force that could protect the country from Muslim Brother encroachment. Taha, a natural oppositionist, had become a government loyalist. Urban opposition to the regime was led by the Communists. The Muslim Brothers were officially allies of Nimeiri, but they sometimes pitched in against him to maintain pressure on the regime (Nimeiri sometimes called them "Satan's brothers"). The Republican defence of the regime led them to attack Communist campaigns against IMF-sponsored price rises in the early 1980s. They also claimed, more hesitantly, that Nimeiri's decision to divide the south and destroy the 1972 peace deal was supported by "a large body of Southerners". They expressed the hope that Southerners would resolve their differences in a state-appointed commission[18].

Mutual incomprehension

The Muslim Brothers owed much of their support to their appropriation of the Muslim, Arab identity developed in central areas of Sudan over centuries. It had previously been the property of the great religious sects. However, their religious institutions were vulnerable to the claims of reformist movements like the Muslim Brotherhood, whose allegiance to the sacred texts could undermine those institutions. Taha's Republicans subverted the Muslim Brothers' mastery of the written sources of Islam with another fluent and literate interpretation of Islam. Each party was arguing in idioms which the other did not fully understand, and this no doubt added to the fury of the debate. An indication of this furious incomprehension was the 1979 trial in El Obeid of a man who threatened al-Amin Ahmad Nur, a Republican brother: "You want to be God ... and we will kill you"[19]. The accused, al-Jili Zayn al-'Abidin, was referring to Taha's claim that the devout worshipper could become God. A *shari'a* judge testified that he knew nothing of the facts, but that the defendant deserved a vote of thanks for doing his religious duty in threatening to kill a blasphemer. This attempt to turn a criminal defence into a *shari'a* prosecution was explicitly rejected by the civil judge who heard the case. He said that the law that applied in his court was the secular 1973 penal code, and not the Qur'an. Al-Jili was convicted and the Republicans rejoiced at the vindication of secular law.[20]

Perfect man

In the 1950s and 1960s Taha wrote his first books, and he wanted to deal with the reform of Islamic legislation. He used a Sufi idiom to explain and justify the changes he proposed in *shari'a*, and argued that the change was justified because of higher modern standards of knowledge, or because of changes in the mode of production[21]. In his letters to the press and to individuals, he acknowledged that: "the most effective instrument for the purification of Islam is the appearance and guidance, in the Islamic world, of the muslim who has first purified Islam in himself"[22]. This more personal and esoteric explanation became more significant over the next few years. For example, in 1971, he brought out the fourth edition of his "Second Message" which made clear that his legislative proposals, could only come about through a *rasul* (messenger, a traditional ascription of Muhammad). "The messenger of the second message ... is the one to whom God granted understanding from the Qur'an and authorised to speak"[23].

Taha, who conceived of theology as "higher" than law, only began to broach theological and spiritual topics in the early 1970s. In 1971, he wrote a long book, *al-qur'an wa mustafa mahmud wal-fahm al-'asri* ("The Qur'an and Mustafa Mahmud and contemporary understanding") a Sufi response to a Qur'an commentary by Mustafa Mahmud. The commentary was serialised in an Arabic magazine and generated controversy around the Middle East. Apart from a prison memoir written in 1984, Taha's last book was written in 1976. He sometimes had to leave Omdurman for the Butana village of Arbaji in order to find the time to write them[24]. In 1973, he was banned from public speaking: although his work-load was diminished by the ban, he found himself too busy to visit the shrines of Sufi saints or even write. The production of Republican literature was delegated to Republican committees and individuals, who would summarise the outcome of Republican debates in a writing style modelled on Taha's own.

Everybody's special

By the mid-1970s Taha was an elderly man surrounded by a large, devoted audience – up to 300 people would attend his weekly meetings. They treated him like a Sufi *shaykh* – lowering their gaze as they approached him. The deferent young Republicans were slightly nonplussed by the carefree affection with which Taha's older, non-Republican friends would greet him[25]. Taha might have been a furious polemicist, but he was a convincing religious leader partly because he was able to focus himself on the individual in front of him – he persuaded many people he spoke to that the person in front of him that was the most important person to him. Taha believed that everyone had talents, and that human authenticity and perfection was attained by "discovery and effervescence of these talents, until they all express the self together"[26]. Taha's attentive manner was perhaps the talent through which he found self-realisation. People sought his company at dawn, and he was still receiving guests in the middle of the night.

> Everyone feels at home in his presence. It's not that he's trying to be accessible, he is accessible. It's not that he's trying to be courteous, it's just a way of being ... it was effortless and relentless[27].

Many who experienced this attention still feel gratitude, but Taha had his critics. In the late 1970s, Girgis Iskander wrote to Taha to say that Taha was misleading his followers by promising paradise. He attacked Taha's polemical methods and his vehement rejection of the Muslim establishment, his use of the courts, his reliance on Nimeiri, and his pamphleteering approach to social change that only led to breaches of the peace[28].

The star of David

Taha acknowledged Girgis Iskander's letter, but never got round to a reply. It did not change a drift towards a yet more esoteric understanding of life, on the one hand, and a yet more vehement confrontation with Muslim Brothers on the other. In August 1979, there were food riots after IMF cuts on food subsidies took effect. What did the Republicans do? They took to the streets on Christmas day, with a pamphlet with the star of David on its cover, entitled *'awdat al-masih* ("The return of Christ"). Many Republicans see this book as a point in the movement's history when it began to embrace mystery more wholeheartedly than ever before. The book used the figure of the "Muhammadan messiah", an equivalent to the idea the perfect man, promising his imminent arrival, to unite the Christian, Muslim and Jewish faiths in a world system that would express all their virtues:

> The notion of the Super Man, which contemporary man finds extremely interesting and artistically inspiring, deeply illustrates this longing for the coming of the ultimately able man whose coming is dictated by immediate living necessities[29].

Had the Republicans gone mad? Or were they responding to Sudan's economic gloom with a toke of millenarian opium? There were other groups in Sudan pushing millenarianism at the time – the Niassiya, originating in west Africa, promised every follower a chance of reaching *qutbaniya*, another of the technical terms of Muslim mysticism for the trip to the absolute. Awad al-Karsani lists some of the movements at the University of Khartoum which preached the end of the world[30]. 'Abdelwahab El-Affendi, a historian with links to the Muslim Brotherhood, recalls a clever student of French there who, he says, listened to too much Republican mysticism, went mad and called himself Abu Zafira, the Mahdi. El-Affendi does not put Taha in the same category:

> Taha had a special mission ... his followers believed in this – it surfaced at university. One of them said the mission will happen whether you accept it or not. But they're not the same as Abu Zafira, who lost touch with reality. There's a difference between [that] and having a plausible theory which justifies distance from reality[31].

The one and only

Taha continued with his drift into abstraction. In 1982, the Sudanese pound lost a third of its value, the regime tried again to remove food subsidies and faced uncontrollable riots. At one of his weekly meetings, Taha announced a new message to the Republicans. Much of his previous teaching democratically suggested that every person had the germ of their own authenticity, *asala*, within them, and that this authenticity would be revealed in an encounter with God that made them authentic, *asil*. In 1971, he dedicated a book as follows:

> To the person that humanity awaits
> whose appearance they expect
> the *insan* [human being]
> and so, to men and women
> do you dream of him?
> he is within you
> the Qur'an will reveal him[32].

In 1982, Taha said that this authenticity was still available for all, but that he believed only one person would attain it in this life[33]. *Waqtajiya* Republicans who were waiting for the time of the imminent messiah saw this as a sign of hope, a clarification of past teaching, but many Republicans found the idea difficult to grasp. Some Republicans feared that the movement was becoming a cult[34]. Republicans discussed the arrival of the perfect man at length, and then took to the streets with a pamphlet, *al-taqlid!! wal-asil!! wal-usala'!!* ("Tradition!! the authentic one!! and the many authentic people!!"). Taha's new message clearly implied that he was the sole candidate for human perfection. Surprisingly, this may explain his continued support for Nimeiri at a time when Nimeiri was dropping his commitments to all the achievements which Taha held dear. For Taha, Sudan was "the most spiritual country in the world", and it had an enormous spiritual vocation[35]. He carefully watched the times, waiting for the messianic dawn. Perhaps he believed that Nimeiri's chaotic time was somehow connected to the time for perfection.

Pyramid and person

In the 1960s Taha used pyramids to express the diversity, upward movement and final unity of life and history. By 1982, Republicans were using a more expressive and obscure evolutionary symbol. The perfect man, *al-insan al-kamil* of Sufi theosophy, was the symbol of creation:

God allowed the body of the perfect man to rise from the level of
vegetable to the level of animal, to the level of human, and it is the
highest level of all[36].

The perfect man, for Taha, was the apotheosis of humanity who would
bring about the end of time. Republicans wrote about this person in
imprecise and highly coloured language. They associate the perfect
man with the messiah, the "Muhammadan reality" (the pre-existence
of the prophet Muhammad), and with "the laudable station", *al-maqam
al-mahmud*, mentioned in a Qur'an verse that encouraged Muslims to
perform the supererogatory night prayer which was part of Republican
spiritual training[37]. The phrase in the Qur'an is ambiguous, and is
consequently used by Muslims of different traditions to talk about the last
things: perhaps it had a special meaning to Republicans because *mahmud*,
laudable, was Taha's name. Taha could have used the persona of the
Mahdi to talk about the last days, but that title is associated with God's
vengeance on the wicked: he preferred the more eirenic perfecter.

Throughout their history, Sufis of a literary bent tried to express
their psychological states in symbols. To say God has a human form
runs counter to the transcendental theme that dominates the Qur'anic
description of God, a theme that fits the *shari'a* picture of obedience to a
mysterious sovereign. Sufis looked for more than obedience, and tried to
express how God could be known. They accepted the *shari'a* tradition's
assertion of inaccessible divine transcendence – this characteristic of God
was "the essence". But they asserted that there were knowable aspects
to God, descending from this essence, and one of these emanations was
al-insan al-kamil, the perfect man. This person is a perfect expression
of the essence, not the essence itself[38]. This complex theosophy had
wide effects in Sudan and the Muslim world. It gave Muslims a kind of
religious love poetry, and established the importance of religious feeling
against obedience. Sufi poems saw the prophet not as a legislator, but
someone whose "saliva is sweeter than fresh water"[39]. The effect of this
religious passion differed with time and place and person. For members
of the *shari'a* tradition, Sufism could inject feeling into their religious
life: for people at the non-literate periphery, the figure of this perfect
man had an attraction which legal treatises could not rival. The links
between Muhammad's perfection and the perfection of his followers are
obscure, but they were part of an imaginative repertoire that Taha and
his audience understood.

Taha believed that he could, through a process of trial and error, identify himself with the perfection of God through Muhammad, conceived by the Sufis as the organising force behind creation. His *asala* (authenticity) was a proof of his progress, but the perfection he hoped for would transform more than just himself. None of the people interviewed for this work ever heard Taha claim he was the perfect man, although many believed that he had a duty to aspire to be him[40]. In 1980, the Muslim Brothers accused Taha of claiming "that he was the perfect man and that he would judge [all] people on the day of resurrection"[41]. The Republicans said this claim was never made, and accused the Muslim Brothers of slander[42].

Nevertheless, Taha seems to have drifted from a concern with law to a concern with mystery. Was this a change of direction for the movement? Many of Taha's followers look on developments in Taha's thoughts as clarifications, not changes. They hold that Taha had worked out all his ideas in his 1946 *khalwa*, and was slowly initiating his followers and Sudan into his strange ideas. He revealed new ideas to audiences whom he felt were ready for them. According to this view, Taha sought and received the permission of Sufi saints to spread his message, and began the gradual process of educating his followers, and then Sudan and the world, about the new *shari'a*. Finally, he would be able to explain his new theosophy, Sufi self-realisation for the masses. This syllabus for utopia was interrupted by Muslim Brothers, who forced Taha into complex explanations about his prayer life (*risalat al-salat*, 1966) before he had begun his legal work in his "Second Message" (1967). Throughout the 1970s and 1980s, Taha began to write and speak about messiahs and perfection, and this process reached its peak after the late 1970s.

Another view might say that Taha's vivid spiritual experience in the 1940s helped him reach some conclusions about the need to change *shari'a* and to express his sense of self-realisation in striking Sufi language. The sources surveyed for this book are not comprehensive, but it would appear that Taha's view of abrogation first saw the light of day in 1967. Taha's change of symbols in the 1970s – from pyramid to perfect man – may have marked a new stage in his self-realisation. It is very difficult to judge Taha's personal feelings, because he voiced them in circumlocutions: "Our Sufi friends say ..." was one code for his opinion[43]. Another difficulty is that Taha wrote no books after 1972, because he devoted himself full-time to the spiritual formation of his followers. This was the period when Taha's mysticism became most pronounced, but the texts dealing with it were mostly written by Republicans and then edited by Taha[44].

It is tempting to interpret the movement's messianic turn to its increasing political marginality or even the politically bewildering effects of IMF economics. Yet there are reasons for avoiding such conclusions. Taha had spent many years trying to understand if his Sufi ideas were for the masses, and he seems to have gradually come to the conclusion that they were. In any case, Taha's had isolated himself to some extent from economic troubles through his asceticism. 'Abdelwahab El-Affendi remarks that Taha embodied moral integrity in the machiavellian world of Sudanese politics, and this sincerity is another reason not to dismiss Taha[45].

Republicans may have counselled other-worldliness when food prices made Sudan unbearable, but they had little to gain from their political stand. One remarkable feature of the movement is its exceptionally low attrition rate to the Muslim Brothers. That movement expressed the political and economic aspirations of Sudan's growing middle class. It offered substantial political and material rewards in a time of economic disaster. After the Iranian revolution, some Sudanese leftists, not least of them Nimeiri, began to affiliate themselves to the Muslim Brothers. Republicans were a highly educated group who could reasonably expect to prosper if they joined up for the Muslim Brother political project: none did.

The movement retained internal tolerance in spite of its shrill attacks on opponents, and in spite of its extravagant messianism. Some members sincerely believed that Taha was about to be transformed into the perfect man, others believed that he had solved an intractable contradiction between Islam and modernity. Women followers of Taha looked on him as a guarantor of their human dignity. Yet they could share their movement with less committed people, the movement's circle of friends, who came along for its social activities, hospitality, even for free food at the Republican houses[46]. The movement had little ethnic or class diversity, but it allowed for a diverse range of experiences, and no-one was pressed to accept more than they could believe. When the Republicans had their debates, Taha would welcome opinions contrary to his own, perhaps feeling that his stated opinions swayed too many of his supporters.

Conclusion

Taha's work in the 1960s used Sufi legal scepticism and Islamic modernist disaffection with *shari'a* rules to challenge the Muslim Brothers. His literate and activist Sufism was a good target for the Muslim Brothers, who needed to delegitimise Sudanese Sufism in order to legitimise their own view of Islam, which aspired to the *shari'a* tradition and linked Sudan to the Arab and Muslim world. In the 1960s, he made tactical alliances with the left and with progressive forces. When Nimeiri set up his left-inspired single party system, got rid of the patricians and made peace with the south, Taha was unwavering in his support, and forgave Nimeiri's excesses. He saw Nimeiri as a person who could help him bring about his magically inclusive Sufi version of Sudan.

When Nimeiri turned to the Muslim Brothers and the patrician movements for support, Taha more or less kept faith with the president, but ratcheted up the polemic against the Muslim Brothers. His movement became caught up in a struggle to preserve and develop a Sufi vision of Sudan.

The situation in Sudan deteriorated in the late 1970s, and Taha moved to a more mystical and (in historical respects) more familiar Sufi challenge to *shari'a* piety and theology. Taha's pamphleteering theosophy accompanied his increasingly strident attacks on Muslim Brothers and their allies. He believed that the years spent by the Republicans publicising his novel ideas had borne fruit, and that his attacks on the wider *shari'a* system had a chance of success. Yet the content of his teaching in the 1980s is sometimes alarmingly mystical. Messianism and millenarianism had a political currency in Sudan at the time. Political actors who used these themes stepped up their confrontation with Taha. Taha accepted the challenge serenely; he may have been wondering if it was all going to end, perfectly.

Chapter 16

The perfect ending

Do you think 'Abdullahi that people will to our way by persuasion? The way you wish? No, it's going to be a transformation, like the flip of a coin.

This chapter looks at Taha's last conflict with his political enemies, and relates it to the religious, social and economic turbulence of Sudan in the mid-1980s.

Banks, guns and shaykh Ahmad's dream

In 1983, the May regime was in serious difficulty. After a period of low rainfall that had lasted the 14-year length of the regime, and increasingly hampered its progress, drought began in the west. Increasing pressure on food subsidies brought serious rioting to the towns. In the south, war began in earnest in protest at the government's decision to nullify the south's federal status.

How did people respond to these events? In Darfur, people worked out poor-man's strategies for survival[1]. In the dry borderlands with the south, former Mahdist fighters were turned into farm labourers; they and their tribal groups acquired small arms from the war-zones of Africa in preparation for war[2]. In the cities, Communists called for opposition to the regime's economic policies from wall newspapers and pamphlets[3]. Muslim Brothers in the restive unions participated in the demonstrations against the regime[4]. Muslim Brothers dominated the political scene, at once the chief allies and opponents of Nimeiri, who was trying to manoeuvre between them, the army, his remaining southern supporters, and his coterie of loyalists in the bureaucracy and security services. Banking was booming – eight new financial institutions were created

204 ISLAM'S PERFECT STRANGER

in 1983 and 1984[5]. The new Islamic banks dominated the cash sector of Sudan's economy. Muslim Brothers built support in the military with courses on Islamic ideology for officers.

It was 1404, four years into the fifteenth Muslim century. Some Muslims influenced by Mahdist and Shi'a thought attach a mystical significance to that century, which is believed to herald the last days. With life getting bleaker, many Sudanese took to reflection on the end of things. West African migrants expressed their sense of the turbulence of the time by relating it to a foreseeable end. Roneo copies of *"Shaykh Ahmad's dream"*, a pre-modern narrative about the corruption before the last days, began to circulate in Khartoum[6]. In February 1983, the state *ifta'* council, which issued *fatwa*s or official *shari'a* opinions, officially denied the truth of a prophecy that calamity would strike Sudan that month[7]. And Taha had just announced that he was the only *asil*.

Al-Nayl Abu Gurun, who saw Taha in his dream in chapter nine, had become a singer, and then a judge, and finally turned to his Sufi family and spiritual ambitions. In 1978, he published *sirat al-mustaqim* ("The straight path"), a book about prayer which attacked Taha. His *tariga* believed that in the fifteenth century, a Mahdi would be chosen from the Sufis who had reached the highest spiritual station, and he may have seen Taha as a competitor for this station[8].

Nimeiri too had been influenced by the year 1400, when there was Islamic revolution in Iran and Islamic disturbances across Africa and Arabia, and he began to wonder if he might be part of the end of the world[9]. Nimeiri was getting religious – he had given up whisky, and began to sack judges for drinking[10]. But he was not a Muslim Brother: he sought his guidance from the small *tariga shaykh*s around Khartoum, where he visited *wali*s and danced at *zikr*[11]. Al-Nayl Abu Gurun was one of his presidential advisers. Nimeiri used the indefatigable Muslim Brothers to prop up his system, sponsoring and frustrating them as political exigency required: they in turn posed as allies and opponents of the May regime as they saw fit. But the only supporters who saw Nimeiri through to the end were his coterie of bureaucrats and security men, and Abu Gurun's coterie.

TV preacher

'Umar Muhammad al-Tayyib was the first vice-president and head of the State Security Organ (SSO). Like Nimeiri, he was a soldier with a weakness for Sufi celebrities[12]. He was a Nimeiri loyalist, rather than a fellow traveller of the Muslim Brothers, but he had a mosque in the capital where Muhammad Najib al-Muti'i was a regular preacher. Muti'i was an Egyptian firebrand – he had run a mosque in a poor Cairo suburb which had witnessed thousands of arrests after armed clashes between Christians and Muslims[13]. Now he was far from the Egyptian jails where his fellow rioters languished, developing relationships with Muslim Brothers and their allies in Sudan. He taught *hadith* in the Islamic University and a diploma course in *da'wa* (Islamic mission or ideology) to military officers. Muti'i was hostile to Christians and to Muslims who did not share his ideas about Islam. His television series brought his brand of Egyptian TV evangelism to the people of Sudan, attacking Republicans, Christians and Sufis – the last were an old target of the *shari'a* tradition and its radical modern exponents which most Muslim Brothers were wise enough to avoid attacking[14].

Muti'i was in a different league from the Republicans, who were still printing their roneos. Television had been extended across Sudanese cities from the mid-1970s, and in 1983 there were over 100,000 sets in the country[15]. The new media were the preserve of the state, and the state had excluded Taha from every place of communication – mosques, clubs, newspapers – except the street. In 1946, Republican roneos were near the cutting edge of political technology, but the movement never developed beyond them – Republicans were reluctant to abandon the combination of written word and personal encounter that pamphleteering implied. However, Republicans were unable to rebut Muti'i's attacks:

> [Republican] young men and women mix together in distributing pamphlets ... each girl travels with a boy to underdeveloped areas, crossing the desert wastes of Sudan ... a half-naked, tender skinned buxom girl, for they have taken off their beautiful Sudanese *tob* and exchanged it for a mini or a micro-skirt[16].

Muti'i had a keen eye for the female figure, but he misled people about the chaste white *tob*s of the Republican sisters. He declared that Republicans could be killed with impunity[17]. The Republicans turned to the regime to save them. A pamphlet entitled *al-hawas al-dini yuthir al-fitna li-yasil ila al-sulta* ("Religious fanaticism stirs up discord to take power") came out in May 1983. It criticised the failure of al-Tayyib, as security chief, to protect them from Muti'i, who preached in his mosque:

> The spearhead of the campaign of organised distortion against
> Republican thought is an Egyptian legist who works as a professor at
> Omdurman Islamic University (Muhammad Najib al-Muti'i). He has
> preached in al-Taqwa mosque whose flock includes the vice president.
> He began his distortion campaign with [al-Tayyib] ... which has given
> him the courage to step up his campaign against us in this mosque
> and on the television, stage by stage[18].

Al-Tayyib responded to the pamphlet by confiscating the movement's
printing facilities, books and the tent in which exhibitions were held. He
began to arrest leading Republican brothers and sisters in the capital,
Kosti, Medani, El Obeid, Dongola, Kassala and Port Sudan. Taha was
detained on the thirteenth of May 1983. He was held in an SSO detention
centre, the home of Bona Malwal, a former minister, who was held next
door. It was comfortable, and according to Bona Malwal, there was
little harsh treatment[19]. Taha was joined in detention by an acquaintance
named Khalil Osman, one of Sudan's richest men.

Khartoum Republicans were held in two wings of Kober prison.
The Republicans had a strong sense of hierarchy, with every delegation,
team, house or region having its own leader, and this hierarchy followed
them into jail. Sa'id Shayib led one wing, and Jalal al-Din al-Hadi the
other. The *waqtajiya*, Republicans who had the highest expectations
of Taha and his future spiritual status, saw the moment as a blessing.
Ibrahim Yusuf kept a diary where he described his chance to re-live
the spiritual retreat that Taha underwent in Kober after 1946[20]. More
"rationalist" Republicans, like Abdullahi An-Na'im, saw it differently:

> I saw it as a political experience – not rejecting the spiritual dimension
> – but Ibrahim Yusuf saw it as a transformative, symbolic experience.
> I felt the Sufi feeling that to ask hardship of God is not really good.
> We should ask to be merciful and compassionate and to avoid
> suffering[21].

Some Republicans believe that al-Tayyib met Muti'i and his friends
from the radical Islamist movements in the Republican palace to run
a campaign against Taha[22]. Others felt that the SSO was responding to
Republican provocation with a short period of detention, just as they
had done in 1977. However, later that month a new political rationale to
Taha's detention appeared – he was a warning to other Muslim groups
in the country who might oppose new *shari'a* legislation proposed by
Nimeiri. In September, the Republicans were joined by Sadig al-Mahdi

and Mahdist prisoners: he had been jailed after a speech against the new laws (see below). Sadig al-Mahdi was the real threat to Nimeiri – he had his inherited support, but he did not acquiesce in the new laws, as did the Khatmiya leadership. Even Communists mooted his name as an alternative to Nimeiri. Sadig himself encountered Taha in his detention centre. According to Sadig al-Mahdi's account of the meeting, he questioned Taha's self-absorbed support for "one of the worst dictatorships in Africa"[23]. But, says Yusuf Hasan, a close associate of Sadig's, their discussion was good-natured[24].

New legitimacy

Nimeiri used his relationship with small-scale Sufi *tariqa*s as a base for his new, Islamic legitimacy, which replaced the legitimacy conferred on him by the 1973 peace deal. Many southern leaderships were still prepared to deal with him, but he had to juggle them with the other alliances he had made. In 1983, he broke decisively with most Southerners, announcing the redivision of the south in July, and replacing the secular laws based on the 1973 constitution with a version of *shari'a* in September[25]. Southern officers from the Sudanese army mutinied, and formed the Sudan People's Liberation Army (SPLA), which began a rebellion in the south against Nimeiri, co-opting southern tribes to the cause. One Muslim Brother minister explained that Nimeiri was going to hand over the government to his movement, "But we told him that he should hand over the south to us as he found it before 1972. We know how we will deal with [the Southerners]"[26].

Nimeiri's decision to implement *shari'a* was a complex one. In 1977, the Muslim Brothers persuaded him to set up a committee to oversee the modification of laws in line with the *shari'a*. He produced a book on the Islamic way in 1980 – highly praised in a Republican response[27]. He drew closer to the small-scale Sufi *shaykh*s. There was an underlying antagonism between the Sufi *tariqa*s, with their traditional practices, and the Muslim Brothers, who wanted to reconfigure Sudanese power structures, replacing Sufi patrician leadership with an urban, professional leadership with prestigious connections to the wider Muslim world. In May 1983, Nimeiri attended the Abu Gurun festivities for the *mi'raj*, or night journey of Muhammad, where al-Nayl Abu Gurun agreed to produce a new, Islamic penal code for Sudan. One *shaykh* promised that the childless Nimeiri would have a son if he returned to the true path[28]. The decision to implement *shari'a*, according to Zein, was taken in

May 1983, with the support of Abu Gurun's small scale Sufi leadership. Nimeiri bypassed, and "stunned" the Muslim Brothers, who nevertheless decided to back the measures[29].

The pervasive debate about the place of *shari'a* in modern Islamic states and societies was noted in chapter 12. These states had different historical experiences of *shari'a*. In Middle Eastern cities, *shari'a* was a set of institutions, laws and rules which had framed a relatively stable class structure and regulated commerce and family life. Sudan's experience of *shari'a* was different. Some modern radical exponents of the *shari'a* tradition make the unsupported claim that the Funj sultanate was a *shari'a* state[30]. Spaulding suggests that *shari'a* courts were a largely urban phenomenon in pre-colonial Nile valley, and that their influence was resisted by the Sufi mainstream[31]. *Shari'a* attained importance in Sudan because Turkiya and British colonialists regarded it as a prestigious and authoritarian religious form, and used it bolster their own legitimacy. The Mahdi took up the centralising potential of *shari'a* when he built his state. However, the colonialists were interested in the legitimating power of *shari'a* institutions rather than the normative content of *shari'a* – their laws were drawn from western codes and were intended to facilitate colonial commerce. Modern radical Islamists accepted *shari'a* institutions but felt keenly the absence of enforceable *shari'a* law[32]. Their campaigns for *shari'a* envisaged extending the jurisdiction of an existing institutional structure, and sometimes smacked of tokenism. Zein, who broadly supports Nimeiri's *shari'a* experiment acknowledges this:

> It was understood that the degree of seriousness and sincerity of Islamization would be measured by the implementation of the part of the *hudud* that was considered by the West as inhumane ... and contrary to the declaration of Human Rights which was accepted by Sudan[33].

Abu Gurun and his associates saw Sudan's legal deficiencies as an absence of Islamic laws and an absence of Islamic punishments. Accordingly, they attached Islamic punishments to crimes defined in the terms of western jurisprudence – strikers would be lashed, for example[34]. Other political groups, even those committed to *shari'a*, were not so sure that *shari'a* laws or punishments alone could transform a starving country. Sadig al-Mahdi explained to a crowd of his Mahdist supporters: "If a man's family is starving and he steals to feed them, we cannot rule that his hand should be cut off"[35].

Laws for the rich and poor

Nimeiri's version of *shari'a* was not a law for the poor. The new rules jeopardised women and marginalised groups who did not fit in the *shari'a* system, as the Republican sisters discovered in jail. Asma and Sumaya Mahmud, Batoul Mukhtar and Huda Osman were for a time the only politicals in Omdurman women's prison. The women in with them were mostly from poor backgrounds, and many had fallen foul of the new rules on alcohol. Brewing *marissa* was still a traditional occupation for poor urban women, and many did not understand what they had done wrong:

> God, we brought up our children up on this *marissa*, and the children
> of the prison guards too![36]

Shari'a rules against alcohol consumption have different effects. In Sudan, they criminalised a diet that was associated with the rural and the African. State intervention in diet has been noted before – the colonialists' preference for wheat was taken up by Sudanese elites (see chapter 11). Sudan spent hard currency on wheat farming and imports, while European livestock ate Sudanese sorghum[37]. Diet could be used to mark class divisions, and the *shari'a* ban on fermented nutrients was used to distinguish between the poor people from marginalised ethnic groups and the city tastes of the Muslim Brothers. When an air hostess from an important family was jailed for smuggling alcohol, she was freed in two days, whereas the Republicans witnessed pregnant women miscarrying as a result of the floggings they received for their brewing activity. Asma Mahmud recalls:

> No-one asked after them, no-one cared for their health and treatment,
> their families. They were just put there like animals. This was an
> experience. It was important – it showed you what really happened
> in Sudanese society[38].

Asma coped with the experience by writing letters to her father, telling him about the dreams of wild animals she was having, and reading and summarising his books. Amna Lutfi had to cope with freedom while her husband and two daughters lay in jail – she only saw them every few weeks[39]. In Kober, prisoners wrote and prayed, for many Republicans the period was a happy time[40]. Taha wrote a religious and political essay, *dibaja*, in 1984, and a number of letters to the Republicans from his own separate detention centre, his "blessed retreat"[41]. Affectionate and

spiritual, he encouraged them to remember that the blessed present was
full of concealed meaning. It was easy for these letters and messages to
slip in and out of Sudan's porous prison system, and Taha's letters were
passed around lovingly:

> If we are doing any work, or meeting someone significant, or if we
> have to give a talk or debate, for example, we must not be impatient
> for our *shari'a* [the personal *shari'a* of worship, or the law of perfect
> freedom] to come, nor should we live outside the present moment. We
> live in the moment of meeting, the moment of talking, the moment
> of debating, busy in readiness for what we love to say, before there
> comes the time [when the world is perfected][42].

In some ways, it was harder for Republicans on the outside. They provided
for the prisoners' families, and kept up the pressure on the regime. They
went out to preach and distribute pamphlets, not knowing if they would
come back at night. Although they would not pray in mosques, they
began to attend mosques in order to listen out for signals of the regime's
intentions[43].

Abrogation theory hits the headlines
At the beginning of 1984, Nimeiri offered Taha and the sisters their
freedom. Taha refused to accept it without the release of the rest of the
brothers, but he told the sisters to leave jail. Republicans on the outside
managed to publish a booklet on the September laws, *al-mawqif al-
siyasi al-rahin* ("The present political situation"). It looked at Republican
history and the happy days of the 1972 peace accord. The pamphlet was
one of the few Republican attempts to analyse the social problems of
marginalised groups in Sudan. It discussed women brewers, sorghum
prices, prostitution, starving villagers in Darfur, and the attrition of
Southerners' rights[44]. The September laws (as Nimeiri's *shari'a* was known)
gave Republican fixations about law and society a dramatic credibility.
Republicans established their case for a change in law by quoting classical
writers from the *shari'a* tradition, such as the exegete Ibn Kathir (d 1373)
to show that the *shari'a* tradition made compulsion part of religion, and
could not be sustained in a multi-religious state like Sudan[45]. Ibn Kathir,
for example, claimed that the Qur'an's sword verse "Kill the unbelievers
wherever you find them" (4:84) is definitive and final:

> Every pact of the prophet, peace and blessings be upon him, with
> any of the polytheists, is abrogated ... as ibn 'Abbas says, there is no

longer any pact or protection for polytheists since [this verse] was revealed[46].

In fact, Nimeiri maintained legal protection for Noble Spiritual Beliefs (which many Sudanese Muslims carelessly identified with polytheism). But for 'Awad al-Jeed, his legal draftsman, "it was a sin to protect those beliefs"[47]. Abrogation theory was being discussed in unlikely places: a pastoral letter from the Catholic archbishop of Khartoum exhorted his flock to keep away from Nimeiri's theatres of punishment. Jesus, said archbishop Gabriel Zubeir Wako, abrogates harsh laws[48].

Constitutional chaos

Nimeiri claimed that his presidential decrees were in effect a new Islamic constitution. However, he could not get parliament to revoke the 1973 constitution and shelved the proposal. Two Republican judges, (one of whom was a woman, Rashida Muhammad Fadul) claimed that the presidential decrees, with their *shari'a* discriminations against women and non-Muslims, violated the constitution, but their legal challenge failed in court[49]. Meanwhile, criminal justice was in turmoil: Nimeiri introduced emergency courts and then Instant Justice courts; some judges refused to co-operate, and Nimeiri replaced them with unqualified Muslim Brothers, who used the courts to settle scores with other factions. The country was treated to a carnival of floggings, amputations and executions, as the economy collapsed, corruption widened, and the IMF refused to bail out the regime with more loans. Famine deaths in Darfur were counted in tens of thousands, and different militias contested the highly militarised south, with the SPLA gaining the upper hand. There were waves of strikes and demonstrations, and Philip Ghaboush, the leader of the Nuba Mountains political movement, was arrested for allegedly threatening a Nuba uprising in the armed forces[50].

Taha's release

Nimeiri had little room to manoeuvre: he had the support of the United States of America (USA), the Muslim Brothers, and his coterie of loyalists. Sometimes he said he would abolish the September laws, and sometimes he jailed cronies for corruption. But he had a stranglehold on political dissent – in December 1984 he could even afford to free Sadig al-Mahdi and his followers, who kept quiet on release. A weak Sadig was a good counterbalance to the Muslim Brothers. Nimeiri also decided to release Taha.

Muhammad 'Ali Malik and 'Abdallah al-Dabi were two former sso officers who became Republicans in the mid-1970s. They had to explain to their colleagues the Republican belief that state security was about awareness raising, not repression, and they were soon gently moved on. But now al-Tayyib, the vice president and sso chief, decided to negotiate through them. On the eighteenth of December, they were taken from Kober prison to Taha's detention centre. Taha welcomed them with hot sweet lemon, told them not to be bitter, and look for the hand of God behind it all. He said they should ask al-Tayyib for an explanation for the detention, and for the return of the printing press. Taha said that if there was to be a release, it must simultaneously include all the Republican detainees in the cities around Sudan. The two ex-security men went to 'Umar Muhammad al-Tayyib's office. Al-Tayyib was like a baby in a general's uniform, says Muhammad 'Ali Malik, all tears and affection, telling them how much he respected Taha's mission to the Sudanese people. He spoke of his Sufi regret for the political exploitation of *shari'a* and said that he had been forced to detain Taha. Al-Tayyib worried that Taha might not accept release. Muhammad 'Ali Malik and 'Abdallah al-Dabi conveyed Taha's wishes to al-Tayyib. Taha and the Republicans detained in different cities were released on the nineteenth.

The two Republicans sensed that there was a conspiracy afoot, and that their old boss al-Tayyib was trying to distance himself from it[51]. Taha knew that the regime wanted to finish him off. He told the Republicans to prepare for struggle, he told some of his friends to be careful because the regime was "planning something big".

Back to work

After the happy reunions, the Republicans went back to their old activities – meeting in Taha's house and then getting into buses to the centre of Omdurman or Khartoum where they would hold *zikr* in public squares and stations, and sell books. Taha led the processions, dressed in his simple white Sudanese clothes and skull-cap. On the twenty-fifth of December, Christmas, the Republicans published a short pamphlet entitled *hadha ... aw al-tufan* ("Either this or the flood"). Taha told the brothers and sisters, who met at his home daily, that only those who were convinced of the truth of the pamphlet, and who were ready to face the consequences of distributing it, should join in the distribution efforts. Busloads of Republicans accepted the challenge and distribution went ahead, preceded as ever by half an hour or more of *zikr*. Their efforts were concentrated around the university, and some of them were arrested.

Either this or the flood[52]

The pamphlet was a lucid and brief denunciation of the September laws. It said the laws deviated from mainstream *shari'a* law, and, echoing al-Sadiq al-Mahdi's speech at Aba, said that it was not right to amputate the hands of thieves in the current economic conditions. The laws "humiliated and insulted the people", and it was "futile to claim that a Christian person is not adversely affected". Taha invoked mainstream *shari'a* because the September laws were drafted carelessly, and made major departures from orthodoxy. But he also called for his heterodox and reworked version of Islam, the only way to guarantee the rights of non-Muslim citizens:

> The rights of southern citizens in their country are not provided for in *shari'a* but rather in Islam at the level of fundamental Qur'anic revelation, that is, the level of *Sunnah*.

The pamphlet called for the repeal of the September laws and the end of the war and the revival of Islam through education. There was no long excursus into gnostic Sufism. According to Ibrahim Yusuf, the pamphlet had a good reception, and dominated the discussions of the Republicans each evening. (A few months before someone outside the movement had been jailed for possession of Republican material, so even acceptance of the pamphlet must have implied the reader's approval)[53].

A day in court

At the end of December, senior Republicans learned from the attorney-general al-Rashid al-Tahir (a lapsed Muslim Brother now close to Taha) that the minister for criminal affairs, a Muslim Brother named Muhammad Adam 'Isa, had instructed prosecutors to press capital charges of sedition, inciting unlawful opposition, and membership of an illegal organisation against some Republicans detained for breach of the peace. Republicans led a procession through the capital and held a *zikr* circle outside the court, to keep up the spirits of the accused, only to find that the case had been adjourned for a week. The president had to sanction the capital charges. They went back to distributing the pamphlet, conscious of the popular astonishment at their tenacity[54].

The redeemer

Republicans spent several days celebrating Sudan's independence day (the first of January). On the fourth, Taha gave his last interview to *al-Jami'a* magazine. He spoke about presidential and parliamentary government,

Islamic banks and the nationalist struggle. But that night, Taha retreated into the private Sufi discourse that had nourished the Republicans in their detention. "The time has come for our knowledge to be incarnated" he told them, and reminded them of how Sufi *wali*s redeemed their people from the power of plague:

> *Sayyid* Hasan [al-Mirghani] died in a plague, and the plague stopped. In 1915, *shaykh* Taha [wad 'Abd al-Sadig] in Rufa'a died from the meningitis that spread wildly, and no-one escaped without death or disablement. *Shaykh* Taha died and the sickness stopped. This story is regularly told among the Sufis, but the secularists find it hard [to grasp]. Now, you must redeem the Sudanese people from the humiliation and degradation that has come on them ...[55]

Many Republicans had high expectations of Taha; some even thought he was going to be the perfect man, or messiah. Not to discourage such speculation is to encourage it, and Taha did no more than keep silent. If someone asked him if he was the perfect man, he answered "I hope to be"; if someone asked him if he was a Republican, he gave the same answer[56]. On the night of the fourth of January, Taha made his most explicit statement about his aspirations; he said "I am not the perfect man, but I hope to be"[57]. Taha's prosecutors, it will be seen, tried to link him to far-away gnostics like al-Hallaj, but Taha drew comparisons with Sudanese Sufism instead. Sudan, the heart of Africa, the most spiritual place in the world, was the place for a perfect man, he believed, a man in the redemptive tradition of *shaykh* Taha wad 'Abd al-Sadig whom he may have met as a small boy (see chapter two).

Arrest

At noon on the fifth, sso men with submachine guns escorted the elderly mystic to the police cells in Omdurman. He was interviewed by a police officer and the public prosecutor. He accepted full responsibility for the pamphlet and gave them a talk on Republican history and *shari'a*. Taha was happy to be jailed with non-political prisoners in the police cells. Instead of looking for special treatment, as he had done in Kober in 1946, he bothered himself about the conditions of his fellow detainees, asking the Republican lawyers to be sure to help them out[58].

The trial

Taha went to the dock on the seventh, with four Republicans arrested the week before: Khalid Babikr Hamza, Muhammad Salim Ba'shar, 'Abd al-Latif 'Umar (one of his four deputies), and Taj al-Din 'Abd al-Raziq. Nimeiri sanctioned capital charges and applied the bizarre section 458(3) of the penal code, which allowed the court to impose any *hadd* (Qur'an-specified penalty such as flogging or stoning; the singular of *hudud*) in the absence of specified punishments[59]. Sudan's confused and incomplete legal system had always allowed judges to fill legislative vacuums with their own initiative, but this chaotic capital case even had judges making up *hudud* – a highly restricted set of punishments which in mainstream *shari'a* can only be mandated by the Qur'an.

It was hard to find judges who could cope with such laws. The man chosen was Hasan Ibrahim al-Mahalawi, a relative of Abu Gurun not yet qualified as a judge. The Republicans, many coming from outside Khartoum, again processed through the streets to the court, which had to be moved to a larger courtroom to accommodate the crush. A policeman went through his investigation of the offence and submitted the sole piece of evidence, Taha's pamphlet, to the judge, who read it nervously. Ibrahim Yusuf felt that even the prosecutor was moved. The process took less than an hour, and when the judge turned to the defence case, Taha and his co-accused denounced the September laws and announced their boycott of the proceedings. Taha spoke at the end:

> I have repeatedly declared my view that the September 1983 so-called Islamic laws violate Islamic *Shari'a* law and Islam itself. Moreover, these laws have distorted Islamic *Shari'a* law and made them repugnant. Furthermore, these laws were enacted and utilized to terrorize the people and humiliate them into submission. These laws also jeopardize the national unity of the country. These are [my] objections from the theoretical point of view.
>
> At the practical level, the judges enforcing these laws lack the necessary technical qualifications. They have also morally failed to resist, placing themselves under the control of the executive authorities which exploited them in violating the rights of citizens, humiliating the people, distorting Islam, insulting intellect and intellectuals, and humiliating political opponents.
>
> For all these reasons, I am not prepared to cooperate with any court that has betrayed the independence of the judiciary and allowed itself to be a tool for humiliating the people, insulting free thought, and persecuting political opponents[60].

There was nothing that al-Mahalawi could say except that he would pass judgement the next day, and there was nothing the Republicans could do except publish Taha's court-room speech in a pamphlet. That same night, Nimeiri announced that he had pardoned Philip Ghaboush and 200 of his Nuba supporters from Western Sudan, who were facing state security charges for an alleged conspiracy to mutiny[61].

Sentence

The morning of the eighth, Republicans marched in procession to the court, only to be met by security forces. They made it to the court after some protest. Al-Mahalawi started off his judgement with a discussion of Taha's Sufi secrets:

> It is true that the Qur'an has intricacies and secrets with which God favours those of his servants he wishes to favour, when he reveals to them the truths of things. [Such a servant] sees things not as ordinary people see them: these are individual states of consciousness which should not be propagated because they are favours, and because propagating them stirs up discord among believers[62].

An-Na'im comments that al-Mahalawi seemed to be groping his way towards an apostasy conviction when he suddenly concluded by convicting all five men of the crimes against the state[63]. He passed death sentences for sedition, but said the accused could be reprieved if they recanted. This was a clear conflation of security laws with the *shari'a* law of apostasy.

Judicial review

The death sentence had to be reviewed by a higher court, and that court met on the twelfth of January with al-Mukashafi Taha al-Kabbashi presiding. He was from a Sufi family, but had joined the Muslim Brothers. Ahmad Mahjub Hajj Nur, a Muslim Brother with a reputation for savage sentencing, and Muhammad Sirr al-Khatim were sitting with him. Taha had been tried by a small-*tariqa* Sufi: for al-Mahalawi, his crime was to reveal secrets to the unworthy. For the Muslim Brothers, his crime had always been that he believed those secrets. The Muslim Brothers were not prepared to discuss Taha's abrogation theory, his direct challenge to *shari'a* rules. Instead, they concentrated on his spiritual secrets, locating him in a distant Sufi challenge to *shari'a* theology, and caricaturing his Sufi dreams of perfection (linked to Sudan's religious mainstream) as an ancient heresy. The Muslim Brothers wanted to use the trial to delegitimise Sufism, a necessary part of their strategy to win over the constituencies of Sudan's Sufi patricians. They did not want to allow Taha to put forward his proposal to delegitimise *shari'a*. So when the Muslim Brother judges came to review the bizarre verdict, they made sure to add the unbelievable secrets to it. The judges brought new evidence to the case, picking through Republican works of the late 1980s which dealt with incarnation and authenticity (*asala*)[64]. They used his references to the incarnated life of God, the Muhammadan messiah or the station of Mahmud, as evidence that he was reviving heresies. Like the protagonists of the 1968 trial, the judges sought to play out the ancient Islamic role of infuriated *shari'a* rigorists against Taha's Sufi martyr. In 922, the theosophist al-Hallaj faced a *shari'a* judge who insisted on taking his wild statements literally, and had him crucified. But Taha did not seem to want the role of al-Hallaj[65]. He confined his few public remarks to denouncing the inadequacies and injustices he saw in Nimeiri's version of *shari'a*, and in traditional *shari'a*.

The appeal judges relied heavily on the apostasy charge implied by al-Mahalawi, (for which Taha and his followers had not been tried), but they confirmed the sentences for the state security charges and sentenced them to "the *hadd* of apostasy"[66]. Apostasy was not one of the September laws, but the appeal court judges simply used the sweeping provisions of section 458(3), which allowed them to make up *hadd* punishments as they pleased. Most of the review was taken up with the apostasy of the accused. They quoted extensively from the records of Taha's 1968 trial and the condemnations from foreign *shari'a* authorities.

Who pulled the trigger?

The Muslim Brothers supported the trial and sentence, but they were not the main force behind the affair. Several months later, when crowds stormed through the Republican palace, they found a memo from Abu Gurun to Nimeiri, telling him not to miss a golden opportunity to get Taha[67]. Abu Gurun's disciple al-Mahalawi gave an indication of his master's concerns about Taha in his condemnation of Taha's democratic approach to Sufi secrets. Why was this an offence?

It was suggested in chapter seven that many of the leaderships of Sudan's small-scale *tariqa*s had gradually been co-opted into the colonial state. This process was continued by Nimeiri's ministry of religious affairs, who used the leaderships as a means of extending control over rural areas of the northern Nile valley. This process helped these leaderships to identify the spiritual elitism of their Sufi heritage with the class structures of state society. For men like Abu Gurun and al-Mahalawi, the Sufi secrets shrouded in the impenetrable symbolism of classical Sufi poetry, were a mark of spiritual and social eminence. Taha's attempt to communicate them was a threat to that eminence.

Taha's offence may have been more personal. It was noted above that 1980s Sudan was full of wild eschatological rumours, and that some of Sudan's leaders were wondering if they might have a role in the last things. Taha claimed a high spiritual station for himself, but his claims may have been contested by men like Nimeiri and Abu Gurun. Zein suggests that Abu Gurun may have wanted the Sufi secrets for himself:

> Ustaz Mahmud was popularly perceived as an eminent Sufi Saint who was a dangerous competitor to their [Abu Gurun's] *tariqa*. Furthermore, Ustaz Mahmud himself claimed that he was seeking to reach that *maqam* [the high spiritual station which Abu Gurun believed qualified a Sufi for the status of Mahdi – Taha used the term messiah or perfect man][68].

The political motivation for the trial is more straightforward: it kept pressure on Sadig al-Mahdi to stay quiet, and sent a signal to worldwide representatives of the *shari'a* tradition that Nimeiri was one of their number. The sso was unhappy with the sentence, they worried about international reactions, and arrested hundreds of Republicans[69]. Human rights lawyers flew into Khartoum to plead for clemency, and Communists and some Republicans discussed how they could thwart the execution. But many Republicans refused to plead for clemency. Some believed that it would be a betrayal of Taha's long-standing rejection of the authority of state over belief[70]. Others believed that Taha's spiritual power was more than a match for Nimeiri and his gallows.

The hanging

On the fifteenth of January, Taha was sentenced to immediate execution, without possibility of repentance. He was judged an incorrigible heretic, but his four co-accused were given a month to recant. Nimeiri confirmed the judgement the next day, with a bullying defence of his actions on state television two days later: anyone who tried to "interfere in the course of justice will receive an appropriate punishment"[71]. Nimeiri's confirmation of sentence was based again on *shari'a* apostasy law, but like others involved in the bizarre legalities, he did not mention the offence by name.

Asma did not believe it would happen. She went to visit her father to tell him so, but he just looked at her. She felt some comfort when she looked at his eyes, but she still believed that something would stop it, or that heaven would intervene[72]. Muhammad 'Ali Malik also got to see him. The doctor who examined Taha noted an abnormal physical calm about him. Taha was wearing the same prison *'araqi* that he wore in Kober in 1946. He looked down on his white robe as Muhammad 'Ali Malik left, and his last words to him were: "Mmhuh, the noblest uniform"[73].

'Abd al-Mun'im 'Abd al-Latif Sa'd was a prison warder who volunteered to guard Taha. He wanted to see history in the making. At four o'clock on the seventeenth, the prison authorities informed Taha that he was "going to the next world in the morning"[74]. He had no requests, but his diabetes troubled him, and there was no toilet in the condemned cell, just a palm mat and a blanket. Sudan's capital had an uneasy night. The Muslim Brothers were preparing for a feast, but many Sudanese who had been fed hundreds of lurid trials for drinking, corruption, and the novel offence of attempted fornication, felt restless and dismayed at this new show.

The next morning, the eighteenth of January 1985, crowds gathered around the prison walls. They were mostly Muslim Brothers, including Hasan al-Turabi, but some foreign journalists came to watch a Muslim state dramatically assert its "fundamentalism". Some Republicans came, convinced that Taha would not die, but transform himself and the world to perfection. Some were arrested for shouting that he would not die[75].

Taha's historian-warder described Taha's last moments: "They took him to the gallows' square, and he climbed up with firm steps and a lion heart. They lifted the cover [over his face] and there was a man smiling at fate. Peace on the nation that bore a man like Mahmud"[76]. The Muslim Brothers gathered in the gallows square shouted "God is great, God is great, Islam is the answer", as the elderly man, his head and body covered in a sack, fell through a gallows' trapdoor[77]. Abu Gurun's student dream of Taha had come true.

Taha dropped to his death: one of the journalists felt sick and left before a doctor examined his body. A helicopter lifted him off to a secret desert grave[78]. Some of the Muslim Brothers slaughtered sheep to celebrate, and many of Taha's followers were filled with a dismayed perplexity which they have yet to resolve. There were no prayers, shroud or washing for his apostate body, and he had died a death like Jesus', just as he had predicted during his retreat.

Chapter 17

Aftermath

This chapter concludes this account of Taha's life by looking at events in the months after his execution, and then by assessing Taha's contribution to Islamic thought and to Sudan.

Penitence

Two days after Taha was executed, his four co-accused met in Kober prison to talk about the offer of recantation which had been appended to their conviction for sedition. Some Republicans believe that Taha had told them not to follow him to the gallows. They decided to recant.

Observers of Sudan in 1985 often commented on how far events in Khartoum were divorced from the realities of life in the hinterland. While men like al-Kabbashi defended the true faith from the horrors of gnosticism, many ordinary Sudanese were thinking about food. Up to ten million people were affected by the drought in the country, half of them severely affected. Over a million people displaced by hunger converged on Khartoum. In the south, war and famine lethally coincided. In Darfur, people ransacked termite hoards for food. In Khartoum, however, merchants hoarded grain to speculate on prices. When the central bank realised what was happening, they ordered commercial banks to shorten credit lines for food stocks. The Islamic banks stepped in to offer the hoarding merchants the longer credit needed to make up to 400% annual returns on sorghum stocks[1].

The four recanting Republicans wrote letters to Nimeiri declaring that they had "repented of all their words". This was not enough: they had to submit to interrogation from their appeal judges, a Muslim Brother minister and representatives of the religious affairs ministry. The televised session was opened by 'Abd al-Jabbar al-Mubarak, a consultant to Faisal Islamic Bank, and anti-Republican polemicist. "God loves the penitent sinner" said al-Mubarak to Khalid Babikr[2]. He and his fellow convicts had to read a recantation:

> I declare my repentance to God almighty and great, and my recantation of all my thoughts and opinions which I took from the infidel apostate, Mahmud Muhammad Taha, who deceived me with his thought and took me out of the confession of Islam, until God hanged him dead[3].

'Abd al-Latif 'Umar, the water-seller who had learned to read through the movement, could not say the words, and tried some casuistry about the five pillars of Islam being enough to return him to the faith. One judge told him that if he did not recant, he would be taken to the gallows directly. In the end, all four men read out the confession, twice. 'Abd al-Latif sobbed, and his prosecutors cried "praise be to God".

Redemption

The four hundred Republicans detained on the eve of Taha's execution were freed within a week. 'Umar Muhammad al-Tayyib, the security chief, was unhappy about the execution and feared Taha's supporters might resort to suicide attacks, although this was never considered by the detainees. Abdullahi An-Na'im, then a well-connected Khartoum academic, was invited to discuss their release. Some Republicans believe that Taha had indicated that his fellow convicts should recant, and Abdullahi An-Na'im was allowed to discuss the matter with Sa'id Shayib, who was still at large, and who felt that there should be no more martyrdom. An-Na'im met Abu Gurun, 'Awad al-Jeed and Badriya Sulayman (one of Abu Gurun's coterie) and they negotiated a recantation which did not include references to infidels or apostates, but included an undertaking not to propagate Taha's views. The recantation was debated in the police cells, each holding 20 or 30 Republicans. All but four Republicans signed – many were persuaded that Taha wanted them to do so, and that they were disavowing their pride, that stopped them from recanting, rather than disavowing their beliefs[4].

Was Taha a redeemer?

The Economist Intelligence Unit (a business publication) wrote extensively about Taha's execution in its quarterly review. Its analysis suggests that Taha succeeded in his aim to "redeem the Sudanese people from the humiliation and degradation that has come on them"[5]. The

EIU presented evidence indicating that the outcry over his death led to a decrease in *hadd* sentencing. In the 16 months before Taha's death, 70 people convicted of theft had hands amputated; in the four months after it, there were only two[6]. Four Ba'athists on the same sedition charges as Taha's got eighty lashes rather than death, even though their trial, under al-Kabbashi, had the same examination of the Islamic correctness of their ideology, rather than the facts of the case[7]. The execution led to a London meeting between the patrician parties and the SPLA which galvanised opposition to the May regime.

Taha was speaking for many Sudanese when he wrote his last pamphlet, "Either this or the flood". He was in a unique position to articulate a widespread sense of dismay at Nimeiri's version of *shari'a*. His belief that he had a mission to explain the truth and even to redeem Sudan was not fanciful. The country was seized by a "paroxysm of remorse", and the professional syndicates who organised themselves to present letters of protest about his trial and execution went on to lead a successful popular uprising against Nimeiri in April that year[8]. The USA, which had been shoring up Nimeiri's debts for several years, began to withdraw support, and many other governments condemned the execution. Nimeiri thought he was being wise in tyranny when he destroyed a weak opponent to demonstrate his power, but from beyond the grave, Taha destroyed him.

Republican responses

Like many other commentators, Republicans make the connection between the execution and the fall of Nimeiri. When Nimeiri was replaced in April, they published *ma dha qal al-'alim 'an al-ustadh mahmud* ("What the world has said about *ustaz* Mahmud"), which reproduced reports from around the world. *Jeune Afrique*, with his picture on its glossy cover, called him an African Gandhi. Taha was given sympathetic write-ups in the pan-Arab press. One Egyptian Christian resigned from the Nile valley parliament (an attempt at Egyptian-Sudanese unity) in protest[9]. The Arab Organisation for Human Rights adopted the anniversary of Taha's death as Arab human rights day.

Taha's conviction was overturned by the supreme court, in a suit raised by his lawyer daughter Asma Mahmud. She did not want any compensation, although the Mahdi family and even some Communists claimed large reparations from the government that replaced Nimeiri's.

However, the Republicans initially decided not to revive their movement after the death. Sadig, a Republican who conducted a survey of the movement two years after the execution found less than a third of respondents wanted to start again[10]. Forty-four percent of his interviewees had begun to doubt their Republican beliefs, while 40% said that the execution strengthened their belief in a man who had stood by his[11].

Sadig's sample found that 68% of informants cited Taha's "attractive personality" as a reason for joining[12]. This personal link to the movement meant that Republicans often had sharply differing expectations of Taha. For some, he was the leader of a social movement that had become part of their life; for others, he vindicated their feminist or socialist ideas. Those with the highest expectations of Taha believed he was a Sufi master who might become a messiah. Taha's death brought out these differences.

Sociable movement

Sadig's 1988 study found that less than a third of his Republican informants wanted to revive the movement. Almost all (23 out of 25) proponents of revival cited the need to maintain social links, an indication of the group loyalty that Taha had built, and of the difficulty in returning from Republican to kinship networks. In Taha's successful social movement, people sang the same songs; celebrated Christmas and Muslim feasts; went on trips or missions together. Some lived a common life in busy religious houses, and many married each other. This friendly human bustle was silenced by the execution, and it was a loss to those Republicans who were attracted to the movement's warmth and companionship, rather than its legal or spiritual preoccupations. Some Republicans felt that Taha was the only thing that stopped them from becoming secularists, and when he died, some of them took the obvious step. Others ceased to identify themselves as Republicans and went back to mainstream social and religious life.

Civil rights movement

Taha's inclusive and tolerant manner made space for people who were less than completely committed to his ideas. But many of his followers were deeply impressed by his reworking of *shari'a*, and saw his constitutional ideas as the main reason for joining up. For them, Taha was a murdered pacifist and a moral exemplar.

> By accepting his fate in that manner, Ustadh Mahmoud demonstrate
> that belief and action can combine in the life of a human being into a
> single consistent pattern, even up to the ultimate test[13].

For some of these civil and gender rights activists, Taha's death eventually
worked as a tragic and forceful reminder that there was more work to
be done. They became involved in the campaign led by professionals
and unionists to protest the execution, a campaign that brought down
Nimeiri in the end. Abdullahi An-Na'im was associated with that
campaign, and has subsequently written extensively on human rights in
different cultures, developing Taha's distinction between Qur'anic ethics
and *shari'a* law in the context of wider debates about law and rights.
During their 1985 incarceration, all the Republicans were adopted as
prisoners of conscience by Amnesty International and many of them
went on to work in the international human rights system. Their works,
often in English, analyse the ideas of modern exponents of the *shari'a*
tradition with the same mixture of serenity and anger that was a feature
of Republican writing all along. A few briefly involved themselves in
armed struggle against the Islamist regime that took over the country
in 1989.

Jesus

Fatma Ibrahim, a Communist who was involved in protests before
Taha's execution, recalls one Republican academic who refused to join
her protests because he believed Taha would not die. Some Republicans
were *waqtaji*s, that is, they believed that Taha's candidacy for perfection
was going to be successful. Their demonstration in the gallows square
on the eighteenth of January was not against the execution, but against
death itself. Nimeiri was trying to kill the messiah. Some Republicans lost
their faith in Taha after the execution, but others began to draw parallels
between Taha and Jesus, and build up the hope that the execution was
not the end.

Shubbiha

Shubbiha is a near-untranslatable Arabic word. It appears once in the
Qur'an (4:157), in its story of the crucifixion of Jesus. Arberry translates
it in a circumlocutory phrase:

> Yet they did not slay him, neither crucified him, *only a likeness of that
> was shown* to them[14].

Most Muslims take this passage to mean that Jesus was not crucified, but snatched away to heaven, from where he will return. "The Return of Christ" in Sudan was an established Mahdist reference, it was also a Republican book. Certain anomalies in the execution brought some Republicans to believe that Taha had not been killed. Why did only one person, a doctor, see his corpse? Why was he flown away in a helicopter? Why was he buried in the desert? Why did the post-Nimeiri search for the secret grave come up with nothing?[15] Ibrahim Yusuf gives a moving and messianic account of Taha's last days; Fatma Yusuf Guway makes explicit parallels:

> There are seven similarities between the *ustaz* and Christ.
> 1. He said, a day will come when people will deny me, and his followers denied him
> 2. Barabbas is like Philip Ghaboush, the man of violence who was saved
> 3. A rich man was imprisoned with Christ, and the *ustaz* was imprisoned with a man who had factories, Khalil Osman
> 4. The *ustaz* was hanged, and then he was crucified for 20 minutes in Kober prison
> 5. *Ustaz* Mahmud was smiling when he went to the gallows, and Christ sighed "Why have you forsaken me"
> 6. The *ustaz* was taken away in a helicopter, just as Christ was lifted up
> 7. Nobody knows where the *ustaz* is buried.
> He left a will where he said he would die the death of Christ ... But the *ustaz*'s smile on the gallows was a higher thing than the sigh of Christ on the cross[16].

For some Republicans, there is a hope that Taha will return, like the Muslim Jesus. Others look for him in the prayers in the last third of the night. Although many Republicans have written about Taha's legal opinions, few have tried to write down this hope. Yasir Sharif makes some allusions:

> I myself heard the *ustaz* say "I am not the perfect man but I hope to be". I now claim that the teacher, God sanctify his secret, took the place of the perfect worshipper in struggle, at ten o'clock on the eighteenth of January 1985, before the view of thousands, meeting God with a smile of contentment and joy, in spite of his fettered limbs. Peace be upon him, among the immortal![17]

Conclusion

The introduction to this book offered to assess Taha's political and
religious success, to explain Taha's life as a legal reformer, and to relate
that to Sudan's complex legal systems, and to Sudan's diversity.

Muslim Brothers lose

In January 1985, for the first time in 12 years, the Muslim Brothers
lost elections for control of Khartoum University students' union[18].
In March, Nimeiri rounded up two hundred leading Muslim Brothers,
blaming them for the country's ills. Abu Gurun, his Sufi counsellor, was
retained in government. Nimeiri left the country for medical treatment
a few weeks later, and urban demonstrators, led by the committee for
Taha's defence, thronged the streets. 'Abd al-Rahman Suwar al-Dahab, a
general related by marriage to the Mirghani family, took over in April to
prevent further bloodshed.

Muslim Brothers win

A chain of events led from the gallows to the fall of Nimeiri. But although
Taha may have redeemed his people from Nimeiri, the Republicans were
not the winners. Suwar al-Dahab did not repeal the September laws,
and his cabinet included at least one acknowledged Muslim Brother,
Bashir Haj al-Tom. Without getting rid of the discriminatory laws, the
regime could not expect to meet the SPLA's conditions for dialogue; the
Muslim Brothers were able to use their intransigence on legal reform
to call for a military solution to the south. There, a malign combination
of militia rivalry, speculation on grain, and government connivance led
to famines that broke world records of mortality[19]. Nevertheless, the
Muslim Brothers, now called the National Islamic Front (NIF) won 51
seats in parliamentary elections the next year, on 18% of the vote. The
imprisonment of their leadership (including Hasan al-Turabi) helped
distance them from Nimeiri; some also distanced themselves from
Taha's execution[20]. Although a minority, they dominated the flailing
parliamentary regime led by Sadig al-Mahdi, and were openly active in
the army.

Muslim Brothers win everything

In 1989 the allies that the Muslim Brothers and their NIF party had
cultivated in the military took control of the country in a coup d'état, just
as a peace agreement with the SPLA was about to be concluded. No-one

expected the new military government to last more than a few months, but in the event, it turned itself into the most durable regime since the colonial period. The Islamist security forces that were the cornerstone of its power were prepared to use the excesses of violence usually reserved for the peoples of Sudan's periphery against Khartoum's middle classes, in secret jails in Khartoum. Al-Turabi helped to draft a new version of *shari'a* law enacted in a 1991 penal code that deviated less ineptly from mainstream *shari'a* than did the 1983 September laws. (Although the Islamist regime mastered violence more thoroughly than Nimeiri's, it seldom implemented *hudud* punishments in Nimeiri's theatrical way).

Al-Turabi, the godfather of Islamist politics in Sudan was marginalised by an alliance of military officers and his own disciples in the late 1990s, when the economic crisis that had lasted the length of the regime eased. The Islamist security men were able to set up a new patrimonial system based around commercial and industrial development in the northern Nile valley of Sudan, and eventually based on the oil they began to extract from southern oilfields. Their grip on the economy eclipsed that of the old patricians, and ended some of the structures inherited from the colonialists. The violence, corruption and schism of the regime's first decade discredited its religious claims, and the departure of al-Turabi made the regime turn to its ethnic base in the Nile valley north of Khartoum for support.

Al-Turabi thought that the answer to Sudan's diversity was to impose an Islamist cultural project on the country – to link citizenship to Islamic affiliation. In some respects, he was reprising the Mahdi's Islamic centralism – he has antecedents in western Sudan, and was able to develop a limited and provisory alliance between some Muslims in the west and in the northern Nile valley by invoking Islam.

However, the most widereaching component of the Islamist project was over a decade of *jihad* – a policy of war, enslavement, rape and cultural annihilation in the south (Hajj Nur, one of Taha's judges, died in the *jihad*). The war against the south brought immense suffering and tenacious resistance from millions of ordinary Southerners. The Islamists did not win, but by the end of the twentieth century, incentives for the regime had been decisively skewed by the commercial exploitation of southern oilfields.

The SPLA, which fought remorselessly against the Khartoum regime (and often against itself) was able to conclude in 2005 a peace deal with the northern regime that allowed it to keep *shari'a* in the north in return

for a southern right to self-determination (*shari'a* was still too important
to the regime's legitimacy to be sacrificed). The deal, characterised by the
subtlety and toughness of John Garang, then leader of the SPLA, set out a
clear division of national resources between its two parties. However, the
agreement paid little attention to most other marginal groups in Sudan.
That exclusion was one of the reasons behind the decision of some
groups in Darfur to mount a military challenge to the state. The deal
also preserved the notionally Islamist security state, that has relinquished
neither arbitrary violence nor its system of economic control.

The flawed, profound peace deal reflected many of Garang's ideas
and gave space for secularism in the south. Southern resistance had led
to a qualified acknowledgement of Sudan's diversity that no northern
intellectual had managed to achieve. It also led to a relaxation of security-
force control in northern cities; the return of opposition politicians who
had spent over a decade in exile; and the emergence of civil society and
human rights organisations in the capital. The Republicans were one of
the groups that re-emerged as a result. Republicans would still meet for
shared devotions in private houses and they began occasionally to engage
in public politics. They are still a tiny group, but they are still important:
their attempt to reconceptualise Sudan's diversity in Islamic terms
provides an intellectual framework that is still attractive or even necessary
for some Muslim intellectuals. Their aura of incorruptible sincerity is
probably an important counterweight to the religious grotesqueries that
the overwhelmingly devout northern Sudanese Muslims have endured.

Taha's political failure

Although Taha beat Nimeiri, the Muslim Brothers won in the end. The
reasons for this are complex. First, Taha's utopian Islam had none of the
political astuteness of the Muslim Brothers, with their soldier and banker
friends. Karsani suggests that the Republican movement collapsed because
it was a group of intellectuals wrapped up in the person of Taha[21]. This
may be true, but another reason for the movement's inability to survive
Taha's death was that the man himself chose a strategy that did not
include political success among its aims. Taha wanted to educate people
to freedom and he believed that purpose was best served by perfecting
his self-expression in Republican dialogue. The Muslim Brothers and
the Communists before them attained power within a generation of
their founding because of their tactical use of the military and their
engagement with economic life in Sudan. Taha renounced those tactics

early in his life. Taha had an unfeigned faith in the effective power of civil society, but the history of Sudan in the 1970s and 1980s suggests that this faith may have been misplaced. The Muslim Brothers, a single disciplined and forceful group, were able to over-run civil society. They understood that influence over civil society was not a major component of their success. Having a bank, and friends in the army, were far more important than scout troops.

Another reason for Taha's political failure was that his challenge to the Arab-Muslim state was at the same time too innovative and too dependent on inaccessible classical texts. Taha was aware that many Muslims of his generation were searching for a new ethical framework that reworked the *shari'a* tradition and dispensed with some of its discriminatory norms. He sensed that ancient Muslim traditions of legal scepticism could be modernised to provide a comprehensive reworking of Islamic law. But his critique was too total for it to win wide acceptance; and the sources for his critique were too inaccessible for most Sudanese.

Finally, Taha was sometimes too focused on Khartoum politics to revolutionise Sudan. He was able to challenge the state's mysterious claim to indispensability with his faith in the power of ordinary people. But he accepted the value of the state as a midwife for his utopia, even a state like Nimeiri's. He did not see that effective challenges to Sudan's narrow and unrepresentative state lay in the southern rebellion and the resistance of ordinary Southerners faced with a project that aimed at their cultural annihilation. Perhaps if Taha had tried to draw lessons from other parts of Sudan his Sudanese Sufi critique of the state would have been more grounded and politically usable.

Between Damascus and Kashmir

The Muslim Brothers were the vanguard of a movement to free Sudan of multi-cultural complications. Their wealth and status were tied up with Islam and Arabism. Muslim Brothers and their allies reworked a longstanding ideological theme: that Arabness and Middle Eastern, metropolitan forms of Islam were more prestigious than other religions and cultures on offer in Sudan, and that Arabised Muslims had first rights to control the wealth of the country, and that the use of a constructed Arab-Muslim past was an inescapable part of the state's legitimacy. At the recantation of Taha's co-accused, Hajj Nur gave a fascinating account of the Muslim Brothers' aspiration for a non-African Sudan:

Sudan is different from **neighbouring countries** because its people
agree on one doctrine, the doctrine of *sunna*. They may differ in their
sects and orders, but **all of them**, in their different sects and parties
and groups agree on the doctrine which the prophet (peace be upon
him) taught ... if we look at **neighbouring countries**, they have
Shi'ites and Sunnis. Syria has Shi'ites and Sunnis. Iraq has Shi'ites and
Sunnis, Iran, Pakistan, India – in all these countries Muslim groups
are divided ... This division has even entered east and west Africa ...
but **our country** has stayed free of this [division] until Republican
doctrine came along [emphasis added][22].

Hajj Nur seems to be trying to shove Sudan somewhere between
Damascus and Kashmir. No-one is an African in Sudan, and the
country is full of men schooled in the books he reads. Hajj Nur's telling
geographical and cultural solecism was not challenged by anyone in the
small, oppressive, strobe-lit room in Kober. The Muslim Brother picture
of Sudan had an appreciative audience.

Sudan of the heart

"Sudan is placed in Africa in the place of the heart, and its shape is like
a heart", said Taha in 1974[23]. Although a fluent interpreter of Middle
Eastern traditions, and a gifted Arabic speaker, Taha often identified
himself as African[24]. While the Muslim Brothers sought refuge in
monocultural simplicity, Taha (like most Sudanese) could live with
different constituents of his own identity and those of Sudan too. His
first publication called for economic development for the south, and his
last called for political rights and peace for the south and for Christians:

> It is not enough for a [non-Muslim] citizen today merely to enjoy
> freedom of worship. He is entitled to full rights with all other citizens.
> The rights of southern citizens in their country are not provided for
> in *Shari'a* but rather in Islam at the level of fundamental Qur'anic
> revelation[25].

Taha could acknowledge the cultural complexity that Muslim Brothers
denied. He could see that complexity resolved in a Sufi utopia, while their
Islam would be used as a fast track to national unity or state consolidation.
Hajj Nur's Sudan might have lain in some imaginary Persia, but Taha's
Sudan lay between earth and heaven.

Like the Muslim Brothers and their allies, Taha was an Islamist; that
is, he sought to extend the role of Islam in state and society. Although
his version of Islam for the south was unrecognisably different from the

war that eventually claimed the life of Hajj Nur, he still believed that all
Sudan's cultures, and all the world's cultures, had an Islamic vocation,
that would they would discover through years of development. Francis
Deng, a southern academic, ends a positive account of Taha's ideas with
an equivocal summing-up:

> the Republicans might have been more successful in promoting
> identification with Islam than the more coercive models that operated.
> Depending on whether such a tolerant process of assimilation into
> the Islamic mold would have been a good or bad thing for the South,
> the suppression of Taha's perspective meant that an opportunity to
> develop a more comprehensive, integrative sense of national identity
> was lost. Its failure, however, also helped preserve the identity of the
> South as a culturally and religiously diverse entity[26].

Bona Malwal, a southern politician and friend of Taha's, admits that
Southerners would be obliged to dismiss him like any other missionary
who tried to raise them to a "higher" culture or religion[27].

This book has portrayed Taha as someone who accepted the
differences in Sudanese society. For Taha, diversity was the base of a
pyramid whose peak was unity. He did not accept that diversity was an end
in itself, any more than *shari'a* was. Does this mean that Taha's ideas were
another form of hegemonic discourse, like the other religious ideologies
available in Sudan? Malwal and Deng certainly give that impression.
Perhaps they are too quick to group Taha with other Islamists in Sudan.
Other groups were prepared to sacrifice Sudanese diversity in order to
promote the coherence of the state, and to win its wealth and power for
a dominant or aspiring elite. Taha, in contrast, was prepared to sacrifice
linguistic and cultural diversity to promote or even perfect individual
self-expression. Taha engaged with Sudan's diversity in his 1955 work on
the constitution, and then again in his Republican delegations that toured
Sudan in the 1970s and early 1980s. Members of those delegations give
widely differing evaluations of the experience 20 years later. All of them
believed at the time that they were trying to coax Sudanese people into
a new understanding of society and self, and all of them adapted their
identities to some extent, in order to make themselves attractive to their
interlocutors. However, some now wish that their efforts had aimed at
mutual understanding rather than clear explanation.

Perhaps the opportunity for a more extensive Republican dialogue
with Sudan might have come if political circumstances had not led to
the confrontation with the exponents of the *shari'a* tradition. Sudan's

drift towards *shari'a* alarmed the Republicans, who involved themselves in uncompromising and shrill attacks on Muslim Brothers and their allies, simultaneously seeking self-expression in disconcertingly mystical discourse that may have divorced them from the outside world. However, it would be unfair to define Taha by these drifts towards the private language of spirituality and the jargon of *shari'a* jurisprudence. The movement prized dialogue, its meetings were open to all and based on free discussion. Public encounters always had a propaganda motive, but the Republicans were living in times when their ideas were sharply contested and daily discussed. In a less febrile atmosphere, dialogue might have superseded propaganda.

This book has accepted some criticisms of Taha's hegemonic approach to ideology. But here, a possible anachronism must be noted. Taha wrote most of his works in the 1950s and 1960s, and the few decades that separate then from now also separate the modern and the post-modern. In Taha's day, "comprehensive ideology" was celebrated with more gusto than "diversity", and although Taha the Muslim thinker was always looking for total solutions, he was sincerely committed to the local and the personal. Sudan's diversity is now a popular theme of Sudanese intellectuals. Perhaps Taha's open mind, and his relentless polemic against the state system that could not live with his right to free expression, has led other Sudanese to accept some of his ideas (see below).

Legal reformer
Reworked *shari'a*

Taha's writings on *shari'a* are intense and sometimes impenetrably mystical, but this book suggests that his criticisms of the *shari'a* tradition were unprecedented and far-reaching. *Shari'a* laws were derived from ancient texts, and they were incorporated into a legal system that stressed their immutability for ideological reasons. Although Muslims and their subjects worked out ways of extracting concessions from the *shari'a* edifice, they were never able to challenge the laws explicitly. Taha was able to mount that challenge using an ethical legal scepticism that drew heavily on the Sufi tradition. Unlike previous Sufis, who challenged the ideological and theological trappings of *shari'a*, Taha challenged the laws themselves, using Muslim sources to construct a new set of laws and rights, that would lead to a utopia.

Patrician fudge

Taha chose to pay attention to abrogation, a theory that had important implications for a country where *shari'a* was a contested part of the idiom of the state. However, the abrasive novelty of his teaching was too great for it to gain wide acceptance. Too Islamic for the secularists, and too heterodox for the Muslims, is 'Abdelwahab El-Affendi's judgement[28].

Taha tried to invest in methodological cast-iron rather than political viability. A politically viable solution to the problem of *shari'a* discriminations against women and non-Muslims in a multi-religious, dysfunctional state, would probably have to come from the Muslim establishment. Their private reluctance about the *shari'a* state in the 1960s was noted in chapter 11. In the 1990s, the Islamists overwhelmed their power bases, and they started to deal with the secularist SPLA, the only effective opposition to the regime. They enigmatically committed themselves to "the non-use of religion in politics" in 1994[29]. Sadig al-Mahdi wrote tracts denying the modern validity of *jihad* and proposed greater political participation for women[30]. Hasan al-Turabi, after his political defenestration, reinvented himself as a spokesman for human rights, democracy and feminism. Republicans point out that patricians and Islamists who try to rework *shari'a* need to fudge their methodology. Perhaps this fudge is more palatable to Sudanese public opinion than Taha's wholesale reconstruction of the *shari'a* system. Abdullahi An-Na'im accepts that other actors have more politically viable legislative proposals than did Taha, but that their methodological evasions leave them vulnerable to attack from more radical exponents of the *shari'a* tradition. The Republican task, he says, was not to create a political constituency that would accept their ideas, but to get those ideas straight.

> The difficulty with Sadig fudging is that it is subject to challenge and when challenged it will regress, if you don't have the methodological foundations. [Hasan al-] Turabi and Sadig [al-Mahdi] have similar ideas [to those of Taha]. Republicans would say that people like Sadig and Turabi are just dishonest because they know that their premise does not give the conclusion they claim. Sadig and Turabi would say, "but it is immaterial because the people we are dealing with are not interested in the consistency of our reasoning ... [The Republicans on one hand and Sadig and Turabi on the other represent] two approaches. It's better and proper for someone like the Republicans to do what they do and for others to do what they do [best][31].

Ustaz Mahmud

Most of the people who were interviewed for this book were asked how they might write a biography of Taha. Many of them were friends or followers, and wanted to stress their loyalty and admiration for him. Some wanted to emphasise his stand for women's rights, others wanted to explain his spirituality. Many people would like to place Taha in Sudan's informal canon of saints, or a great tradition of Muslim or Sudanese thinkers. One informant said that although there was a time in his life when he wanted nothing more than to get on television and talk and talk about Taha to everyone, he now felt that his devotion to the man was better expressed by reading his works devoutly, and looking in them for signs to explain his life and the world.

This book has tried to present Taha as a Sudanese man who had a particularly wide range of sympathies and experiences. His family was descended from one of the first Muslim leaders in Sudan, he lived as a farmer and an *effendi*, was an orphan and a father, participated in some of Sudan's huge migrations, lived in towns and hamlets, travelled around much of the Nile valley, made money and gave it all away (twice) and built up a large body of devoted supporters. Taha's mystical imagination sometimes drew him away from ordinary life, at other times he hurled his Sufi hopes and songs at the Sudanese people and then listened patiently for a response. His decision to publicise his aspirations for the highest spiritual station probably meant that he received the response he was listening for. He saw the gallows as a test of his ability to worship God without fear of death or any human being.

Sudanese flatterers of authority are often reminded mockingly that they have begun to fear people, and do not fear God. Fearing God alone is a popular virtue for Sudanese Muslims, and a large number of them came to admire Taha's reckless fear. For him, the gallows may have been a test of his gigantic spiritual aspiration as well – perhaps God would vindicate him, perhaps he would be transformed. He probably went to his death hoping to be the perfect man, but not believing it. He only believed it was yet another attempt at perfection:

> Taha would say, "it's like a golf ball, you can hit it as many times as you like, but it only scores if it falls into the hole. If he is a candidate, it is proved by his success, or disproved by his failure[32].

Taha certainly has a place in Sudanese and Muslim tradition, which he earned by his devoutness, his recklessness, and his intellectual and spiritual curiosity, and his gruellingly polemical approach to opponents. Taha's utopianism is probably worthy of more respect than most people credit it with. It was evidence of a readiness to rethink Sudan's problems from scratch, and articulated a widespread uneasiness about the legal fetishism of 1980s Sudan.

However, I would find it hard to place Taha in a great tradition or a canon of saints. I have tried to avoid the temptation to explain Taha in terms of textual tradition. Instead I have tried to relate him to place and time, the ephemeral, eclectic and profound present where he tried to live.

The most compelling remnant of his personality that I encountered in interviews with followers and acquaintances was his ability to see the significance of the person in front of him, and communicate that significance to that person graciously and attentively. Taha may have a claim to intellectual immortality for his unprecedented reworking of *shari'a*, and he may have his claim to sainthood through his death. It would be no dishonour to Taha to say, however, that he was one of over a million Sudanese who have died over the past 30 years because state, culture, economic power, and religion have not been working right. Probably some of them confused Sudan with utopia, and probably many of them, like Taha, hoped all their lives for a perfect ending. Taha was different because he spent so much time, and gave so much of himself, trying to find an answer to Sudan's big questions, but it would be almost quoting the man to say that he, like every one of those people, was an end in himself.

Endnotes

Introduction

1   Taha, *The Second Message of Islam*, (henceforward *Second Message*) 1987:117

Chapter 1

1   Interview, Sayyida Lutfi 17/6/1998
2   Interview, Ahmad Omer 3/12/1997
3   Interview, 'Ali Lutfi 5/12/1997
4   Interview, Muhammad 'Ali Malik 6/12/1997
5   "Diet in the Gezira irrigated areas of the Sudan", Culwick papers, Sudan Archive, Durham (henceforward SAD/) 428/5/45,54
6   Dirar 1993:48
7   Interview, Sayyida Lutfi 17/6/1997; Muhammad nd:29,41
8   Bedri 1980:121
9   "Blue Nile Trek", 1908, Thomson papers, SAD/404/5/11
10 "History of Football in Sudan", Garrett papers, SAD/479/8/184
11 Letter, Batoul Mukhtar 25/8/1998
12 Jackson 1955:94
13 Interview, Asma Mahmud 28/11/1997. *Ustaz* is a respectful title for a teacher or professional, and Mahmud Muhammad Taha's followers all use the term to refer to him.
14 Interviews, Ahmad Omer 3/12/1997, 'Ali Lutfi 5/12/1997, Sayyida Lutfi 17/6/1997.
15 Interview, Ibrahim Yusuf 13/6/1997
16 Interview, Asma Mahmud 28/11/1997
17 Hasan 1976:62f
18 Interview, Al-Baqir Mukhtar 10/2/1997
19 El Hassan 1993:11
20 Tribal history of the Butana, narrated by the Shukriya shaykh 'Awad al-Karim Abu Sinn to the local British district commissioner. Acland papers, SAD/777/14/34
21 MacMichael 1, 1922 :198
22 Interview, 'Ali Lutfi 5/12/1997
23 *Faki* is a Sudanese word that relates to two Arabic terms, *faqih*, legist; and *faqir*, poor man or ascetic.

24 Kenyon 1991:141
25 Interview, 'Ali Lutfi 5/12/1997
26 See al-Tayib 1963:60
27 "Handing over notes" 1934, Longe papers, SAD/641/5/40
28 Wingate 1905:275
29 Interview, Sayyida Lutfi 17/6/1997
30 Interview, Sayyida Lutfi 17/6/1997
31 "Diary", 1923, Robertson papers SAD/531/1/48f
32 Interview and video record, 'Ali Lutfi 5/12/1997
33 Bedri 1980:183
34 Speech text in Ibrahim Yusuf papers
35 Bedri 1980:202
36 Bedri 1980:107
37 Bedri 1980:182
38 Interview, Ahmed Omer, 3/12/1997
39 Gordon Memorial College (henceforward GMC) "Report and Accounts" 1935, SAD/556/8/30
40 Interview, 'Abdallah al-Dabi, 5/12/1997
41 Dirar 1993:106ff
42 Interview, Amna Lutfi, 28/11/1997

Chapter 2
1 Spaulding 1977
2 Hargey 1981:8f
3 Evans-Pritchard 1971:267
4 Arkell 1955:177
5 Ewald 1990:181f
6 James Bruce, a seventeenth century traveller to Sennar, quoted by Mahmoud in Westerlund and Rosander eds, 1997.
7 Karrar 1992:16
8 Osman 1990:60
9 *Tabaqat*, quoted by Mahmoud, in Westerlund and Rosander ed, 1997:167
10 Mahmoud, in Westerlund and Rosander eds, 1997:167
11 "Preliminary Note on the Tribal History of Medani District and the Gezira", Henderson papers, SAD/660/10/41
12 McHugh 1994
13 see Al Karsani in Daly ed, 1985
14 Spaulding 1979:332
15 Sikainga 1996:8
16 Spaulding and Kapteijns in Craig ed, 1991:92
17 Lovejoy 1983:203
18 Bjørkelo 1989:111
19 Bjørkelo 1989:62
20 Spaulding 1982:6
21 Shuqayr 1972:555
22 "Handover Notes for Rufa'a" Sept 1932, Longe papers, SAD/641/4/6
23 Interview, Khalid Muhammad al-Hasan 23/11/1997
24 Encyclopaedia of Islam, new edition, 1 26

25 Interview, Al-Baqir Mukhtar 10/2/1997
26 Mire in Willis ed., 1985:115.
27 "Statement of an ex-slave in Kabkabeiya", Dupuis papers, SAD/402/5/17
28 Hargey 1981:13
29 Hargey 1981:20
30 One slave was called Bakhita (Lucky) by her captors because she survived a particularly
    vicious slave raid. She ended up in an Italian household in Khartoum, went to Italy,
    became a nun and was beatified in 1993.
31 Spaulding 1982:12
32 Interview, 'Ali Lutfi 5/12/1997
33 Spaulding 1973
34 Toledano 1982:62f on nineteenth century Istanbul and Jeddah prices; Austen, in
    Savage, ed, 1982:216f, on seventeenth and eighteenth century Cairo prices.
35 Hargey 1981:14
36 Ahmed 1992:4
37 Tillion 1983:30
38 Spaulding in Hay and Wright eds, 1982
39 Spaulding 1992
40 Al-Shahi and Moore eds, 1978:101ff
41 Spaulding 1982
42 Hill 1959:43
43 Hill 1959:36
44 Schuver 1996:106
45 Spaulding 1973:33
46 Mamdani 1996:17
47 Mamdani 1996:37f
48 El Zubeir Rahma Mansur 1970:31
49 Abu Shouk and Bjørkelo 1996:xxviii
50 Brenner in Levtzion and Voll eds. 1987:44
51 Levtzion in Levtzion and Voll eds. 1987:35
52 Lovejoy and Hogendorn 1990:219
53 Trimingham 1949:94
54 Osman 1990:37ff
55 Quoted in al-Bashir 1972:24
56 Al-Bashir 1972:32. For an alternative view, see Osman 1990:68
57 Haj al-Mahi, quoted in Osman 1990:71
58 Haj al-Mahi, quoted in Osman 1990:329
59 Hofheinz in O'Fahey ed, 1994:243
60 Warburg in Lovejoy ed, 1981:247
61 Kapteijns 1985:78
62 Slatin 1898:51
63 Smirnov 1974:91
64 Johnson 1993:51
65 Smirnov:1974:102
66 Nugud 1995:91
67 Holt 1970:256f
68 Al-Gaddal in Naqr ed, 1981:156f
69 Abu Shouk and Bjørkelo 1996:xxxi

70 In the early 1870s, one Egyptian pound was the monthly wage of a domestic servant, twice the wage of a farm labourer, or the price of a cow. Bjørkelo 1989:113
71 Trimingham 1949:181f
72 Ismail and Makki 1990:192
73 McHugh 1994:186
74 Al-Karsani in Daly ed., 1985:86
75 Text of Al-Afghani's articles in *L'Intrangiseant*, December 1883, in Kedourie 1966:74ff
76 al-Bashir in El Naqar ed, 1981:189
77 Daly 1986:194-7
78 Mahmoud 1984:17f
79 Sikainga 1996:43
80 Daly 1986:63
81 Daly 1986:125
82 McHugh 1994:186
83 Bekheit in Hasan ed 1971:259
84 Daly 1986:401
85 Daly 1986:149
86 Greenwood, 1941:189
87 Hayder Ibrahim Ali quoted by Makris in Ali ed, 1995:53

Chapter 3
1   Interview, Al-Baqir Mukhtar, 10/2/1997
2   Beshir, 1969:10, McHugh 1994:85ff
3   Beshir 1969:15
4   McHugh 1994:191
5   See 'Abd al-Hamid 3, 1949:101, Beshir 1969:21 for different views.
6   Beshir 1969:194ff
7   See Bray, Clarke and Stephens 1986:60
8   Daly 1986:383
9   Cromer, quoted in Daly 1986:242
10 Beshir 1969:31
11 Kitchener letter 1898, quoted in Beshir 1969:213
12 Interview, 'Ali Lutfi 5/12/1997
13 Bedri 1980:120
14 Bedri 1980:162
15 Interview, Sayyida Lutfi 17/6/1997
16 Interview, Saadia 'Izz al-Din 23/11/1997
17 Interview, Khalid Muhammad al-Hasan 23/11/1997
18 Letter, Girgis Iskander, 7/8/1997
19 GMC "Report", 1933, SAD/555/6/6
20 "Sudan Education Ladder", Education Department, 1927, Cox papers, SAD/662/2/1
21 Letter, Girgis Iskander, 7/8/1997
22 Cromer letter, quoted in Daly 1986:246, see also page 382
23 Interview, Asma Mahmud 28/11/1997
24 Interview, Mahmoud Amin Siddig 3/12/1997
25 Interview, Khalid Muhammad al-Hasan 23/11/1997

240   ISLAM'S PERFECT STRANGER

26 Beasley 1992:181, Bedri 1980:164
27 Interview, Khalid Muhammad al-Hasan 23/11/1997
28 Letter, Girgis Iskander, 15/8/1997
29 Sikainga 1996:104
30 Sikainga 1996:123ff
31 Text in Sikainga 1996:207f
32 Sikainga 1996:83
33 Hillelson 1918:26
34 Thesiger 1987:201
35 "Diary" 1922, Robertson papers , SAD/531/1/9-10.
36 Bedri 1980:199
37 "Handover notes for Rufaa", September 1932, Longe papers, SAD/641/4/6f
38 "Handover notes for Rufaa", September 1932, Longe papers, SAD/641/4/6f
39 "Handover notes for Rufaa", September 1932, Longe papers, SAD/641/4/2
40 "Handover notes for Rufaa", September 1932, Longe papers, SAD/641/4/2
41 Interview, 'Ali Lutfi 5/12/1997
42 MacMichael 1934:269
43 "Handover notes for Rufaa", September 1932, Longe papers, SAD/641/4
44 See Hourani 1991:336
45 Lane 1895:39. The writer describes the nineteenth century house. There are few
    remaining examples of houses from earlier periods, but those which do are similar to
    nineteenth century houses (Noor in Hyland & Al-Shahi ed, 1984:61)
46 See O'Fahey and Spaulding, 1974:80
47 Letter, Girgis Iskander 15/7/1997
48 Dirar 1993:108
49 Interview, Al-Baqir Mukhtar 10/2/1997

Chapter 4
1   Education department, "Sudan Educational Ladder", 1927, Cox papers,
    SAD/662/2/1
2   Education department, "Sudan Educational Ladder", 1927, Cox papers, SAD/662/2/1.
    Sudan's currency, the Egyptian pound, was worth a few pence more than the pound
    sterling.
3   Letter, Girgis Iskander 7/8/1997
4   "Report of the De La Warr Commission", 1937, Cox papers, SAD/665/2/39
5   GMC "Report and Accounts for 1936" SAD/Sud.A.PK1528.4 Gor, page 17
6   GMC, "Report" 1935, SAD/556/8/8
7   GMC "Report and Accounts for 1936" SAD/Sud.A.PK1528.4 Gor, page 17
8   Bray, Clarke and Stephens 1986:87
9   GMC "Syllabus" 1927, SAD/666/11/2
10 GMC "Report and Accounts for 1932" SAD/Sud.A.PK1528.4 Gor, page 18
11 GMC "Report and Accounts for 1933" SAD/Sud.A.PK1528.4 Gor, page 20
12 GMC "Report and Accounts for 1936" SAD/Sud.A.PK1528.4 Gor, page 17
13 GMC "Report and Accounts for 1932-1936" SAD/Sud.A.PK1528.4 Gor
14 GMC "Report and Accounts for 1936", SAD/Sud.A.PK1528.4 Gor, page 33
15 GMC "Report and Accounts for 1935" SAD/Sud.A.PK1528.4 Gor, page 31
16 Interview, Mahmud Amin Siddiq, 3/12/1997
17 Letter, Girgis Iskander, 31/7/1997

18 Letter, Girgis Iskander, 27/7/1997
19 Interview, Mahmud Amin Siddiq, 3/12/1997
20 Daly 1991:70
21 Atiyah 1946:179
22 Interview, Al-Baqir Mukhtar 10/2/1997
23 Atiyah 1946:179
24 Atiyah 1946:141ff
25 GMC "Report and Accounts for 1936" SAD/Sud.A.PK1528.4 Gor, page 31
26 Letter, Girgis Iskander 1/8/1997
27 'Abd al-Rahim 1969:124
28 Shibeika 1965:503
29 El Hassan 1993:72ff
30 Al-Karsani 1987:398
31 Bjørkelo and Abu Shouk 1996; Bedri 1980:83
32 Spaulding and Kapteijns in Craig ed, 1991:95
33 Sikainga 1996:79ff
34 Kurita in Hag el-Safi 1989:27
35 Adu Boahen 1990:254
36 Niblock 1987:166
37 Ewart report on political agitation, 1925, quoted in Daly 1986:291
38 *Hadarat al-Sudan* editorial, 1924, quoted in Mahmoud 1984:134f
39 See Beshir 1974:81f
40 Kurita in Hag el-Safi ed, 1989
41 Beshir 1974:103
42 Makris in Ali ed 1995:54
43 See Zubeida 1993
44 Sanderson 1976:77
45 "History of Football in Sudan", Garrett papers, SAD/479/8/10
46 el Shoush 1963:22ff
47 el Shoush 1963:32
48 El-Affendi 1991:35
49 I am grateful to Girgis Iskander for making this point clear
50 Muhammad Muftah el-Faituri in el Shoush 1963:35
51 In 'Abd al-Rahim 1969:114
52 'Abd al-Halim Muhammad in al-Fajr, 1937, quoted in el-Amin 1981:15. See chapter 5 for more on their politics.
53 'Abd al-Rahim 1969:113; el-Amin 1981:13
54 Letter, Girgis Iskander, 1/8/1997
55 Interview, Al-Baqir Mukhtar, 10/2/1997
56 See el-Amin 1981
57 Letter, Girgis Iskander 7/8/1997

Chapter 5
1 GMC, "Report and Accounts for 1933", SAD/Sud.A. PK1528.4 Gor. page 21
2 Daly 1991:84f
3 "Report of the De La Warr Commission", 1937, Cox papers SAD/665/2/52
4 Interview, Al-Baqir Mukhtar 10/2/1997
5 Sikainga 1995:39

6   Beshir 1969:196, Daly 1991:84
7   Beshir 1974:156
8   Interview, Yusuf Lutfi 3/12/1997
9   Interview, 'Ali Lutfi 5/12/1997. The date of this event is not clear.
10   Interviews, Mahmud Amin Siddig 3/12/1997; Yusuf Lutfi 3/12/1997
11   RB, *al-sifr al-awwal* 1976:16f
12   Interview, Abdullahi An-Na'im 8/11/1997
13   Interview, Yusuf Lutfi 3/12/1997
14   Interview, Mahmud Amin Siddiq 3/12/1997
15   Interview, Mahmud Amin Siddiq 3/12/1997
16   Interview, 'Ali Lutfi 5/12/1997
17   Fawzi 1957:34. The country saw a number of strikes by labourers and workers in Sudan's nascent industries in the 1930s and 40s, Beshir 1974:192
18   El-Amin 1981:17
19   Sikainga 1995:40
20   Daly 1991:130
21   Letter, Girgis Iskander, 31/7/1997
22   Hill 1965:113
23   Interview, Amna Lutfi, 28/11/1997
24   Interview, Ali Lutfi, 5/12/1997
25   Interview, Sayyida Lutfi, 17/6/1997
26   Beasley 1992:347, 352
27   Interview, 'Ali Lutfi 5/12/1997
28   Letter, Batoul Mukhtar 25/8/1998
29   Interview, 'Abd al-Rahman Ali al-Shaykh 17/6/1997
30   Interview, 'Abd al-Rahman Ali al-Shaykh 17/6/1997
31   Letter, Girgis Iskander 4/10/1997
32   Interview, Amna Lutfi 28/11/1997
33   Interview, Al-Baqir Mukhtar 10/2/1997
34   Lichtenthaler 1993:14
35   Galal al-Din in Pons ed, 1980:429
36   Interview, Mahmud Amin Siddig 3/12/1997
37   "History of Football in Sudan", Garrett papers, SAD/479/8/17
38   Interview, Yusuf Lutfi 3/12/1997
39   "Circular, strictly confidential" 1946, Morgan papers SAD/408/1/41
40   Interview, Al-Baqir Mukhtar 10/2/1997

Chapter 6
1   For more detail, see 'Abd al-Rahim 1969, Niblock 1987, Khalid 1990 and Daly 1991
2   Figures from Niblock 1987:86ff
3   Osman and Suleiman in Robson and Lury ed, 1969:439
4   Dirar 1993:62
5   Sudan Political Intelligence Summary (henceforward SPIS) 56, Jan-Apr 1946 in Public Record Office file (henceforward PRO/) FO/371/53328
6   SPIS **56**, Jan-Apr 1946 in PRO/FO/371/53328
7   Case studies in d'Almeida Topor et al 1992
8   SPIS 1947 series, **3**, April-May 1947, in PRO/FO371/63047
9   "History of Football in Sudan", Garrett papers, SAD/479/8/87

10 Interview, Yusuf Lutfi, 3/12/1997

11   RB *ma'alim 'ala tariq tatawwur al-fikra al-jumhuriya khilal thalathin 'aman 1945-1975*, **2**, 1976:58 (henceforward *ma'alim*)

12 Interview, Mona Zanoon Gubara 12/7/1998

13 Interview, Mahmud Amin Siddig 3/12/1997

14 Interview, Yusuf Lutfi 3/12/1997

15 RB, *al-sifr al-awwal* 1976:25

16 RB, *al-sifr al-awwal* 1976:16

17 RB, *al-sifr al-awwal* 1976:21f

18 RB, *al-sifr al-awwal* 1976:20.

19 Telegram 1/10/1945 in PRO/FO/371/53257.

20 Part of the text of *al-nadhir al-'uryan* is reproduced in RB, *ma'alim*, 1, 1976:5

21 Republican pamphlet dated 18/2/1946, in RB, *ma'alim*, 1, 1976:36

22 Letter, Al-Baqir Mukhtar 17/9/1998

23 Interview, Mahmud Amin Siddig 3/12/1997

24 Republican pamphlet dated 18/2/1946, in RB, *ma'alim*, 1, 1976:36

25 Quoted in Ibrahim Yusuf papers.

26 "Memoirs", W C McDowall, SAD/815/8/13

27 "Memoirs", W C McDowall,, SAD/815/8/21

28 SPIS 57, May-June 1946 in PRO/FO371/53328

29 "Report by the Governor-General on the Administration, Finances and Condition of the Sudan in 1947", 1949:16

30 "Report by the Governor-General on the Administration, Finances and Condition of the Sudan in 1947", 1949:16

31 Text of article in *al-Ra'y al-'Amm* 26/6/1946 in Ibrahim Yusuf papers

32 *Al-Ra'y al-'Amm*, 26/6/1946, in Ibrahim Yusuf papers

33 SPIS 58, July-August 1946 PRO/FO371/53328

34 Telegram from a nationalist in El Obeid, in RB, *ma'alim* 1, 1976:31

35 Sadig 1988:56

36 SPIS 58 July-August 1946, PRO/FO371/53328

37 Interview, Yusuf Lutfi, 3/12/1997

38 Interview, Mahmud Amin Siddig, 3/12/1997

39 Interview, Asma Mahmud, 29/11/1997

40 SPIS 58, August-September 1946 in PRO/FO/371/53328

41 SPIS 61, November 1946, reports the Republican departure from the front. PRO/FO371/53328.

42 Text of *al-nadhir al-'uryan*, in RB *ma'alim* 1 1976:5

43 A 1980 study of over 3,000 women from Northern Sudan found that 98% were circumcised and over 83% were infibulated. El Dareer 1982:1

44 Pridie et al 1945

45 'Abd al-Tahir in Pridie et al, 1945

46 'Abd al-Rahman al-Mahdi in Pridie et al 1945.

47 Sudan Government Gazette, Legislative Supplement, 762, 15/2/1946 (Civil Secretary, noting the discussions of the standing committee on female circumcision, 2/4/1949, in PRO/FO371/ 73668)

48 Sanderson 1981:74

49 Beasley 1992:287

50 Beasley 1992:406

51   "Note of a camp-fire debate on female circumcision held on 26/8/38 ..." Newbold papers, SAD/761/4/10

52   Beasley 1992:405ff

53   RB *ma'alim* 1, 1976:40

54   "Diary" 23/9/1946, Johnson papers, SAD/751/11/3

55   RB *ma'alim* 1, 1976:41

56   "Diary" 23/9/1946, Johnson papers, SAD/751/11/4

57   SPIS 59, August-September 1946, PRO/FO371/53328. Turabi's involvement is noted in Lybarger 1997:31

58   Interview, 'Abd al-Rahman Ali al-Shaykh, 17/6/1997

59   Interview, Ahmad Omer, 4/12/1997

60   "Diary" 23/9/1946, Johnson papers, SAD/751/11/5

61   Interview, 'Abd al-Rahman Ali al-Shaykh, 17/6/1997

62   Interview, 'Ali Lutfi 5/12/1997

63   Ali ed 1992:11

64   Interview, 'Ali Lutfi 5/12/1997

65   RB, *ma'alim* 1 1976:46

66   SPIS 61, November 1946, PRO/FO371/53328

67   SPIS 59, August-September 1946, PRO/FO371/53328.

68   Trimingham 1949:268

69   SPIS 1947 4 in PRO/FO371/63047

70   Sanderson 1981:93

71   Sa'id Muhammad Ahmad al-Mahdi quoted in RB *ma'alim* 1 1976:49

72   Muhammad al-Mahdi al-Majdhub poem, November 1946, in Asma Mahmud papers

73   Bayart 1989:155

74   Kenyatta 1961:130ff

75   Interview, Fatma Ibrahim 21/8/1997

76   Lybarger 1997:32

77   Interview, Sayyida Lutfi 17/6/1997

78   Khalid 1990:87

79   "Note on Present Set up of Political Parties in Sudan," Secretariat Central Office, 28/10/1951 in PRO/FO371/90114

Chapter 7

1   Taha, letter to *al-Sha'b* newspaper, on his return to public life, 27/1/1951, text in Ibrahim Yusuf papers

2   Luce papers, SAD/828/3/10-14

3   Interview, Muhammad 'Ali Malik 6/12/1997

4   Interview, Muhammad 'Ali Malik 6/12/1997

5   *Al-Ra'y al-'Amm* newspaper, 24/10/1946, quoted in RB *ma'alim* 1, 1976:47

6   "Regulations as to Sudanese who leave their masters" 1907, in Sikainga 1996:196

7   Letter, Batoul Mukhtar 25/8/1998

8   Interview, Ahmed Omer 12/1997

9   Letter, Al-Baqir Mukhtar, 17/9/1998

10   SPIS 61, November 1946, in PRO/FO371/53328

11   Interview, Ibrahim Yusuf, 13/6/1997

12   McHugh 1994:86

13   Karrar 1992:125ff

14 See Marlow 1997:9
15 See for example Qamar-ul Huda, 1996
16 Trimingham 1949:132
17 Interview, 'Ali Lutfi 5/12/1997
18   Interview, 'Ali Lutfi 5/12/1997
19 Interview, 'Ali Lutfi 5/12/1997
20 Siddiqi 1993:55
21 Saeed Sheikh in Sharif ed, 1 1993:582ff
22 Taha, quoted by Ibrahim Yusuf, interview 13/6/1997
23 Karrar 1992:126
24 Interview, Ibrahim Yusuf 13/6/1997
25 Interview, Ibrahim Yusuf 13/6/1997
26 Letter, Girgis Iskander 19/8/1998
27 Interview, Ibrahim Yusuf 13/6/1997
28 Taha, letter to *al-Sha'b* newspaper, 27/1/1951. Text in Ibrahim Yusuf papers
29 Interview, Abdullahi An-Na'im, 8/11/1997
30 El-Affendi 1991:51
31 Grand qadi Abu Gusaysa in *Al-Ra'y al-'Amm* newspaper 21/11/1968, quoted in Da'ud 1974:98f
32 Taha, quoted by Abdullahi An-Na'im. Interview 8/11/1997
33 Interview, Khalid Muhammad al-Hasan 24/11/1997, see also An-Na'im in Taha, *Second Message* 1987:17n. It has not been possible to examine this will, but several informants have attested that it covers these topics.
34 Interview, Khalid Muhammad al-Hasan 23/11/1997
35 Interview, Yusuf Lutfi 3/12/1997
36 Interview, Sayyida Lutfi 17/6/1997
37 This comes from a newspaper article, written after Taha's death, in the papers of Yusuf Lutfi. Date and author are missing from the clipping..
38 Interview, 'Ali Lutfi 5/12/1997
39 Mukhtar told this to Elnur Hamad, interview 29/11/1997
40 Interview, 'Ali Lutfi 5/12/1997
41 Interview, Yusuf Lutfi 3/12/1997
42 Interview, 'Ali Lutfi 5/12/1997
43 See Foucault 1991:301
44 Remarks by Taha to Abdullahi An-Na'im, interview 10/11/1997
45 Niblock 1987:62ff
46 Interview, Abdullahi An-Na'im 10/11/1997
47 Text of letter to *al-Sha'b*, 28/1/1951 in Taha, *rasa'il wa maqalat* 1973:8
48 Interview, Ibrahim Yusuf 13/6/1997
49 Interview, 'Ali Lutfi 5/12/1997
50 Sadig 1988:59
51 Interview, Al-Baqir Mukhtar 10/2/1997
52 Interviews, 'Ali Lutfi 5/12/1997 and Amna Lutfi 28/11/1997. Sudanese spouses seldom use each other's first name, but call each other "the father of" (*abu*) or "the mother of" (*umm*) their eldest son.

Chapter 8

1 Interview, 'Ali Lutfi 5/12/1997
2 Interview, 'Ali Lutfi 5/12/1997
3 Interview, Amna Mahmud 28/11/1997
4 Interview, Amna Mahmud 28/11/1997
5 Interview, 'Ali Lutfi, 5/12/1997
6 Khalid 1990:152
7 See 'Abd al-Rahim, 1969; Beshir, 1974; Daly 1991
8 RB, *al-sifr al-awwal* 1976:16
9 Sikainga 1996:168
10 SPIS 1948 **7**, September 1948, in PRO/FO/371/69251
11 Legislative Assembly debate on the Constitution Commission, quoted in 'Abd al-Rahim 1969:198
12 Sikainga 1996:170f
13 See el-Amin 1996
14 Text of a 1948 circular in a police note on the SMNL quoted by el-Amin in Middle East Studies 33 (1) 1997:131.
15 SPIS 1947 3, in PRO/FO371/63047
16 Al-Gaddal in Mamdani and Wamba-dia-Wamba eds, 1995:92
17 Warburg 1978:154
18 See El-Affendi 1991:42ff
19 El-Affendi 1991:57
20 SPIS 1948 1 in PRO/FO371/63047
21 El-Affendi 1991:29
22 El-Affendi 1991:153f
23 RB *ma'alim* 1, 1976:55
24 Taha, *qul hadhihi sabili* 1976:12
25 Taha, *qul hadhihi sabili* 1976:16
26 Taha wrote an open letter to the director of UNESCO in 1953 called for a world government. Taha, *rasa'il wa maqalat* 1973:32; RB, *ma'alim* 1, 1976:7
27 Interview, Al-Baqir Mukhtar 18/8/1998
28 Interview, 'Ali Lutfi , 3/12/1997
29 Letter to *Sawt al-Sudan* in Taha *rasa'il wa-maqalat* 1973:38
30 "Note on the Present Set-up of Political Parties in Sudan", Central Office Secretariat, 28/10/1951 in PRO/FO/371/90114
31 SPIS 8 1954, PRO/FO371/108328
32 Interview, 'Ali Lutfi, 3/12/1997
33 El Affendi 1991:65
34 Interview, Ibrahim Yusuf 13/6/1997
35 See al-Turabi 1991:27ff, El-Affendi 1991:40ff, Zayn al-'Abidin 1991:5ff
36 Interview, 'Ali Lutfi 3/12/1997
37 See Hale 1996b:170
38 "The Sudanese Parties and Sects - December 1951", Foreign Office Research Department paper in PRO/FO/371/90113
39 Interview, Amna Lutfi 28/11/1997
40 Interview, Sayyida Lutfi 17/6/1997
41 Interview, Sayyida Lutfi 17/6/1997
42 Shalgami 1991:65

43 Niblock 1987:338.

44 Niblock 1987:31

45 Niblock 1987:33

46 I G & M C Simpson in Craig ed 1991:274

47 Letter, Girgis Iskander 4/9/1997

48 Interview, Ibrahim Yusuf 13/6/1997

49 Interview, Elnur Hamad 30/11/1997

50 Letter, Girgis Iskander 11/9/1997

51 In 1956, the Sudanese pound replaced the Egyptian one as Sudan's currency. It was tied to the dollar, and was valued at over $2·50 until the late 1970s.

52 Letter, Girgis Iskander 16/8/1997

Chapter 9

1 See "Report of the Sudan Electoral Commission"1953, for Mahdist objections to the campaign. PRO/FO371/108336

2 SPIS November 1953 in PRO/FO371/102702

3 Speech by prime minister Isma'il al-Azhari in August 1954, quoted in Sanderson and Sanderson 1981:340

4 Taha, *usus dastur al-sudan* (henceforward *usus*)1968:12

5 Taha, *usus* 1968:26

6 Taha, *usus* 1968:40

7 1953 election returns in Niblock 1987:72f; 1986 election returns in Keen 1994:151, compared to 1956 and 1983 census figures in Ministry of National Planning 1983

8 "Some Notes on the Southern Sudan Education (Wau)", 10/2/1955; 'Abd al-'Aziz al-Sayyad, quoted in Sanderson and Sanderson 1981:338

9 Taha, *usus* 1968:53

10 Taha, *usus* 1968:23f. I am grateful to Al-Baqir Mukhtar for pointing out this passage.

11 Taha, *usus* 1968:12

12 Taha, *usus* 1968:60

13 Khalid 1990:129

14 RB, *ma'alim,* 2 1976:10

15 Letter, Girgis Iskander, 3/3/1998

16 Shalgami (1991) reproduces accounts of participants in the Joda incident.

17 Letter, Girgis Iskander 3/3/1998

18 Speech of Communist trade union leader in Kosti, quoted by Shalgami 1991:115

19 Shalgami 1991:116. Shalgami quotes a statement of *al-hizb al-jamhuri*, the Republican Party, but it is possible that he refers to the Republican Socialist Party, a short lived group which had three representatives in parliament.

20 Letter, Girgis Iskander 3/3/1998

21 Osman and Suleiman in Robson and Lury ed 1969:444

22 Recollections of Abdullahi An-Na'im of Republican views at the time - interview 10/11/1997

23 Interview, Asma Mahmud 28/11/1997

24 Interview, Elnur Hamad 29/11/1997

25 Text of letter to John Voll in Taha *rasa'il wa maqalat* v 2, 1971:7. This was written about fifteen years after the period under discussion, and it is one of the few English texts that Taha produced. However, Taha's remarks tally with remarks he made to Girgis Iskander in the 1950s, and so his own words are quoted anachronistically here.

26 Letter, Girgis Iskander 23/1/1998
27 Ibn al-'Arabi, quoted in Affifi 1939:93
28 Interview, Al-Baqir Mukhtar 6/7/1998
29 Interview, 'Ali Lutfi 5/12/1997
30 Interview, Abdullahi An-Na'im, 10/11/1997
31 Letter to John Voll (in English) in Taha, *as'ila wa ajwiba* **2**, 1971:7
32 Interview, Abdullahi An-Na'im, 10/11/1997
33 Interview, Ibrahim Yusuf 13/6/1997
34 Letter, Girgis Iskander 10/9/1997. Girgis Iskander does not believe that Taha claimed any sort of divine status in his conversations, only that he (and possibly others) would gain that status. Letter, 14/2/1998
35 Hofheinz, in O'Fahey ed, 1994:243
36 Interview, Al-Baqir Mukhtar 18/8/1998
37 Eltayeb 1995:210
38 Interview, 'Ali Lutfi 3/12/1997

Chapter 10
1   See Voll in Warburg and Kupferschmidt ed, 1983:133
2   Interview, Ibrahim Yusuf 13/6/1997
3   Interview, Ibrahim Yusuf 13/6/1997
4   Interview, Ibrahim Yusuf 13/6/1997
5   Women have secondary rights in marriage, divorce, child custody, legal testimony and inheritance. *Shari'a* can also be taken to exclude women from production and formal authority over adult males.
6   Letter, Girgis Iskander,4/10/1997
7   *Al-Ra'y al-'Amm* 22/1/1960, quoted in Da'ud 1974:75
8   Da'ud 1974:77.
9   Interview, Ibrahim Yusuf 13/6/1997
10 Osman and Suleiman in Robson and Lury ed 1969:444
11 See Simonse 1992:302ff for accounts of relationships between traditional leaderships and Northern bureaucrats.
12 Report of an interview between Abboud and bishop Allison, 24/8/1960, Allison papers SAD/803/11/2
13 RB *ma'alim* **1**, 1976:5
14 Text of a letter to Nasser on the revolution in Iraq, 1958, in RB *ma'alim* **2** 1976:27
15 RB, *al-mawqif al-siyasi al-rahin: hawl hawadith al-sa'a,* ("The current political scene: on the events of the hour," henceforward *al-mawqif*) 1984:13
16 'Umar 'Abd al-Rahim Adam in Ali ed, 1995:184
17 Many of them are reproduced in Taha, *rasa'il wa maqalat* 1973
18 Taha, *al-islam* 1968:13
19 Taha, *al-islam* 1968:23ff
20 Taha, *al-islam* 1968:35
21 Taha, *al-islam* 1968:36
22 Taha, *al-islam* 1968:45
23 Jalalayn 1987:95
24 Taha, *al-islam* 1968:45
25 Taha, *al-islam* 1968:48
26 Interview, Ibrahim Yusuf 13/6/1997

27 RB *ma'alim* **2**, 1976:12
28 Interview, Ibrahim Yusuf 13/6/1997
29 Information from Al-Baqir Mukhtar,18/10/1998
30 Interview, 'Ali Lutfi 5/12/1997
31 Interviews, 'Ali Lutfi 5/12/1997, and Mahmud Amin Siddig 3/12/1997
32 Letter, Al-Baqir Mukhtar 17/9/1998
33 Interview, Asma Mahmud
34 Interview, 'Ali Lutfi , 5/12/1997. Other informants date this event to Taha's retreat in Rufa'a, 1948-1951, when he was widely criticised for neglecting his family.

Chapter 11
1   Quoted in Khalid 1990:199
2   El Tayeb 1971:50
3   Ministry of Culture and Information 1974:48ff
4   Interview, Ibrahim Yusuf 13/6/1997
5   Taha, *al-thawra al-thaqafiya*, 1972:8
6   Interview, Mona Zanoon Gubara 12/7/1998
7   Interview, Asma Mahmud 28/11/1997
8   Interview, Abdullahi An-Na'im 8/11/1997
9   Interview, Abdullahi An-Na'im 8/11/1997
10 Taha, *tariq muhammad*, nd:28f
11 RB, *waqa'i' qadiyat bursudan* (henceforward *waqa'i'*) 1, 1975:39
12 Letter to British foreign ministry from ambassador R W D Fowler, PRO/ FO371/190421
13 Akolawin in Hasan ed, 1971:295
14 Letter to British foreign ministry from ambassador R W D Fowler, PRO/ FO371/190421
15 Khalid 1990:237
16 Bekheit in Hasan ed, 1971:264
17 Statement of the National Council for the Islamic Constitution in 1968, quoted in Taha, *al-dastur al-islami, na'm wa la* (henceforward *al-dastur*) 1968:21
18 Da'ud, 1974:3
19 al-Maydan 15/11/1965, quoted in Da'ud, 1974:13-14
20 Interview, Bona Malwal 19/8/1997.
21 Interview, Fatma Ibrahim 21/8/1997
22 Sadig 1988:68
23 Khalid 1990:246
24 El-Affendi 1991:60ff
25 Radio address by Sadig al-Mahdi 17/12/1965, quoted in Warburg 1978:117
26 Adam in Ali ed, 1995:171ff
27 Text of communiqué in British embassy note on political parties, 6/4/1966. PRO/ FO371/190419
28 Harir in Harir and Tvedt eds, 1994:155ff
29 See Beshir 1968:96
30 Taha, *mushkilat al-sharq al-awsat* (henceforward *mushkilat*)1968:5ff
31 Interview, Muhammad Ali Malik, 6/12/1997
32 Taha, *mushkilat* 1968
33 Taha, *mushkilat* 1968:5ff

34   Interview, Ibrahim Yusuf 13/6/1997
35   Figure based on party joining dates listed in a 1988 survey - 35 8% of Republicans questioned said they had joined in this period. Sadig 1988:21
36   Interview, Mona Zanoon Gubara 12/7/1998
37   Interview, Abdullahi An-Na'im 8/11/1997
38   Taha, *al-dastur* 1968:3f
39   Taha, *al-dastur* 1968:42
40   *al-Ra'y al-'Amm* 14/11/1968, quoted in RB *mahkamat al-ridda: 'ar al-quda' al-sudani* 1981:8
41   For example, Ibn Farid (a favourite author of Taha's), quoted in Nicholson 1921:239
42   Taha, *al-risala al-thania min al-islam* (henceforward *al-risala al-thania*) 1968, quoted in Zaki 1985/6:152
43   Taha, *al-risala al-thania* 1968, quoted in Zaki 1985/6:152
44   Taha, *al-risala al-thania* 1968, quoted in Zaki 1985/6:156
45   Court report in Da'ud 1974:93
46   RB, *ma'alim* 2, 1976:24
47   Text of al-Sadiq's judgement in Da'ud 1974:97. Ibn 'Abidin is a name given to two Ottoman legists of the nineteenth century.
48   Fluehr-Lobban 1987:70f
49   RB, *mahkamat* 1981:13
50   Interview, Mahmud Amin Siddig 3/12/1997
51   Ibrahim Yusuf papers
52   Da'ud 1974:99
53   RB *waqa'i'* 1 1975:39
54   RB *mahkamat* 1981:11
55   Zaki 1985/6:98
56   Zaki:1985/6:153, Al-Husayni 'Abd al-Majid Hashim in Zaki 1985/6:11
57   Letter, Girgis Iskander, 4/9/1997
58   see O'Fahey in Brenner ed., 1993:30ff
59   Mansur Khalid, quoted in *waqa'i'* 1 1975:26
60   RB *mahkamat* 1981:14f
61   Interview, Abdullahi An-Na'im 8/11/1997
62   Interview, Abdullahi An-Na'im, 11/11/1997
63   Interview, Asma Mahmud 28/11/1997
64   El Tayeb 1971:37f
65   Interview, Abdullahi An-Na'im 17/11/1997
66   Interview, Asma Mahmud 30/11/1997
67   Text of letter to *Sawt al-Sudan* in Taha *rasa'il wa maqalat* 1973:36
68   Coulson 1969:96ff
69   Khalid 1990:213

Chapter 12
1   Shaban 1971:8
2   Al-Shafi'i 1961:123ff
3   RB, *al-din wa rijal al-din 'abr al-qurun* 1975:4
4   Fadel 1996
5   See Lapidus 1996
6   Davison 1973:55

7   Ahmed 1992:65
8   Fadel 1997:185
9   Lapidus 1988:251
10   Ahmed 1992:4
11   al-Barmaki (d 808) quoted in Marlow 1997:38
12   AlSayyad 1991:3
13   Rodinson 1974:62
14   Rodinson 1974:30ff
15   Zubeida 1995:152
16   Sikainga 1996:114 Na'im
17   See Gilsenan 1992:32
18   Toledano 1982:129f
19   Hodgson 1, 1974:350
20   Taha, *Second Message* 1987:109
21   Weiss in Heer ed, 1990:59
22   Rahman 1979 :138
23   al-Ghazali 1959 :16
24   See Osman 1990:37ff
25   "Letter to the Pakistani attorney-general on the matter of Pakistan's constitution and the Qur'an", in *Sawt al-Sudan* 1953; text in Taha, *rasa'il wa maqalat* 1973:38ff
26   Taha, *al-islam* 1968:26
27   See for example al-Turabi 1980
28   al-Turabi 1980:36. I am grateful to Eltayeb Hassan for pointing this out to me
29   Taha, *Second Message*, 1987:33
30   Taha, *Second Message*, 1987:35
31   Burton 1990:20
32   Burton 1990:185
33   Taha, *Second Message*, 1987:139
34   Taha, *Second Message*, 1987:140
35   Taha, *tatwir shari'at al-ahwal al-shakhsiya* (henceforward *tatwir*) 1979:76
36   Taha, *tatwir* 1979:73
37   Taha, *Second Message*, 1987:156
38   Taha, *Second Message*, 1987:132ff
39   Taha, *Second Message*, 1987:137
40   Taha, *tatwir* 1979:45, citing Qur'an 3:159; Taha, *Second Message*, 1987:157
41   2:102, Arberry 1986:13
42   Taha *Second Message* 1987:40
43   Lichtenthaler 1993:24
44   al-Tabari 1, 1968:287f
45   Taha, *tatwir* 1979:73
46   Bell and Watt 1970:108
47   Taha, *Second Message* 1987:125
48   Taha, *Second Message* 1987:125
49   Taha, *tatwir* 1979:79
50   Taha, *tatwir* 1979:40f
51   Kamali 1989:153
52   Taha, *Second Message* 1987:142
53   Taha, *Second Message* 1987:142

54 The work is summarised in Eltayeb 1996:52f and An-Na'im in Taha, *Second Message* 1987:6ff
55 Taha, *tatwir* 1979:9
56 Henri Coudray, quoted in Renaud, nd:3
57 Coulson 1964:49
58 Interview, Abdullahi An-Na'im 8/11/1997
59 Interviews, Al-Baqir Mukhtar 10/2/1997 and Abdullahi An-Na'im 8/11/1997; see Al-Shahi in Cunnison and James eds, 1972
60 Noredenstam 1968:104f, 200f
61 Makris 1996
62 Sikainga 1996:120
63 An-Na'im 1990:59
64 Lapidus 1988:195
65 Interview, Abdullahi An-Na'im, 10/11/1997
66 Taha, *tatwir* 1979:46
67 Taha, *risalat al-salat* 1979:10
68 Taha, *risalat al-salat* 1979:11
69 Dar in Sharif ed, 1 1993:362
70 Taha uses two words usually translated as "human" - *bashar* and *insan*. The latter is the highest humanity which was Muhammad's experience and is the vocation of all men and women. Taha, *tatwir* 1979:39
71 Taha, *risalat al-salat* 1979:13
72 Taha, *al-marksiya fil-mizan* (henceforward *al-marksiya*) 1977:21f
73 Taha, *al-marksiya* 1977:17ff
74 Ewald 1990:181f
75 "Positive laws and heavenly laws" 25/8/1952 in Taha *rasa'il wa maqalat* 1973:22vf
76 Taha, *al-risala al-thania* nd:43
77 See for example RB *lajnat ta'dil al-qawanin bija'liha lihadd al-khamr ta'ziran tuzayyif al-shari'a wa tu'awwaq ba'th al-din* 1979:11
78 Taha, *Second Message* 1987:107
79 Affifi in Sharif ed, 1, 1993:418
80 Taha, *Second Message* 1987:39
81 Zaki 1985/6:128ff
82 Taha, *tatwir* 1979:89
83 Taha, *al-marksiya* 1977:8
84 Taha, *tatwir* 1979:20
85 Taha, *tatwir* 1979:35
86 Taha, *tatwir* 1979:48
87 Taha, *al-risala al-thania* nd:11
88 Interview, Abdullahi An-Na'im 11/11/1997

Chapter 13
1 Text in Khalid 1985:47
2 Fuller histories of the period in Niblock 1987, Khalid 1990
3 Interview, Al-Baqir Mukhtar
4 Interview, Abullahi An-Na'im 8/11/1997
5 RB, *ma'alim* 2, 1976:45. The 'Arakiya are a localised Gezira tariqa.
6 RB, *ma'alim* 2, 1976:52

7   RB, *ma'alim* 2, 1976:55

8   RB, *ma'alim* 2, 1976:57

9   Interview, Omer El Garrai 25/11/1997

10   Ministry of Culture and Information 1974:55

11   RB, *al-sulh khayr* ("Reconciliation is good") 1977:12

12   See Howard 1988

13   Interview, Omer El Garrai 25/11/1997

14   Ministry of Culture and Information 1974:55

15   For example, text of lecture in RB *al-ustadh mahmud muhammad taha yuhaddith al-nisa' fi huquqihinn* ("Ustaz Mahmud Muhammad Taha speaks to women about their rights"), 1976

16   Interview, Yusuf Hasan 14/6/1997

17   Manuel 1988:17

18   Sadig 1988:29

19   Interview, Ibrahim Yusuf 13/6/1997

20   Audio tape 21/6/1979

21   Osman 1990:123

22   Quote in Renaud, nd:2

23   Interview, Mona Zanoon Gubara 12/7/1998, letter, Elnour Hamad 12/4/1998

24   Figures in Hale, 1996b:129

25   Abu Nasr 1965:157ff

26   Interview, Fatma Yusuf 5/12/1997

27   Howard 1988:88

28   Interview, 'Awatif 'Abd al-Gadir

29   Interview, Asma Mahmud 29/11/1997

30   Interview, Asma Mahmud 29/11/1997

31   Howard 1988:90

32   Interview, Al-Baqir Mukhtar

33   Interview, Yusuf Lutfi 3/12/1997

34   Interview, Al-Baqir Mukhtar 17/6/1997

35   Interview, Asma Mahmud 30/11/1997

36   Interview, Abdullahi An-Na'im 8/11/1997

37   Interview, Elnour Hamad 30/11/1997

38   Interview, Asma Mahmud 30/11/1997

39   Taha, quoted by Elnour Hamad, interview 30/11/1997

40   Letter, Elnour Hamad 12/4/1998

41   Eltayeb 1995:210

42   Letter, Girgis Iskander, 4/10/1997

43   Taha, *tatwir* 1979:59

44   Interview, Asma Mahmud 30/11/1997

45   Interview, Steve Howard, 23/11/1997.

46   Henri Courday quoted in Renaud, nd:4

47   Dirar 1993:106f

48   See Howard 1988

49   Taha, *al-din wal-tanmiya al-ijtima'iya* (henceforward *al-din wal-tanmiya*) 1974:16ff

50   El Hassan 1993:85

51   An-Na'im in Taha, *Second Message* 1987:8

52   Interview, Abdullahi An-Na'im 17/11/1997

53 Text of letter in RB, *al-din wa rijal al-din 'abr al-sinin* (henceforward *al-din wa rijal al-din*) 1975:40
54 An-Na'im in Taha, *Second Message* 1987:7f, and interview, 8/11/1997
55 Interview, Eltayeb Hassan 21/8/1998
56 Text in Taha, *al-din wal-tanmiya*, 1974:25ff
57 RB, *liqa' idha'i ma' al-ustadh mahmud muhammad taha* ("A radio interview with ustaz Mahmud Muhammad Taha") 1977:8
58 Interview, Eltayeb Hassan 23/8/1998
59 Interviews, Khalid Muhammad al-Hasan 23/11/1997 and 'Awatif 'Abd al-Gadir 25/11/1997

Chapter 14
1 Interview, 'Abdallah al-Dabi 5/12/1997
2 Al-Karsani, nd:4
3 Taha, *ta'allamu kayfa tasallun* 1972:64
4 Interview, Abdullahi An-Na'im 8/11/1997
5 Interview, Omer El Garrai 25/11/1997
6 Interview, Khalid Muhammad al-Hasan 24/11/1997
7 Interview, Al-Baqir Mukhtar 10/2/1997
8 Interview, Abdullahi An-Na'im 11/11/1997
9 Interview, Muhammad 'Ali Malik 6/12/1997
10 Interview, Asma Mahmud 29/11/1997
11 Interview, Khalid Muhammad al-Hasan 23/11/1997
12 Interview, Elnour Hamad 29/11/1997
13 Interview, Al-Baqir Mukhtar
14 Interview, Al-Baqir Mukhtar. Unfortunately, this book is unobtainable
15 RB, *al-ikhwan al-jumhuriyun fi jaridat al-ahram al-misriya* 1976
16 Interview, Muhammad 'Ali Malik 6/12/1997
17 Mubarak 1994
18 Taha deals with this theme in his last interview, published in *al-Jami'a* magazine in May 1985.
19 Interview, Muhammad 'Abd al-Khalig 17/6/1997
20 Interview, Khalid Muhammad al-Hasan 23/11/1997
21 Sadig 1988:26
22 Interview, Khalid Muhammad al-Hasan 23/11/1997
23 Taha, *al-islam* 1968:48; text of letter to Republicans 14/2/1984 , in Yusuf Lutfi papers; interview, Muhammad 'Ali Malik 6/12/1997
24 Interview, Khalid Muhammad al-Hasan 23/11/1997
25 Taha, *usus* 1968:67f
26 Interview, Ibrahim Yusuf 13/6/1997
27 Interview, 'Ali Lutfi 5/12/1997. A 1977 booklet dealing with sectarian misdeeds claimed that Mahdist (Ansar) politics was many times more corrupt than that of the Khatmiya. RB, *al-sulh khayr* 1977:4
28 Sadig 1988:17ff
29 Sadig 1988:18
30 Interview, 'Abdelwahab El-Affendi 31/3/1998
31 quoted in RB *waqa'i'* 1, 1975:8
32 RB *waqa'i'* 2, 1975:26

33 RB *waqa'i'* 18
34 RB *waqa'i'* 18
35 Interview, Al-Baqir Mukhtar, 17/6/1997
36 Letter, Girgis Iskander 17/2/1998
37 Interview, Fatma Ibrahim 21/8/1997
38 Interview, Asma Mahmud 29/11/1997
39 Interview, Omer El Garrai, 26/11/1997
40 Interview, Abdullahi An-Na'im 11/11/1997
41 Interview, Abdullahi An-Na'im 8/11/1997

Chapter 15
1   Khalid 1985:143
2   RB, *al-sulh khayr* 1977:31
3   From a list of Sufi and Mahdist virtues written by an informant who requested anonymity
4   Warburg 1978:40
5   See El Hassan 1993
6   See Al-Karsani in Brenner ed 1993:146
7   Faisal Islamic Bank nd:2ff
8   Shaaeldin and Brown in Barnett and 'Abdelkarim eds 1988:131ff
9   RB, *al-din wa rijal al-din* 1975:16
10 Text of Muslim World League letter in RB, *al-din wa rijal al-din* 1975:38
11 Interviews, Abdullahi An-Na'im, 8/11/1997; and Eltayeb Hassan 23/8/1998
12 See RB, *lajnat ta'dil* 1979
13 RB, *al-sulh khayr*
14 Interview, Khalid Muhammad al-Hasan, 24/11/1997
15 RB, *bank faysal al-islami!?* ("Faisal Islamic Bank!?")1983
16 Muslim Brother activities for the period 1977-1983 are described in RB, *fitnat iran* 1979; RB, *ila mata hadha al-'abath bi-'uqul al-nas wa bi-din allah* ("How long will they fool with people's minds and God's religion", henceforward *ila mata*) 1980; RB, *al-mawqif* 1984; Muti'i, 1986; Ali in Guazzone ed, 1995:198
17 Tadamon Islamic Bank 1984 and Faisal Islamic Bank (Sudan) 1984 gives details of banks' involvement in imports in the early 1980s.
18 RB, *atfa'u nar al-fitna: hawl hawadith al-sa'a* ("Extinguish the fire of conflict: on the events of the hour", henceforward *ila mata*) 1982:18
19 RB *mahkamat* 1981:20
20 RB *mahkamat* 1981:20ff
21 Taha, *Second Message* 1987:167; Taha, *tatwir* 1977:35
22 Taha, *as'ila wa ajwiba* 2, 1971:5 (English text).
23 Taha, *al-risala al-thania* 1971:42
24 Interview, Asma Mahmud 28/11/1997
25 Interview, Abdullahi An-Na'im 17/11/1997
26 RB, *al-taqlid!! wal-asala!! wal-usala'!!* (henceforward *al-taqlid!!!*) 1982:3
27 Interview, Abdullahi An-Na'im 8/11/1997
28 Letter, Girgis Iskander 10/2/1998
29 RB, *The Return of Christ* nd:26 (English version of 1979 pamphlet).
30 Al-Karsani in Brenner ed 1993:149
31 Interview, 'Abdelwahab El-Affendi 31/3/1998

32 Taha, *al-qur'an wa mustafa mahmud* 1971:1
33 RB, *al-taqlid!!* 1982:14
34 Interview, Elnour Hamad 29/11/1997
35 Interview, Steve Howard 23/11/1997
36 RB, *adab al-salik fi tariq muhammad* (henceforward *adab al-salik*) 1982:57
37 RB, *adab al-salik* 1982:50; Qur'an 18:79
38 See Nicholson 1921:77ff for more on the perfect man, and Eltayeb 1995:130ff for more on Taha's views on the subject
39 Haj al-Mahi, quoted in Osman 1990:307
40 Interviews, Abdullahi An-Na'im, Asma Mahmud, Khalid Muhammad al-Hasan, letters from Girgis Iskander.
41 Quoted from a Muslim Brother poster in RB, *ila mata hadha al-'abath* 1980:23
42 RB, *ila mata hadha al-'abath* 1980:23
43 Interview, Abdullahi An-Na'im 8/11/1997
44 I am very grateful to Eltayeb Hassan for clarifying some of the developments in Taha's thoughts.
45 Interview, 'Abdelwahab El-Affendi 31/3/1998
46 Interview, Steve Howard, 23/11/1997

Chapter 16
1   De Waal 1989:172
2   De Waal in Daly and Sikainga eds, 1993:149
3   RB, *atfa'u* 1982:9
4   RB, *atfa'u* 1982:11
5   Tadamon Islamic Bank 1984:8
6   Al-Karsani in Brenner ed 1993:149
7   Zein 1989:125
8   Zein 1989:74
9   See Khalid 1985:259ff; Zein 1989:197
10 Economist Intelligence Unit (EIU), **3**, 1983
11 Zein 1989:64
12 Interview, Abdullahi An-Na'im 8/11/1997
13 Ibrahim Yusuf papers
14 Ibrahim Yusuf papers
15 Frost ed, 1983:317
16 Muti'i 1986:18
17 Interview, 'Abdallah al-Dabi 5/12/1997
18 Part of the text of *al-hawas al-dini* in Muti'i 1986:19
19 Interview, Bona Malwal 19/8/1997
20 Ibrahim Yusuf papers
21 Interview, Abdullahi An-Na'im 8/11/1998
22 Ibrahim Yusuf papers
23 Sadig al-Mahdi lecture, 11/6/1997
24 Interview, Yusuf Hasan 14/6/1997
25 See An-Na'im 1986 for a fuller account of the legislative changes
26 Quoted by Badal in Harir and Tvedt ed, 1993:112
27 See Hamid 1991:201
28 Miller 1996:137

29 El-Affendi 1991:122f
30 For example, Zayn al-'Abidin 1991:5
31 Spaulding 1977
32 For an account of an analogous, but different process in Middle Eastern Islam, see Brown 1997
33 Zein 1989:200
34 Khalid 1990:310
35 EIU 4, 1983
36 A prisoner quoted by Asma Mahmud, interview 30/11/1997
37 Dirar 1993:108
38 Interview, Asma Mahmud 30/11/1997
39 Interview, Asma Mahmud 30/11/1997
40 Interview, Steve Howard 23/11/1997
41 Text of letter, Taha 14/11/83, in papers of Ibrahim Yusuf
42 Text of letter dated 14/2/1984, papers of Yusuf Lutfi
43 Interview, Steve Howard 23/11/1997
44 RB, *al-mawqif* 1984:60ff
45 RB, *al-mawqif* 1984:78
46 Ibn Kathir, quoted in RB, *al-mawqif* 1984:78
47 Quoted in Zein 1989:242
48 "To all Christian faithful", Letter from archbishop Gabriel Zubeir Wako, 23/9/1983, Allison papers SAD/813/4/7
49 An-Na'im 1986:205
50 See Woodward 1988; Daly and Sikainga 1993; Barnett and 'Abdelkarim 1988 for more information.
51 Interviews, 'Abdallah al-Dabi 5/12/1997 and Muhammad Ali Malik, 6/12/1997, Ibrahim Yusuf papers.
52 Text in An-Na'im's introduction to Taha *Second Message* 1987:
53 Ibrahim Yusuf papers
54 Ibrahim Yusuf papers
55 Ibrahim Yusuf papers
56 Interview, Muhammad 'Ali Malik 6/12/1997
57 Interview, Abdullahi An-Na'im 8/11/1997; al-Sharif 1996:14
58 Ibrahim Yusuf papers
59 An-Na'im in Taha *Second Message* 1987:13.
60 in Taha *Second Message* 1987:14
61 EIU 1, 1985
62 RB, *al-kayd al-siyasi wal-mahkama al-mahzila,* 1985:16
63 An-Na'im in Taha *Second Message* 1987:15
64 Al-Kabbashi 1986:85ff
65 For an alternative view, see El Zein nd
66 Text of review in al-Muti'i 1986:265
67 Interview, 'Abdallah al-Dabi 5/12/1997
68 Zein 1989:74
69 Interview, Abdullahi An-Na'im 8/11/1997
70 Interview, Fatma Ibrahim 21/8/1997
71 Hamid 1991:203
72 Interviews, Asma Mahmud, 29/11/1997 and 30/11/1997

73   Interview, Muhammad 'Ali Malik 6/12/1997
74   Sa'd 1985
75   Interview, Abdullahi An-Na'im 17/11/1997
76   Sa'd 1985
77   Sa'd 1985
78   Miller 1996:12

Chapter 17

1   EIU 1985 1
2   Transcript of recantation in al-Muti'i 1986:215
3   Transcript of recantation in al-Muti'i 1986:222
4   Interview, Abdullahi An-Na'im 8/11/1997
5   Ibrahim Yusuf papers
6   EIU 1985 2
7   Al-Kabbashi, 1986:114
8   Khalid 1990:303
9   RB, *ma dha qal al-'alim 'an al-ustadh mahmud,* nd:13
10   Sadig 1988:93
11   Sadig 1988:94
12   Sadig 1988:91
13   An-Na'im in Taha, *Second Message* 1987:19
14   Arberry 1982:95
15   Interview, Abdullahi An-Na'im 17/11/1997
16   Interview with Fatma Yusuf Guway 5/12/1997.
17   al-Sharif 1996 :14
18   EIU 1985 2
19   De Waal in Daly and Sikainga 1993:156
20   El-Affendi 1991:128
21   Al-Karsani in Brenner ed 1993
22   Hajj Nur, quoted in al-Muti'i 1986:248
23   Taha, *al-din wal tanmiya* 1974:19
24   Howard 1988:87
25   Taha, *Second Message* 1987:11
26   Deng 1995:127
27   Interview, Bona Malwal 19/8/1997
28   Interview, 'Abdelwahab El-Affendi 31/3/1998
29   *Africa Confidential* 3/2/1995
30   al-Mahdi 1992b
31   Interview, Abdullahi An-Na'im 11/11/1997
32   Interview, Abdullahi An-Na'im, 17/11/1997

Appendix 1

Constitution of the Republican Party, 1945

Name: The Republican Party

Principal: Total withdrawal [of British forces]

Aims: a. Setting up a free, Republican, democratic, Sudanese government which maintains the present geographical borders of Sudan
b. National unity
c. Promotion of the individual and concern for the worker and the peasant
d. Fighting illiteracy
e. Propaganda for Sudan
f. Deepening relations with Arab and neighbouring countries

Membership: 1. Open to all Sudanese over 18 years of age
2. Open to all citizens born in Sudan, or continuously resident for over ten years

Party funds: To be used for the aims for which the party has been created

Glossary of non-English terms

ansar	Supporters or followers. The word refers to the supporters of the prophet Muhammad, but was taken up by the Mahdi, and became the name of the Mahdist sect.
'Arakiyin	A small, localised Sufi *tariqa* at Abu Haraz on the Blue Nile, one of the oldest in Sudan.
asala	Authenticity. Taha uses it to mean self-realisation, finding the real self.
asil	An authentic person, someone with *asala*.
'awwam	Common people, the mass at the bottom of Sufi and class hierarchies.
Azhar	An ancient university in Cairo; one of the central institutions of the *shari'a* tradition.
Baggara	Cattle nomads based on the northern bank of the Bahr al-Arab, the river which divides north and south Sudan west of the Nile.
Berberine	A British term for tribes of the far north of Sudan, such as the Ja'alis.
Bilaylab	A clan of Taha's Rikabiya tribe, descended from Hasan wad Bilayl.
daym	Urban quarter. Khartoum *daym*s were considered slums in Taha's day.
Dinka (Jieng)	A group of semi-pastoralist cattle herders, the largest tribe in Sudan.
effendi	In the early part of the twentieth century, the word was used to describe a person with a secular education who wore European or Egyptian clothes to his white-collar job.
effendiya	The *effendi*s as a social grouping.
faki / feki	A Sudanese word related to *faqih* (legist) with the anomalous plural *fugara*, relating to *faqir* (a poor man or a Sufi).
fiqh	*Shari'a* jurisprudence; the codification of norms from *shari'a* sources into laws that can be used in courts or elsewhere.
hadd	A punishment stipulated by the Qur'an for an offence specified by the Qur'an. The punishments - stoning, flogging, crucifixion and amputation - are considered to be rights assigned to God, not man, and there is no pardon for a *hadd* offence.

hadith	A record of what the prophet Muhammad said, did or tacitly approved.
haqiqa	Ultimate reality, a common Sufi term.
Hindiya	A large, centralising *tariqa* based near Khartoum.
hudud	Plural of *hadd*.
ijtihad	Independent legal reasoning based on Muslim source texts.
'ilm	Knowledge, science or mysticism.
'ilmiya	Mysticality, or the esoteric quality that Taha finds in exoteric things.
insan	A human being. Taha uses the term to describe humanity as it should be.
al-insan al-kami	The perfect man, or the person who perfects his or herself through a process of failure, forgiveness and success, thus expressing God's presence to others. The figure is associated with the prophet Muhammad and other high spiritual ranks.
irada	Will, used by Taha to describe God's irresistible will.
al-islam al-'amm	General Islam, one of Taha's terms for lower, concessive Islam of the first message
al-islam al-khass	Special Islam, one of Taha's terms for the higher ethical Islam of the second message
Ja'ali	Sedentary Arabised Muslims based on the Nile banks north of Khartoum. They were greatly affected by Turkiya migrations and many of them became *jallaba*.
jahiliya	The period of barbarous ignorance before the time of the prophet Muhammad. Many Muslim reformers, including Taha, refer to a new *jahiliya*, meaning an age when Muslims do not meet the reformers' standards of religious knowledge.
jallaba	Migrant traders, mainly from the northern Nile valley. Many were forced to leave their homes during the Turkiya, and take up petty trade or slaving. In contemporary Sudan, the term is used to describe rich merchants from the Arabised centre of Sudan who often dominate commerce in marginal areas.
jihad	Warfare for the faith; war legitimized by religious ideology. *Jihad* is also used to describe the spiritual struggles of the believer.
Kababish	Camel nomads of northern Kordofan.
kafa'a	Parity; in *shari'a*, a principle that states that spouses should belong to similar social classes.
khawass	The elect or elite, used to describe social and spiritual hierarchies.
khalwa	The place or action of retreat for a mystic. In Sudan, these retreats became community centres and eventually the word was used to describe Qur'anic basic schools.
Khatmiya	One of the largest *tariqa*s in Sudan and the most successful centralising religious organisation of the nineteenth century.
Khedive	A title used by Egyptian rulers in the late nineteenth and early twentieth centuries.
maddah	A hymn singer. Urban *maddah*s are often religious mendicants.
madih	A hymn in praise of the prophet.
malamati	A Sufi school of blame; a Sufi who deliberately commits sins in

order to gain the censure of the world and thereby rely more heavily on God.

al-maqam al-mahmud — The laudable station (Qur'an), a place from which a person is able to address God directly. For many Muslims, this refers to the prophet Muhammad, who will intercede for humanity or for Muslims on the day of judgement from his laudable station. Taha, and other Sufis, saw it as a station which other mortals could reach.

masid — A religious centre (Sudanese Arabic).

merkaz — Local administrative centre.

mi'raj — The prophet Muhammad's night journey to heaven, celebrated by Sufis.

mufti — Senior *shari'a* legist, author of *fatwa*s.

mulah — A stew, often made of dried fermented okra, the simplest Sudanese hot meal.

mu'amalat — Transactions; a division of *shari'a* dealing with commerce and family status; along with *hudud*, *mu'amalat* are the only enforceable parts *shari'a*.

mustawtan — Sudanese of Levantine or Egyptian origin.

nazir / nazir khatt — Village headman or chief of an administrative division (*khatt*).

Noble Spiritual Beliefs — Term used in Sudan's 1973 constitution to describe African traditional religions

Nuba — Linguistically and culturally related inhabitants of the Nuba mountains in Kordofan, whose culture has been little affected by Arabic or Islam.

Nubian — Partially Arabised sedentary Nile cultivators who live on the border between Egypt and Sudan.

qadi (grand *qadi*) — Judge: the grand *qadi* is the senior *shari'a* judge in Sudan.

rasul — Apostle or messenger, a title of Muhammad.

rida — Desire, taken by Taha to mean God's preference for humanity, as distinguished from his irresistible will, *irada*.

Rikabiya — Taha's tribe, which traced its ancestry to the prophet Muhammad.

Sadigab — Sufi *tariqa* set up by Muhammad 'Abd al-Sadig, and the name of a clan of the Rikabiya tribe descended from him.

sayyid / Sayed — Title of a descendant of the prophet Muhammad.

shari'a — Some authorities define *shari'a* as the infallible sources of Islam (the Qur'an and *sunna*); others define it more narrowly as the legislative content of those sources; this book usually defines it as the laws derived from the Qur'an and *sunna* and the tradition of interpretation based on those laws. Taha used the term in different ways.

Shaygiya/Shaygi — A sedentary, Arabised Muslim tribe based in the far north of Sudan.

shaykh / sheikh — Religious or tribal leader.

Shukriya — Camel nomads or semi-nomads of the Butana, the dominant tribe of the region. Their leading family, the Abu Sinns, had wide influence.

Sinnab — Collective name for the Abu Sinn family.

sudani	Sudanese, a word that described non-Arabised groups, often former slaves, in the north of Sudan. It was eventually taken to denote Sudanese nationality.
sura	A chapter of the Qur'an.
sunna	The way of the prophet Muhammad; all that he said, did or tacitly approved. *Sunna* is recorded as *hadith*. Taha believed that Muhammad's own practice was a higher Islam, contrasted to the lower Islam of *shari'a*.
Ta'aysha	One of the Baggara groups of Darfur.
takfir	The act of declaring an opponent an infidel, and by extension an outlaw.
taqlid	Tradition, *shari'a* structures based on tradition rather than independent engagement with legal sources.
tariq	Way, especially a mystical way to God.
tariga / tariqa	Way, a mystical way to God. In many countries, *tariga*s institutionalised a spiritual method and they became religious "orders" or organisations.
Tijaniya	A Sufi *tariga* from West Africa which came to western Sudan in the nineteenth century.
umma	Can be used to mean the world-wide Muslim community, or a Muslim nation, adopted as Mahdist party name.
'ulama'/ulema	*shari'a* legist, especially in reference to a bureaucratised urban class.
ustaz	A respectful term for a teacher or a professional in Sudan.
Wahhabi	A rigorist Arabian form of Islam.
wali	a departed Sufi saint, a departed *shaykh* noted for piety.
waqtajiya	A group of Republicans who stressed Taha's spiritual claims and waited for the *waqt*, or time of his transformation.
wasil	Someone who has arrived at a personal encounter with God.
wusul	The state of a *wasil*
zakat	Qur'anic alms tax of two and a half percent on capital
zariba	Slave raiding stations set up in southern Sudan in the nineteenth century.
zikr	Remembrance or invocation of the name of God; for Sufis, *zikr* is a communal and sometimes ecstatic performance.

Acronyms

DC	District Commissioner
DUP	Democratic Unionist party
EIU	Economist Intelligence Unit
GGC	Graduates' General Congress
GMC	Gordon Memorial College
ILM	Islamic Liberation Movement
IMF	International Monetary Fund
£E	Egyptian pound
£S	Sudanese pound
MP	Member of Parliament
NA	Native Administration
NIF	National Islamic Front
NUP	National Unionist party
PDP	People's Democratic party
PRO	Public Record Office
RB	Republican Brotherhood
SAD	Sudan Archive, Durham
SPS	Sudan Political Service
SPIS	Sudan Political Intelligence Summary
SMNL	Sudanese Movement for National Liberation
SPLA	Sudan People's Liberation Army
SSO	State Security Organ
SSU	Sudan Socialist Union
SWU	Sudan Women's Union
WFL	White Flag League

Bibliography

Archive material

PUBLIC RECORDS OFFICE, LONDON
1. FO371: Foreign Office, Egypt, political correspondence

SUDAN ARCHIVE, DURHAM
The following collections are cited:
1. P B E Acland papers 707, 777
2. O C Allison papers 803, 813
3. G R F Bredin papers 815
4. G M Culwick papers 428
5. S J Claydon papers 631
6. Cox papers 662, 665
7. C G Dupuis papers, 402
8. R C Garrett papers 479
9. Gordon Memorial College papers 555 - 579, 662 - 673
10. K D D Henderson papers 660
11. Mrs W Johnson papers 751
12. J D Longe papers 641
13. W H T Luce papers, 828
14. W C MacDowell papers 815
15. C E F Morgan papers, 408
16. D Newbold papers, 761
17. J W Robertson papers 531
18. S R Simpson papers, 627
19. D S B Thomson papers 404

Official reports

1. "Report by the Governor-General on the Administration, Finances and Condition of Sudan", series (see also Wingate in published sources).
2. "Situation of Human Rights in Sudan", report by Gaspar Biro, United Nations Special Rapporteur for Human Rights in Sudan, submitted to the United Nations Human Rights Commission, Geneva, February 1996

Private papers

1. Asma Lutfi papers: poetry in praise of Taha by Muhammad al-Mahdi al-Majdhub and some Republican pamphlets from the 1960s
2. Ibrahim Yusuf papers: handwritten transcriptions of official documents and private comment on documents relating to Taha's life, as well as a diary of events surrounding Taha's execution.
3. Yusuf Lutfi papers: a selection of Taha's letters, 1950s - 1980s, and press cuttings and book fragments, without citations, dealing with Taha

Other unpublished sources

1. Sadig al-Mahdi, former prime minister and Umma leader, lecture in Cairo 11/6/1997
2. Audio tape of Republican religious songs, by Asma Mahmud and Mahasin Muhammad Khayr, 21/6/1979
3. Video tape of Sadigab ceremony of *mi'raj*, no date
4. Girgis Iskander, private letters from a Coptic doctor who was a friend and schoolmate of Taha's.
5. Batoul Mukhtar Muhammad Taha, private letters from Taha's brother's daughter and the leader of the Republican sisters.
6. Renaud, Etienne, "Mahmud Taha and the Second Mission of Islam", unpublished paper by a Catholic theologian, nd

Interviews

Many of the people interviewed were at one time members of the Republican brotherhood. They are listed as "Republicans". They are described by their relationship to Taha. Some informants requested anonymity.

1. Abdallah al-Dabi, Republican, 7/12/1997
2. 'Abd al-Rahman 'Ali al-Shaykh, Republican from Rufa'a related to Taha, 17/6/1997
3. Abdullahi An-Na'im, Republican, 8/11/1997, 10/11/1997, 11/11/1997, 17/11/1997
4. Abdelwahab El Affendi, academic with links to the Sudanese Muslim Brotherhood, 31/3/1998
5. Ahmed Omer, son of Taha's mother's friend, 3/12/1997
6. 'Ali Lutfi, Taha's wife's brother, 5/12/1997
7. Amna Muhammad Lutfi, widow of Taha, 28/11/1997, 29/11/1997, 30/11/1997
8. Asma Mahmud, daughter of Taha, 28/11/1997, 29/11/1997, 30/11/1997
9. Awatif 'Abd al-Gadir, Republican, 25/11/1997
10. Al-Baqir Al-Afif Mukhtar, Republican, 11/2/1997, 17/6/1997
11. Bona Malwal, journalist and former minister from south Sudan, 19/8/1997
12. Fatma Ahmad Ibrahim, Former Communist MP and leader of Sudan Women's Union, 21/8/1997
13. Fatma Yusuf Gway, Republican from Rufa'a, 6/12/1997
14. Ibrahim Yusuf, Republican expelled for his opinions from the Omdurman religious institute, 13/6/1997
15. Khalid Muhammad al-Hassan Muhammad Khayr, Republican and son of founding member, 23/11/1997, 24/11/1997
16. Mudawi Turabi, journalist, 28/3/1998

17. Mahmud Amin Siddiq, Republican, son of founding member, 4/12/1997
18. Mona Zanoon Gubara, Republican, daughter of founding member, 10/2/1997, 12/7/1998
19. Muhammad Abdel Khalig, writer, 18/6/1997
20. Muhammad 'Ali Malik, Republican from Heglig, 6/12/1997, 8/12/1997
21. Muhammad al-Fatih 'Abd al-Wahhab, Republican, 17/6/1997
22. El Nur Hamad, Republican, 29/11/1997
23. Omer el-Garrai, Republican, 25/11/1997
24. Saadia 'Izz al-Din 'Ali Malik, daughter of party member, 23/11/1997
25. Sayyida Muhammad Lutfi, Taha's wife's sister, 17/6/1997
26. Steve Howard, Republican, 23/11/1997
27. Eltayeb Hassan, Republican, 12/2/1997
28. Yusuf Hasan, secretary for public relations, office of the Ansar sect, 14/6/1997
29. Yusuf Lutfi, Taha's wife's brother, 3/12/1997

Published sources

This list includes books, journals, magazines and university theses and papers. Official sources are listed above. The affixes *al, an, el,* and *d'* are all ignored as far as alphabetical order is concerned

'Abd al-Hamid, 'Abd al-Aziz Amin, *al-tarbiya fil-sudan wal-usus al-ijtima'iya wal-nafsiya allati qamat biha,* Cairo 1949

'Abd al-Rahim, Muddathir, *Imperialism and Nationalism in the Sudan: a study in constitutional and political development 1899-1956,* Oxford 1969

Abusabib, Mohamed A, *African Art: An Aesthetic Inquiry,* Uppsala 1995

Abu Shouk, Ahmad Ibrahim, and Bjørkelo, Anders, eds, *The Public Treasury of the Muslims: monthly budgets of the Mahdist state in Sudan 1897,* Leiden 1996

Adu Boahen, A, ed, *General History of Africa,* 7, Paris 1990

El-Affendi, Abdelwahab, *Turabi's Revolution: Islam and Power in Sudan,* London 1991

Affifi, A E, *The Mystical Philosophy of Muhyid Din-Ibnul 'Arabi,* Cambridge 1939

Africa Confidential, London 1983-1985

Ahmed, Leila, *Women and Gender in Islam,* New Haven, Connecticut 1992

Akolawin, Natale Olwak, "Personal Law in the Sudan – trends and developments", in *Journal of African Law,* 17 (2) 1973

Ali, A I M, *The British, the Slave Trade and Slavery in the Sudan 1820-1881,* Khartoum 1972

Ali, Hayder Ibrahim ed, *al-ustadh mahmud muhammad taha, ra'id al-tajdid al-dini fil-sudan,* Cairo 1992

— *al-tanawwu' al-thaqafi wa bina' al-dawla al-wataniya fil-sudan,* Cairo 1995

d'Almeida Topor, Hélène; Coquery-Vidrovitch, Catherine; Georg, Odile, and Guitart, Françoise, eds, *Les Jeunes en Afrique,* Paris 1992

el-Amin, Mohammed Nur, "The Impact of the Fajr School on Sudanese Communism", in *Sudan Notes and Records* 62, Khartoum 1981

— "The Sudanese Communist Movement – The First Five Years", in *Middle Eastern Studies* 32 (3, 4); 33, (1). London, 1996 & 1997

Arberry, Arthur J., tr. *The Koran,* Oxford 1982

— *Revelation and Reason in Islam,* London 1957

Arkell, A J, *A History of the Sudan from the Earliest Times to 1821,* London 1955

Asad, Talal, *The Kababish Arabs: Power, Authority and Consent in a Nomadic Tribe*, New York 1970

Atiyah, Edward, *An Arab Tells His Story*, London 1946

Al-Azami, M Mustafa, *On Schacht's Origins of Muhammadan Jurisprudence*, Riyadh 1985

Barnett, Tony, and Abbas, Abdelkarim, *Sudan: state, capital and transformation*, London 1988

al-Bashir, al-Tahir Muhammad Ali, *al-adab al-sufi al-sudani*, Khartoum 1972

Bayart, Jean-Francois, *The State in Africa: The Politics of the Belly*, London 1993

Beasley, Ina, *Before the wind changed: people, places and education in the Sudan*, ed Janet Starkey, Oxford 1992

Bedri, Babikr, *The Memoirs of Babikr Bedri*, 2 London 1980

Bell, Richard, and Watt, W Montgomery, *Introduction to the* Qur'an, Edinburgh 1977

Beshir, Mohamed Omer, *The Southern Sudan, Background to Conflict*, London 1968

— *Educational Development in the Sudan 1898-1956*, Oxford 1969

— *Revolution and Nationalism in the Sudan*, London 1974

— *Terramedia: themes in Afro-Arab relations*, Khartoum 1982

Bjørkelo, Anders, *Prelude to the Mahdiyya: Peasants and Traders in the Shendi Region 1821 - 1885*, Cambridge 1989

Boddy, Janice, *Wombs and Alien Spirits: women, men and the Zar cult in Northern Sudan*, London 1989

Braudel, Fernand, *A History of Civilisations,* London 1993

Bray, Mark, and Clarke, Peter B, and Stephens, David, *Education and Society in Africa*, London 1986

Brenner, Louis, ed, *Muslim Identity and Social Change in Sub-Saharan Africa*, Bloomington, Indiana 1993

Brown, NJ, "*Shari'a* and State in the Modern Muslim Middle East", in *International Journal of Middle Eastern Studies* 29, 1997

Bruce, James, *Travels to discover the source of the Nile*, Edinburgh 1964

Burton, John, *The Sources of Islamic Law*, Edinburgh 1990

Chanock, Martin, *Law, Custom and the Social Order: The Colonial Experience in Malawi and Zambia*, Cambridge 1985

Coulson, N J, *A History of Islamic Law*, Edinburgh 1964

— *Conflicts and tensions in Islamic jurisprudence,* Chicago 1969

Craig, G M, ed, *The Agriculture of the Sudan*, Oxford 1991

Cunnison, Ian, *Baqqara Arabs: Power and Lineage in a Sudanese Arab Tribe*, Oxford 1966

Cunnison, Ian, and James, Wendy, *Essays in Sudan Ethnography presented to Sir Edward Evans-Pritchard*, London 1972

Daly, M W, ed, *Al Majdhubiyya and Al-Makashfiyya: Two Sufi Tariqas in the Sudan*, Khartoum 1985

— *Empire on the Nile: The Anglo-Egyptian Sudan 1898-1934*, Cambridge 1986

— *Imperial Sudan: The Anglo-Egyptian Condominium 1934-1956*, Cambridge 1991

Daly M W, & Sikainga, Ahmad AlAwad, eds, *Civil War in the Sudan*, London 1993

El Dareer, Asma, *Women why do you weep? Circumcision and its* consequences, London 1982

Da'ud, Amin, *naqd muftariyat mahmud muhammad taha wa-bayan mawqif al-quda' minhu*, 1974

Davison, Roderic H, *Reform in the Ottoman Empire, 1856-1876*, 1, New York 1973

De Waal, Alex, *Famine That Kills: Darfur, Sudan, 1984-1985*, Oxford 1989

Deng, Francis, *War of Visions: Conflict of Identities in the Sudan,* Washington DC: 1995

— *The Man Called Deng Majok: A Biography of Power, Polygyny and Change*, Yale 1986

Dirar, Hamid A, *The Indigenous Fermented Foods of the Sudan: a Study in African Food and*

Nutrition, Wallingford, 1993

Economist Intelligence Unit, *Quarterly Economic Reports*, London 1983-1985

EIU = Economist Intelligence Unit

Encyclopaedia of Islam, New Edition, Leiden 1960-

Evans-Pritchard, E E, *The Azande*, Oxford 1971

Ewald, Janet J, *Soldiers, Traders and Slaves: State Formation and Economic Transformation in the Greater Nile valley, 1700-1885*, Madison, Wisconsin 1990

Fadel, Mohammed, "The social logic of taqlid and the rise of the *mukhtasar*", in *Islamic Law and Society* 3 (2) Leiden 1996

— "Two women, one man: knowledge, power, and gender in mediaeval Sunni legal thought", in *International Journal of Middle Eastern Studies* 29 Cambridge 1997

Faisal Islamic Bank (Sudan) *Faisal Islamic Bank of Sudan Investment Operations and Banking Services*, Khartoum, nd

— *Annual Report*, 1984

Fawzi, Saad ed Din, *The Labour Movement in the Sudan 1946-1955*, Oxford 1957

Fluehr-Lobban, Carolyn, *Islamic Law and Society in the Sudan*, London 1987

Foucault, Michel, *Discipline and Punish: The Birth of the Prison*, London 1991

Frost, J M, *World Radio and TV Handbook*, London 1983

al-Ghazali *al-munqidh min al-dalal wal-musil ila dhi al-'izza wal-jalal*, Beirut 1959

Gilsenan, Michael, *Recognising Islam: religion and society in the modern Middle East*, London 1992

Greenwood, H L, "Escape in the Grass", *Sudan Notes and Records* 16 1941

Guazzone, Laura, *The Islamist Dilemma: the political role of Islamist movements in the contemporary Arab world*, Reading 1995

Hag el-Safi, Mahasin Abdel Gadir, ed, *The Nationalist Movement in the Sudan*, Khartoum 1989

Hale, Sondra "'The New Muslim Woman': Sudan's National Islamic Front and the Invention of Identity", in *The Muslim World* 86 (2) 1996a

— *Gender Politics in Sudan: Islamism, Socialism and the State*, Boulder, Colorado 1996b

Hamid, 'Abd al-Rahman Muhammad, *man dayya' al-sudan*, Khartoum 1991

Hargey, T M, *The Suppression of Slavery in the Sudan 1898-1939*, PhD dissertation, Oxford 1981

Harir, Sharif, and Tvedt, Terje, *Short-cut to Decay: The Case of the Sudan*, Uppsala 1994

Hasan, Yusuf Fadl, *Sudan in Africa*, Khartoum 1971

— *al-shillukh, asluha wa wazifatuha fi sudan wadi al-nil al-awsat*, Khartoum 1976

el-Hassan, Idris, *Religion in Society (Nemeiri and the Turuq)*, Khartoum 1993

Hay, Margaret Jean, and Wright, Marcia, eds, *African Women and the Law: Historical Perspectives*, Boston, 1982

Heer, Nicholas, ed, *Islamic Law and Jurisprudence*, Seattle 1990

Hill, Richard, *Egypt in the Sudan 1820-1881*, Oxford 1959

— *Sudan Transport: a history of railway, marine and river services in the Republic of Sudan*, Oxford 1965

Hillelson, S, "Arabic Nursery Rhymes", in *Sudan Notes and Records* 1 1918

Hodgson, Marshall G S, *The Venture of Islam*, Chicago 1974

Holt, P M, *The Mahdist State in the Sudan 1881-1898: A Study of its Origins, Development and Overthrow*, Oxford 1970

Hourani, Albert, *A History of the Arab Peoples*, London 1991

Howard, W Stephen, "Mahmoud Mohammed Taha: a remarkable teacher in Sudan", in

Northeast African Studies 10 (1), 1988

Human Rights Watch, *Civilian Devastation: Abuses by All Parties in the War in Southern Sudan*, New York 1994

Hyland, ADC, & Al-Shahi, Ahmed, ed, *The Arab House*, Newcastle upon Tyne, 1984

Isaacman, Allen, and Roberts, Richard, *Cotton, Colonialism and Social History in Sub-Saharan Africa*, London 1995

Ismail, Ellen, and Makki, Maureen, *Women of the Sudan*, Bendestorf, Germany 1990

Jackson, H C, *Behind the Modern Sudan*, London 1955

Jalalayn (Jalal al-Din Muhammad Ahmad and Jalal al-Din 'Abd al-Rahman Abu Bakr), *tafsir al-jalalayn bi-hamish al-Qur'an al-karim*, Beirut 1987

James, Wendy, *'Kwanim Pa: The Making of the Uduk People*, Oxford 1979

Johnson, Douglas H, "Prophecy and Mahdism in the Upper Nile: an Examination of Local Experiences of the Mahdiyya in the Southern Sudan", in *British Journal of Middle Eastern Studies*, 20 (1) 1993

Al-Kabbashi, al-Mukashfi Taha, *tatbiq al-shari'a al-islamiya fil-sudan, bayn al-haqiqa wal-ithara*, Cairo 1986

Kamali, M H, *Principles of Islamic Jurisprudence*, Cambridge 1991

Kapteijns, Lidwien, *Mahdist Faith and Sudanic Tradition: The History of the Masalit Sultanate 1870-1930*, London 1985

Karrar, Ali Salih, *The Sufi Brotherhoods in the Sudan*, London 1992

Al-Karsani, Awad al-Sid, "The Establishment of Neo-Mahdism in the Western Sudan, 1920-1936", in *African Affairs* 86 1987

—— *The Republican Brothers and the May Regime*, unpublished paper, Department of Political Science, Khartoum University, nd

Kedourie, Elie, *Afghani and 'Abduh: an essay on religious unbelief and political activism in modern Islam*, London 1966

Keen, D, *The Benefits of Famine*, Princeton 1994

Kenyatta, Jomo, *Facing Mount Kenya*, London 1961

Kenyon, Susan M, *Five Women of Sennar: Culture and Change in Central Sudan*, Oxford 1991

Khalid, Mansour, *The Government They Deserve*, London 1990

—— *Nimeiri and the Revolution of Dis-May*, London 1985

Khoury P S & Kostiner J, eds, *Tribes and State Formation in the Middle East*, Oxford 1990

Kropotkin, Petr, *Kropotkin's Revolutionary Pamphlets*, ed Roger N Baldwin, New York 1970

Lane, E W, *The Manners and Customs of the Modern Egyptians*, London 1895

Lapidus, Ira M, *A History of Islamic Societies*, Cambridge 1988

—— "State and Religion in Islamic Societies", in *Past & Present* 151 May 1996

Levtzion, Nehemiah, & Voll, John O, *Eighteenth Century Renewal and Reform in Islam*, New York 1987

Lichtenthaler, Gerhard, *Muslih, Mystic and Martyr - The Vision of Mahmud Muhammad Taha and the Republican Brothers in the Sudan: Towards an Islamic Reformation?* unpublished MA dissertation, SOAS, London 1993

Lovejoy, Paul E, *Transformations in Slavery: A history of slavery in Africa*, Cambridge 1985

Lovejoy, Paul E, & Hogendorn, J S "Revolutionary Mahdism and Resistance to Colonial Rule in the Sokoto Caliphate 1905-6", in *Journal of African History* 31 1990

Lovejoy, Paul E, ed, *Ideology of Slavery in Africa*, Beverly Hills 1981

Lutfi, Yusuf, *Yusuf Lutfi papers*, see primary sources

Lybarger, Loren, "Utopian Islam in post-Condominium Sudan: the case of Mahmud Muhammad Taha and the Republican Brothers", unpublished paper, University of

Chicago 1997

MacMichael, H A, *A History of the Arabs in the Sudan, and some account of the people who preceded them and of the tribes inhabiting Darfur*, 1 and 2, Cambridge 1922

—— *The Anglo-Egyptian Sudan* London 1934

al-Mahdi, Sadig, *al-i'tidal wal-tatarruf wa huquq al-insan fil-islam*, 1992a

—— *al-dawla fil-islam*, 1992b

Mahmoud, Fatima Babiker, *The Sudanese Bourgeoisie: Vanguard of Development?* London 1984

Mahmud, Asma, *Asma Mahmud papers*, see primary sources

Makris, G P, "Slavery, possession and history: the construction of the self among slave descendants in the Sudan", in *Africa* 66 (2) 1996

Mamdani, Mahmood, *Citizen and Subject: Contemporary Africa and the Legacy of Late Colonialism*, Princeton 1996

Mamdani, Mahmood, & Wamba-dia-Wamba, Ernest, eds, *African Studies in Social Movements and Democracy*, Dakar 1995

Mangan, J A, *The Games Ethic and Imperialism: Aspects of the Diffusion of an Ideal*, London 1986

Manuel, Peter, *Popular Musics of the Non-Western World*, Oxford 1988

Marlow, Louise, *Hierarchy and Egalitarianism in Islamic Thought*, Cambridge 1997

Marx, Karl, and Engels, Friedrich, *Selected Works* 3 Moscow 1970

Mawut, Lazarus Leek, *The Southern Sudan, Why Back to Arms?* Khartoum 1986

McHugh, Neil, *Holymen of the Blue Nile*, Evanston 1994

Messick, Brinkley, *The Calligraphic State: Textual Domination and History in a Muslim Society*, Berkeley 1993

Miller, Judith, *God has ninety-nine names*, New York 1996

Mitchell, Timothy, *Colonising Egypt*, Cambridge 1988

Ministry of Culture and Information, *Sudan Facts and Figures*, Khartoum 1973

Ministry of National Planning, Census Office, *Sudan Third Population Census, 1983: Preliminary Results*, Khartoum 1983

Mubarak, Khalid, "al-hizb al-shiyu'i al-sudani al-madi wal-hadir wa ihtimalat al-mustaqbil", in *al-Wasat* 27/3/94

Muhammad, Khalifa Ahmad, *ba'd al'ab al-atfal wal-sabiyah fil-sudan*, Khartoum, nd

Mukhtar, Al-Baqir Al-Afif, *Human Rights and Islamic Law: the development of the rights of slaves, women and aliens in two cultures*, PhD thesis, Manchester University 1996

al-Muti'i, Muhammad Najib, *haqiqat mahmud muhammad taha aw al-risala al-kadhiba*, 1986

An-Na'im, Abdullahi Ahmed, "The Islamic Law of Apostasy and its Modern Applicability: A Case from Sudan", in *Religion* 16, 1986

—— "Mahmud Muhammad Taha and the Crisis in Islamic Law Reform: Implications for Interreligious Relations", in *Journal of Ecumenical Studies*, 25 (1) 1988

—— *Toward an Islamic Reformation*, New York 1990

An-Na'im, Abdullahi and Deng, Francis, eds, *Human Rights in Africa: cross cultural perspectives*, Washington 1990

El-Naqar, Omer 'Abd al-Raziq ed, *dirasat fi tarikh al-mahdiya*, 1, Khartoum 1981

Niblock, Tim, *Class and Power in Sudan*, London 1987

Nicholson, R A, *Studies in Islamic Mysticism*, Cambridge 1921

Nordenstam, Tore, *Sudanese Ethics*, Uppsala 1968

Nugud, Muhammad Ibrahim, *'alaqat al-riqq fil-mujtama' al-sudani, al-nasha, al-simat, al-idmihlal, tawthiq wa ta'liq*, Cairo 1995

O'Brien, Jay, & Rosebery, W, ed, *Golden Ages, Dark Ages: imagining the past in anthropology and history*, Berkeley 1991

O'Fahey, R S, *Enigmatic Saint: Ahmad Ibn Idris and the Idrisi Tradition*, Evanston: Northwestern UP 1990

—   "Slavery and the Slave Trade in Dar Fur", in *Journal of African History* 14 (1) 1973

—   *State and Society in Darfur*, London 1980

O'Fahey, R S, ed, *Arabic Literature of Africa, volume I: The Writings of Eastern Sudanic Africa to c.1900*, Leiden 1994

O'Fahey, R S, & Spaulding, J L, *Kingdoms of the Sudan*, London 1974

Osman, Ahmed Ibrahim, *In Praise of the Prophet: the Performance and Thematic Composition of the Sudanese Religious Oral Poetry*, PhD thesis, Indiana University 1990

Pashukanis, Evgeny, *Law and Marxism*, London 1978

—   *Selected Writings on Marxism and Law*, ed P Beirne and R Sharlet, London 1980

Perks, Robert, and Thomson, Alistair, *The oral history reader*, London 1998

Pons, Valdo, ed, *Urbanization and Urban Life in the Sudan*, Hull 1980

Pridie E D, et al, *Female Circumcision in the Anglo-Egyptian Sudan*, Sudan Medical Service, Khartoum 1945

PRO = Public Records Office, see primary sources

Public Records Office, see primary sources

Qamar-ul Huda, "Reflections on Muslim Ascetics and Mystics: Sufi Theories on Annihilation and Subsistence", in *Jusur*, 12 1996

Qutb, Sayyid, *ma'alim fil tariq*, Cairo 1993

Rahman, Fazlur, *Islam,* Chicago 1979

RB = Republican Brothers

Republican Brothers, - *waqa'i' qadiyat hursudan bayn man kan yusamma bil-qudah al-shari'iyin wal-fikr al-jumhuri*, 1-4, Omdurman 1975

—   *al-din wa rijal al-din 'abr al-sinin*, Omdurman 1975

—   *al-zayy 'unwan 'aql al-mar'a wa khulqiha*, Omdurman 1975 (international year of women series 2)

—   *al-wajibat qabl al-huquq*, Omdurman 1975 (international year of women series 3)

—   *al-mar'a wal-tadayyun*, Omdurman 1975 (international year of women series 9)

—   *al-talaq laysa aslan fil-islam*, Omdurman 1975 (international year of women series 14)

—   *al-mar'a wal-da'wa ila al-din*, Omdurman 1975 (international year of women series 15)

—   *al-sifr al-awwal*, Omdurman 1976 (first edition 1945)

—   *ma dha qal al-ustadh Mahmud 'an al-salat*, Omdurman 1976

—   *ma'alim 'ala tariq tatawur al-fikra al-jumhuria khilal thalathin 'aman 1945-1975*, 1 and 2, Omdurman 1976

—   *al-sulh khayr*, Omdurman 1976

—   *al-ikhwan al-jumhuriyun fi jaridat al-ahram al-misriya*, Omdurman 1976

—   *huquq al-mar'a fi - 1. al-din 2. al-shari'a 3. al-fiqh*, Omdurman 1977 (first edition 1975, international year of women series 11)

—   *liqa' idha'i ma' al-ustadh mahmud muhammad taha hawl 1. al-usul wal-furu' 2. al-khayr wal-sharr 3. al-taharrur min al-khawf 4. al-hikma wara' al-'adhab*, Omdurman 1977 (third edition of the text of a radio interview given by Taha in 1975)

—   *limadha wa kayfa kharajat al-mar'a al-jumhuriya lil-da'wa lil-din*, Omdurman 1978

—   *lajnat ta'dil al-qawanin bija'liha li hadd al-khamr ta'ziran tuzayyif al-shari'a wa tu'awwiq ba'th al-din*, Omdurman 1979

—   *fitnat iran* Omdurman 1979

—   *ila mata hadha al-'abath bi-'uqul al-nas wa bi-din allah?* 1980 *'awdat al-masih*, Omdurman 1980

The Return of Christ, Omdurman 1980

mahkamat al-ridda: 'ar al-quda' al-sudani, Omdurman 1981

al-istiqlal jasad: ruhuhu al-hurriya, Omdurman 1981

atfa'u nar al-fitna: hawl hawadith al-sa'a, Omdurman 1982

adab al-salik fi tariq muhammad, Omdurman 1982

al-taqlid!! wal-asil!! wal-usala'!! Omdurman 1982

bank faysal al-islami!? Omdurman 1983

al-mawqif al-siyasi al-rahin, Omdurman 1984

ma dha qal al-'alim 'an al-ustadh mahmud? Omdurman nd (published after Taha's execution)

al-kayd al-siyasi wal-mahkama al-muhzila, Omdurman 1985

Robson, P, and Lury, D A, *The economies of Africa*, London 1969

Rodinson, M, *Islam and Capitalism*, London 1974

SAD = Sudan Archive, Durham, see primary sources

Sa'd, 'Abd al-Mun'im 'Abd al-Latif, "aqwal shahid 'ayan", in *al-Jami'a* May 1985

Sadig, Haydar Badawi, *The Republican Brothers: a religio-political movement in the Sudan*, Unpublished MSc thesis, University of Khartoum 1988

Said, Edward W, *Orientalism*, London 1978

Sanderson, Lilian, "The 1924 Revolution: Its Repercussions upon the Educational System of the Sudan", in *Sudan Notes and Records* 58, Khartoum 1976

Against the mutilation of women: a struggle to end unnecessary suffering, London 1981

Sanderson, L S Passmore, and Sanderson, G N, *Education, Religion and Politics in Southern Sudan 1899-1964*, London 1981

Savage, E, ed, *The Human Commodity: perspectives on the trans-Saharan slave trade*, London 1992

AlSayyad, Nezar, *Cities and Caliphs: on the genesis of Arab Muslim urbanism*, Westport, Conneticut, 1991

Schuver, Juan Maria, *Juan Maria Schuver's Travels in North East Africa 1880-1883*, ed Wendy James, Gerd Baumann and Douglas Johnson, London 1996

Shaban, M A, *Islamic History, AD 600 - 750 (AH132): a new interpretation*, London 1971

al-Shafi'i, Muhammad ibn Idris, *Islamic Jurisprudence: Shafi'i's Risala*, tr Majid Khadduri, Baltimore 1961

al-Shahi, A, & Moore, F C T, *Wisdom from the Nile*, Oxford 1978

al-Shahi, A, *Themes from Northern Sudan*, London 1986

Shalgami, Nasr al-Din Ibrahim, *kosti al-qissa wal-tarikh*, Khartoum 1991

Sharif, M M, *A History of Muslim Philosophy, with short accounts of other disciplines and the modern renaissance in Muslim lands*, 1 & 2, Delhi 1993

al-Sharif, Yasir, "qad tunkir al-'ayn daw' al-shams min ramad", in *al-Ra'y al-Akhir* 2 (8), Fort Worth, May 1996

Shibeika, Mekki, *al-sudan 'abr al-qurun*, Beirut 1965

el Shoush, Muhammad Ibrahim, "Some Background Notes on Modern Sudanese Poetry", in *Sudan Notes and Records* 44 1963

Shuqayr, Na'um, *jughrafiya wa tarikh al-sudan*, Beirut 1972

Siddiqi, M Z, *Hadith Literature: Its Origin, Development & Special Features*, Cambridge 1993

Sikainga, A A, "Labor Activism and Solidarity among the Railway Workers of Atbara (Sudan) 1924 - 1948", in *South Asia Bulletin, Comparative Studies of South Asia, Africa and the Middle East*, 15 (2) 1995

Slaves into Workers: emancipation and labor in colonial Sudan, Austin, Texas, 1996

Simonse, Simon, *Kings of Disaster: Dualism, Centralism and the Scapegoat King in Southeastern Sudan*, Leiden 1992

Sivan, Emmanuel, *Radical Islam: Medieval Theology and Modern Politics*, Yale 1990

Slatin, Rudolf C, *Fire and Sword in the Sudan: A Personal Narrative of Fighting and Serving the Dervishes*, tr F R Wingate, London 1898

Smirnov, S R, *Africa as a Soviet Scientist sees it*, Moscow, 1974

Spaulding, Jay, "The Government of Sinnar", in *International Journal of African Historical Studies*, 6 (1) 1973

— "The evolution of the Islamic judiciary in Sinnar", in *International Journal of African Historical Studies*, 10 (3), 1977

— "Farmers, herdsmen and the state in rainland Sinnar", in *Journal of African History* 20 (3), 1979

— "Slavery, land tenure and social class in the northern Turkish Sudan", in *International Journal of African Historical Studies* 15 (1), 1982

— *The Heroic Age in Sinnar*, East Lansing, Michigan 1985

— "The value of virginity on Echo Island, 1860-1866", in *International Journal of African Historical Studies* 25 (1), 1992

Sudan Archive, Durham, see primary sources

al-Tabari, *jami' al-bayan 'an ta'wil ayat al-Qur'an*, Cairo 1968

Tadamon Islamic Bank, *Annual Report*, Khartoum 1984

Taha, Mahmud Muhammad, *al-ustadh mahmud muhammad taha yad'u ila tariq muhammad*, Omdurman nd (first edition 1965)

— *usus dastur al-sudan*, Omdurman 1968 (first edition 1955)

— *al-islam*, Omdurman 1968 (first edition 1960)

— *al-dastur al-islami na'm ... wa la*, Omdurman 1968 (first edition)

— *al-risala al-thania min al-Islam*, fifth edition, Omdurman nd (first edition 1967)

— *mushkilat al-sharq al-awsat*, Omdurman 1968 (first edition)

— *al-islam bi-risalatihi al-ula la yuslih li-insaniyat al-qarn al-'ishrin*, Omdurman 1969 (text of a 1969 lecture, first edition)

— *baynana wa bayn mahkamat al-ridda*, Omdurman 1969 (first edition)

— *as'ila wa ajwiba*, 1, Omdurman 1970 (first edition)

— *as'ila wa ajwiba*, 2, Omdurman 1971 (first edition)

— *al-Qur'an wa mustafa mahmud wal fahm al-'asri*, Omdurman 1971 (first edition)

— *al-thawra al-thaqafiya*, Omdurman 1972 (first edition)

— *ta'allamu kayfa tasallun*, Omdurman 1972 (first edition)

— *rasa'il wa maqalat*, 1, Omdurman 1973 (first edition)

— *al-din wal-tanmiya al-ijtima'iya*, Omdurman 1974 (first edition)

— *qul hadhihi sabili*, Omdurman 1976 (first edition 1952)

— *al-ustadh mahmud muhammad taha yuhaddith al-nisa' fi huquqihinn*, Omdurman 1976 (text of a lecture given in 1974, first published in 1975)

— *al-marksiya fil mizan*, Omdurman 1977 (third edition of the text of a 1968 lecture, first published in 1973)

— *tatwir shari'at al-ahwal al-shakhsiyya*, Omdurman 1979 (first edition 1971)

— *risalat al-salah*, Omdurman 1979 (first edition 1966)

— *dibajat al-ustadh mahmud muhammad taha*, Sudan 1984 (sic, essay written in detention)

— *The Second Message of Islam,* New York 1987

al-Tayib, Abdulla, "The changing customs of the riverain Sudan", in *Education in Sudan: proceedings of the 11th annual conference of the Philosophical society of Sudan,* Khartoum 1963

Eltayeb, Eltayeb H M, *The Second Message of Islam: A critical study of the Islamic reformist thinking of Mahmud Muhammad Taha 1909-1985*, Unpublished PhD thesis, Manchester University 1995

El Tayeb, Salah el Din el Zein, *The Students' Movement in the Sudan 1940-1970*, Khartoum 1971

Thesiger, Wilfrid, *A Life of My Choice*, London 1987

Tillion, G, *The Republic of Cousins*, London 1983

Toledano E R, *The Ottoman Slave Trade and its Suppression: 1840 - 1890*, Princeton 1982

Trimingham, J Spencer, *Islam in the Sudan*, Oxford 1949

Turabi, Hasan, *tajdid usul al-fiqh al-islami*, Khartoum 1980

— *al-haraka al-islamiya fil-sudan: al-tatawwur wal-kasb wal-minhaj*, Cairo 1991

Warburg, Gabriel, *Islam, Nationalism and Communism in a Traditional Society: The Case of Sudan*, London 1978

Warburg, Gabriel R, & Kupferschmidt, Uri M, *Islam, Nationalism and Radicalism in Egypt and the Sudan*, New York 1983

Westerlund, D, & Rosander, E E, *African Islam and Islam in Africa*, London 1997

Willis, John Ralph, ed, *Slaves and Slavery in Muslim Africa*, 1 and 2, London 1985

Wingate, Reginald, *Reports on the Finances, Administration and Condition of the Sudan 1902*, Cairo 1905

Woodward, Peter, ed, *Sudan after Nimeiri*, London 1991

Yusuf, Ibrahim, *Ibrahim Yusuf papers*, see primary sources

Zaki, Husayn Muhammad, *al-qawl al-fasl fil-radd 'ala mahazil mahmud muhammad taha*, Alexandria 1406 AH (=1985/6)

Zayn al-'Abidin, al Tayyib *al-qanun al-juna'i al-sudani*, Islamabad 1991

El Zein, Gaysar Musa, *Knowledge Versus Action: Social Dynamics and the Hallajjian Model in Sudan*, Institute of African and Asian Studies, University of Khartoum, no date

Zein, Ibrahim M, *Religion Legality and the State: the 1983 Sudanese Penal Code*, PhD thesis, Temple University 1989

Zubeida, Sami, *Islam, the People and the State*, London 1993

— "Is there a Muslim Society? Ernest Gellner's sociology of Islam", in *Economy and Society* 2 (2), 1995

El Zubeir Rahma Mansur, *Black Ivory or the story of El Zubeir Pasha, slaver and sultan*, tr. H C Jackson, New York 1970

Index